Memoirs from the Left

To Constance and our family

MEMOIRS FROM THE LEFT

John Saville

THE MERLIN PRESS

First published 2003 by The Merlin Press Ltd.
PO Box 30705
London WC2E 8QD
www.merlinpress.co.uk

ISBN: 0850365201

British Library Cataloguing in Publication Data
is available from the British Library

Printed in Great Britain by Antony Rowe Ltd., Chippenham

Contents

Part 1: **Student Days**

The undistinguished entrance to the London School of Economics is still in Houghton Street, a nondescript road off the circle which brings together Fleet Street and the Strand. In my day Houghton Street was a through road for traffic, and at the end of the short street where it turned towards Lincoln Inns Fields was the Three Tuns pub, next door to which was Dalla Turcas, a cafe that offered in October 1934 two sausages and chips for sixpence.

LSE was different, in many respects very different, from other institutions of higher learning in Britain. It had evening students who before 1914 outnumbered full-time students by two to one, a proportion reversed by the nineteen thirties; thirty per cent of its day population in this decade were women; when William Beveridge retired as Director in 1937 there were nearly three hundred research students; nowhere else taught the full range of the social sciences; it was in the middle of London, surrounded by libraries, museums, art galleries, theatres, avant-garde cinemas, with pubs, cafes and restaurants in profusion. For its time the library of the School was superb, almost all on open access; and there was a general absence of the trimmings and associated mummery and dressing up, parading in gowns and coloured robes and caps that many today still appear to believe are a necessary and essential part of the higher learning. The atmosphere in common room and refectory was cosmopolitan; above all, public schoolboys were few and the ethos of the British public schools was wholly absent. It would not be appropriate to describe myself as politically aware when I first entered LSE. Yet I joined the Socialist Society within my first two weeks and the Marxist Society soon after, so there must have been some stirrings of ideas within me, much encouraged of course by the environment I now found myself in: by the conversations I listened to, the literature I was voraciously reading, and by Harold Laski's weekly lecture which I soon began to attend regularly.

The history of academic communities in Britain during the twentieth century is not a story of radical thought or progressive action, and most student generations, and certainly their tutors, have been content to enjoy themselves according to their particular tastes. The world outside the Academy has rarely been of continuous interest. The majority of British academics are technicians: often excellent at their particular specialism; quite often seriously interested in their students, and less often competent verbal communicators of their knowledge. Certainly the majority do not form part of an intelligentsia concerned with the wider cultural or political issues in the world beyond their stone or redbrick buildings.

The radicalism of the decade of the thirties was certainly an exception in Britain, among students in particular, and it has been succeeded only by the 1960s and then for different reasons. The 1930s began with the Wall Street crash and the consequent world-wide slump and depression, with massive unemployment in all the world's industrial countries and economic devastation in the non-industrial sectors which today we call the Third World. Most students, however, at least thought they could look forward to salaried employment, and what was probably closer to their political hearts was revulsion against the butchery and blood-letting of the 1914 war. The Oxford resolution of February 1933 was much quoted: That this House will in no circumstances fight for its King and Country. Japan had invaded Manchuria in the autumn of 1931, but more important for British opinion was the outpouring of novels, poetry, plays and reminiscences in the late twenties and early thirties, all revealing a profound disillusionment with the war to end all wars. It is interesting that this literary revulsion and hatred should have come, with only a few exceptions, some ten years after the ending of hostilities. The accounts we have in general, and of student life in particular, do not suggest a flowing stream of anti-war sentiment or activity in the 1920s.

Towards the end of the twenties there now appeared the extraordinary stream of writing about the horrors and stupidities of war which pushed itself into the consciousness of many of the people of Britain. My own introduction had been Wilfred Owen's Poems which I had borrowed from my local municipal library in the summer vacation before I walked into Houghton Street. The collective emotional impact of R. C. Sheriff's *Journey's End,* the writings of Edmund Blunden, Robert Graves, Remarque's *All Quiet on the Western Front,* the neglected Frederic Manning's *Her Privates We* – the list could be much extended – affected profoundly my generation.

In the early and mid-nineteen thirties the various strands of pacifism and anti-war politics and ideas came together. One remarkable illustration was the formation of the Peace Pledge Union. The Rev. Dick Sheppard wrote a letter to the press in mid October 1934 asking for a repudiation of war in any form or for any purpose, and he received 100,000 replies. The Peace Pledge Union (PPU) was established later at an overflow meeting in the Albert Hall. A few months earlier than Sheppard's letter the League of Nations Union had initiated the National Peace Ballot, a statement of five questions relating to collective security, world disarmament and the policy of sanctions against aggressors. The count was completed at the end of June 1935 with quite astonishing results. Eleven and a half million people had voted, and in overwhelming numbers the votes had been given for large scale disarmament and for the application of sanctions to warring countries. This national ballot indicated a much wider audience for a peaceful world than the unconditional pacifism of the PPU.

By this time my political attitudes had changed. I had never been a pacifist, although I remained deeply moved by the ideas and motivation of the anti-war movement and especially by the obscenity of the industrial world selling arms to the colonial world as well as to each other. I was, however, from the earliest days at LSE mixing with students who were politically on the Left: middle-of-the-road Labour to communists. The dominating themes of discussion were the fascist regimes in Europe, now linked increasingly with the threats of new wars, the native fascist movement in Britain and the consequences of the world slump. My first political demonstration was in a march against Mosley in the East End of London, and fascism at home and abroad had begun to dominate our thinking and in its different manifestations this remained true for the rest of the decade.

During my first year the politics of the world situation were beginning to change. In September 1934 the Soviet Union had been admitted to the League of Nations, with a permanent seat on the Council; it was a move which threw communists everywhere into furious debate, and confusion. For years the League of Nations had been regarded by British communists, and the more militant groups within the ILP, as a 'thieves kitchen' of the victorious imperialist powers, and they were now going to have to revise their political attitudes as well as their terminology. In the year that followed the Soviet Union signed a treaty of mutual assistance with France and in the autumn of 1935 Mussolini invaded Abyssinia. The world was becoming more dangerous.

Inevitably, in these first months at LSE I found myself ignorant of much of the detail of the political discussions I was now listening to; but the remedy was all around. The common room provided the national papers including the *Daily Worker*. Books could not be borrowed from the main library but almost all its stock was on open access and it did not shut until quite late in the evening. Among the books that everyone on the Left was reading was John Strachey's *The Coming Struggle for Power*. It had been first published in 1932 with the fourth edition two years later. The merit of Strachey's writings was his lucidity and a wholesome absence of jargon. *The Coming Struggle* was probably his most influential work, on both sides of the Atlantic. Today some parts read in simplistic terms. For contemporaries as for myself Strachey's summary of the world situation in general, and of Britain in particular, offered a remarkably stimulating analysis. Somewhat unexpectedly, it was his discussion of modern literature that introduced me to the poetry of T. S. Eliot and his early poems.

I was from my first weeks at the School reading for many hours in the Library. The concentration was inevitably upon politics and in addition to Strachey's book there were two other volumes that had an especial influence upon me. One was the selected correspondence of Marx and Engels, first published in 1934 from the German edition, with additional letters of particular interest for British readers. Both the translation and excellently compiled editorial notes were by Dona Torr whose name, typically, did not appear on the title page. She was a remarkable woman, of upper-class origin and we were later to become great friends. My second book was Vincent Sheean's recently published account of his travels, and from this I found myself increasingly fascinated with the modern history of China. He covered a number of countries and anti-imperialist movements in his journeys – the Rif in Morocco, Palestinians and Jews in Palestine (Jerusalem in 1929, he wrote, was an Arab city) – but the long chapter that made a lasting impression was his account of China in 1927. Michael Borodin and Madame Sun-Yat-Sen were the central personalities in his story and thenceforth I read everything I could find on the Chinese revolutionary movement. My Chinese interest came out when sometime in my second year I was at a supper party with R. H. Tawney. The purpose of the occasion I have forgotten. We sat at a table for six, with Tawney in the middle, and he began talking about China which he had visited in 1930 and published his story under the title *Land and Labour in China*. He was telling us about the so-called Christian General who baptised his converts – mostly from his own fighting units – with a hosepipe. 'I have forgotten his name,' said Tawney. 'Feng Yu-Hsian,' I offered from my end of the table. 'Good Lord,' exclaimed Tawney, 'how did you know that?'; but I was too embarrassed to offer anything but a mumble. It was in this book that Tawney compared the poverty of the Chinese peasant with a man standing up to his eyebrows in a river: 'a ripple would drown him'. When it appeared in 1937 Edgar Snow's *Red Star over China* was compulsive reading and it was probably the most exciting book I read in these years: a story that made it so difficult to appreciate the degeneration and cruelty that developed in later decades.

It would not have been difficult to feel oneself lonely at LSE. At the end of each academic working day, however long or short it had been, students went into Houghton Street to find their way to lodgings or flats or family homes. The matter must not be exaggerated. Most young students in their early weeks often feel isolated and somewhat forlorn and at LSE, as elsewhere, there were a large number of social, sporting and political groups to join; but digging into the life of a community always takes time.

I played soccer for the LSE first eleven for all my three years. It was twice a week for the first two years in the autumn and winter, but I limited myself to Saturdays only during my third year, a decision which probably meant that I missed playing for the University of London team. I had had some games with them during my second year. Playing soccer meant losing at least half a day's work. I lived at home during all my LSE days. This meant a mile walk to the station, half an hour by steam train to Liverpool Street, then the underground to Holborn and a short walk to Houghton Street. LSE's playing fields were naturally in the suburbs, and the journey to New Malden started at Waterloo. Away games often meant more time in travelling.

I enjoyed the soccer club. Members of athletic clubs in universities tended to be thought of as the 'hearties' in contrast with the non-athletic aesthetes or intellectuals: at least this was how it was often represented in the years between the wars and before 1914. There was some truth in this understanding in my years at LSE but my recollections of the soccer club members suggest that they were ordinary members of the student community, not very political but interested in matters not limited to sport. W. H. Hutt, a professor of economics from South Africa and a fundamentalist in market economy analysis, attached himself when on leave to LSE, and he used often to travel with the soccer club. Hutt, whom I got to know quite well, once told me that never before had he travelled with a university sports team whose members actually talked about their academic subjects on their journeys to matches.

The intellectual liveliness of the student population was the result of different factors coming together to encourage a cerebral energy not limited to the political Left although the latter were no doubt among the more vociferous. The academic concentration upon the social and political sciences against the background of world economic problems inevitably encouraged serious discussion; the darkening threat of fascism and the growing possibilities of new wars could not be ignored; and the growing number of European refugees were important influences. In my own experience a crucial factor was the co-mingling of the undergraduate population with post-graduate students. The LSE doctoral students – most research students were in this category – had their own common room but they were often to be found in our common room on the third floor. More important, we all ate in the same refectory, and since all at the tables were involved in some area of the social sciences conversation with neighbours was not difficult. My closest academic acquaintances among research students were American, of whom there were quite a number. A common language no doubt helped social contact, but in these middle years of the thirties we were all deeply interested in the New Deal and the political personality of Roosevelt. In part this must have been a response to Laski's lectures and writings, but even more because the United States, with all its many problems, and its New Deal politics, seemed so much livelier than Britain. The contrast with the contemptible politics of the British governments, as well as the passivity of the Labour Party, appeared both depressing and enlivening. I took to reading the *Nation* – there would not be many contemporary university libraries which subscribed – and I began to enjoy American fiction. I became as familiar with Faulkner, Sinclair Lewis, Hemingway and Dos Passos as with English novelists of the period.

This mixing of the more sophisticated with the less contributed greatly to the intellectual animation of student life. There were certainly at the undergraduate level a considerable number of bright young women and men, whatever their politics, and all benefited from this intelligent fraternisation. American research students were not my only companions from other countries. Among the political refugees my particular friends, especially in the first year, were Teddy Prager, a leading figure of the Austrian Left in the post-war years, and Manuel Azcarate, a prominent communist in the Spanish Party after Franco's victory. His father was the Spanish Republican ambassador for most of the Civil War years. There was also a significant minority of Indian students, both undergraduate and research, but once I became known as a communist, as I soon was, care had to be taken not to compromise the radicals among the Indian students. The Indian Communist Party was illegal, and we always assumed, which I am sure was true, that there was continuous surveillance on those from the Indian continent. Few Indian students felt that they could advertise their precise political affiliation on the Left. There were some who became known. At Cambridge Mohan Kumaramangalam, the first Indian to become president of the Union, openly acknowledged his membership of the Indian Communist Party; and was jailed after he returned following the outbreak of war. I knew him slightly during his Cambridge years and we became close friends when I was in the British army in India during the last years of the war.

The structure of the B. Sc. (Econ.) degree encouraged reading over a wide range of the social sciences, a much more liberal and sensible approach for a first degree than the increasing specialisations of today. Political history, social philosophy and the history of political ideas were among the additional options to the three compulsory papers in economics and economic history and the three papers of any one specialism. The main teaching in economics was provided by Lionel Robbins and Hayek assisted in other courses by professors and lecturers most of whom were in broad agreement with their seniors. The exceptions among the junior staff were Abba Lerner and Kaldor, but their teaching was limited to specialists. Lionel Robbins, who had been elected to his chair at the age of thirty, offered the main general course. He was a tall, handsome man with a fine presence, and his lectures were lucidly and expertly delivered. The only problem with Robbins, as we on the Left were constantly telling each other, and anyone else who would listen, was that he was formulating his own version of what the subject was about and it had little relevance to contemporary society. There was no place in Robbin's thinking for the expansionist ideas of Maynard Keynes. Robbins held to his views throughout the 1930s and he was much encouraged by the intellectual support of von Mises and Hayek It was during the war years, when he was in Whitehall and in personal contact with Keynes that he began to change certain of his ideas, and in his *Autobiography*, published in 1971, he wrote that he now accepted *au pied de la lettre* the analytical propositions of the General Theory. He further admitted that his book on *The Great Depression*, published in 1934, was one he would willingly see forgotten.

His later statements in the post-war period do not, however, suggest that he understood the world he was living in any more perceptively than during the 1930s. He was always able to communicate some simple practical ideas, however misguided. It was not only for his ideas in a world submerged beneath millions of unemployed that I disliked Robbins – the more I learned about him the less attractive he has become. When C. A. Smith, among the intellectual oddballs of our time, wrote a witty critique of Hayek's ideas in an issue of *Clare Market Review* in the later thirties under the title of 'Dr. Fun Hike', Robbins promptly cancelled a talk he was to give to the Cosmopolitan Society on the grounds that his colleagues should not be attacked in these ways. Now the Cosmopolitan Society was a non-political group whose purposes were to provide a coming together for overseas students and to encourage a mixing with their English brethren. It was a notably petty-minded gesture on Robbins' part. He could certainly be authoritarian from the comments that have occasionally become public. Kaldor noted in his interview with Shehadi that Robbins could make life 'rather unhappy' for those in the department who took different views from himself; and his reputation on the famous committee on higher education which bears his name was not wholly of a sympathetic liberal-minded chairman. I have always thought his intellectual reputation has been somewhat sanitised, and I noted with interest that Dahrendorf, in the LSE centenary history volume he was asked to write, thought it worthwhile to quote Hayek saying of Robbins that 'he had really very few original ideas'. Now Dahrendorf is a remarkably shrewd personality and in spite of his eminence in English academic life cannot be considered as part of the Establishment, of the Great and the Good that someone like Lord Annan supposed himself to represent; and the comment from Hayek on Robbins did not just slip in when Dahrendorf was half-asleep.

Hayek was always recognised as a more sophisticated theorist than Robbins. He was always more difficult to understand, only partly because of his accent in his lectures. But for myself and my contemporaries on the Left Hayek was damned by the withering review of *Prices and Production* by Keynes in *Economica* in November 1931. Keynes began by saying that the book was one of the most frightful muddles he had ever read. 'It is' he continued, 'an extraordinary example of how, starting with a mistake, a remorseless logician can end up in Bedlam'. Piero Sraffa was similarly dismissive in several places. This was not a devastation we were likely to forget. We were never offered Keynes as necessary or essential reading in our undergraduate courses and since Robbins et al were the examiners for our Finals there was no choice but to immerse ourselves in Wicksteed, Wicksell, Knight and, of course, their own writings. Keynes' *General Theory* was published in 1936 at the remarkable price of five shillings but there was no point in reading it for examination purposes. Naturally we discussed Hayek at length. One of my contemporaries was an unreconstructed fundamentalist of the economy of the free market. His name was not Arthur Seldon in those days, a fact which he forgot to mention in his entry for *Who's Who*. I thought him a nice man, very bright, quite modest but perhaps somewhat mousey. I was wrong about this last because Seldon, who remained undeviating in his ideas, came into his own from the 1970s with the growing influence of the free market ideas of the Institute of Economic Affairs of which he was a leading figure; and he was able to celebrate the developing inequalities of income and the other social misdemeanours of the Thatcher governments by accepting a CBE in the eighties.

I joined the student Communist Party towards the end of my first term. It is not difficult to understand why young people in the mid-thirties chose the Communist Party rather than the Labour Party. The catastrophe of 1931 was still in everyone's mind and from 1933 there was the new and frightening menace of fascism in Germany. The weak experience of the Labour Party and the right-wing trade union leaders in this decade before the war has remained with me throughout my life. The most wicked decision of these years, however, was undoubtedly Labour's support for the infamous Non-Intervention policy of the British and French governments – and especially of the British government. Support by Labour was withdrawn after eighteen months but by that time the scale of fascist intervention was considerable and the Spanish Republic was already on the way to defeat and the terrible decades which followed.

There were about twenty-five to thirty members of the LSE student Communist Party group at the time I joined. Membership figures always appeared somewhat imprecise, partly because of the uncertain numbers of evening students but more perhaps because people always seemed to be drifting in and out. I suppose at the maximum, which would be around 1937-38, there were between eighty or ninety members but these totals would include quite a number who were not very active, and whose membership might often be somewhat short-lived. There was always a very lively core who conducted their affairs in a notably intense manner and in the earlier years of the thirties sometimes in a conspiratorial atmosphere; some parts of which were no more than late adolescent play-acting. There were, however, more serious aspects of party membership. The general view that capitalism was a degenerate and declining system was contrasted with what was believed to be the bright star of Socialism in the Soviet Union. These beliefs were pervasive and powerful influences and they were greatly strengthened by the personalities of the Communist leadership of whom Harry Pollitt was outstanding.

Analytical narratives of the Communist experience in Britain are rare, in personal terms especially. There are the well-known accounts by the disillusioned of which those by Douglas Hyde and Les Cannon are among the best known; and there is the excellent, critical record by Malcolm MacEwen – *The Greening of a Red* – which deserves a much wider audience than it has so far received. The experience related by Raphael Samuel on the background to Communist Party recruitment and commitment is more commonly known. Raphael, tutor for decades at Ruskin College, Oxford, and a personal friend for as long, wrote three articles in 1985-7 that were published in *New Left Review* (Nos. 154, 156 and 165) under the general title 'The Lost World of Communism'. With the greater part of these writings I remain in disagreement, for what is offered is a mixture of his own personal experience, and events and happenings within the

Communist Party itself: a rambling and often inchoate political sociology. The concluding section of the first part was entitled 'Family Communism' and it was an account of his own life in his early years. For his mother's generation he wrote: 'Communism, though not intended as such, was a way of being English, a bridge by which the children of the ghetto entered the national culture'. For Raphael himself: 'Like many Communists of my time, I combined a powerful sense of apartness with a craving for recognition, alternating gestures of defiance with a desire to be ordinary and accepted as one of the crowd. If one wanted to be charitable, one might say that it was the irresolvable duality on which British Communists find themselves impaled today.' This last sentence was written in 1985 when the communist movement in Britain had already largely fallen apart, after years of decline.

I do not deny the validity of Raphael Samuel's own personal history, especially in his younger days, as he has set it down in these pages of *New Left Review*. The historian in him, however, might have acknowledged that it was a very unusual story, typical of some, perhaps many, Jewish comrades but not in any way relevant to the working-class militants who were joining the Communist Party at the time that Raphael was growing up in the 1940s. Nor was it appropriate for most of the non-Jewish intellectuals who were also becoming members. Anyone familiar with the social history of the American Communist Party, above all in the New York area, will recognise many similarities with Raphael's personal experience; but to apply his own history to the engineering shop stewards who joined in the decade before 1945, or miners or dockers – to suggest that they needed a sense of 'belonging' or a craving for 'recognition' – can only be described as absurd.

I joined the Communist Party with a growing sense of excitement at the widening intellectual horizons that Marxism offered. There were many things, inevitably, that I knew little or nothing about in the communist tradition, but I had enjoyed my schooldays within a comfortable and happy family life and I did not feel deprived or starved in any way. It seemed to me a very matter-of-fact decision. I was undoubtedly much influenced by the personalities I had come to know who were themselves members of the student Party. I mention these matters because there were undoubtedly some for whom joining the Communist Party was akin to religious conversion and for whom the Party, in capital letters, was equivalent to a religious order. This has been a common belief, hence the title of such books such as *The God that Failed*.

To work in any organisation of the political Left requires a dedication beyond the normal requirements of everyday life. There must be a conviction, however narrow or broad in scope, in the moral rightness of the activity one is engaged in. At its most uncomplicated it is a simple belief in right and wrong, and no one denies that adherence to a given set of beliefs always involves varying degrees of self-sacrifice and the subordination of self to what are accepted as higher purposes. Certainly this is true of left-wing politics, which in a capitalist society necessarily operate within a permanently hostile atmosphere. But this is an old country, with a native radicalism among ordinary people that goes back a very long way in history. The Communist Party grew out of these traditions, a source of both its strengths and its weaknesses.

It can certainly be acknowledged that there were those inside the Party whose political commitment took the shape and meaning of religious conviction. They were not a few; but in Britain, within my personal experience, most communists stopped short of that intense religiosity which Doris Lessing so beautifully portrayed in her short story 'The Day that Stalin Died'. The nearer one was to the Russian revolution of 1917 the more difficult it seems to have been to break with those early traditions. The record of the British Communist Party is not perhaps typical but not many who left at some point along their political career did so with a bitterness and rancour that remained in the years that followed. There was criticism but compared with the history of ex-communists in the United States or France the refrain of 'the God that failed' has not been very commonly heard. I estimate, and the calculation is a rough one, that at least four-fifths of the communist students of my generation had moved out of membership by 1950 or the early fifties. These were the years when in spite of the heroism of the Soviet peoples during the war – the major factor in the defeat of fascism – the nature and character of the Soviet regime were becoming increasingly known; and against the background of the tensions of the Cold War the exodus can be understood.

To join the student communist party at the end of 1934 was to belong immediately to a network of comrades and friends whose intellectual sophistication was both encouraging and intimidating. Students in their second year – Finalists were rarely seen – appeared to have read everything and were familiar with ideas and theories still beyond young neophytes. In my case it was Jean Macdonald – her family name – and James Jefferys whom I looked to as counsellors and instructors. Jean was already living with Peter Floud, whom she later married, and it was her shining intellectual abilities as well as her physical attractiveness that kept me shuffling my intellectual feet whenever we met. James Jefferys was somewhat different. We had a common interest in sport and he taught me to appreciate what is now called traditional jazz. His own intellectual record, after a somewhat indifferent start at school, was outstanding. Like Jean and in the same year he obtained an outstanding First, and he then went on to complete his Ph.D. in two years with a thesis that remained required reading for the next thirty years. In 1938 he was awarded one of the four scholarships to Harvard. In these years he became my closest friend.

The student party group organised its internal meetings with due respect for those who thought they were engaged in something equivalent to radical-revolutionary politics. Meetings always began with a political survey and in the discussion members were only expected to speak once, usually from prepared notes. It was a useful training for street corner meetings or for future teachers. There was always a 'contact list' reported on: this being the names of other students thought to be potential recruits with their 'minder' (although this description was not then used) offering the latest assessment. On the whole they were sensible and practical meetings largely concentrating on political work within the School, and their elementary discipline of behaviour in debate and discussion would have benefited many of the academic committees I was to endure in my next six decades. Looking back on these years the most important shift in my thinking, given what was still only a basic understanding of Marxism, was the sense of belonging to a world movement dedicated to an unyielding opposition to injustice and oppression. For many years now I have come to characterise Rajani Palme Dutt as an utterly disastrous influence within the British Communist Party, but his positive influence on me in the 1930s was the continuous discussion of colonialism and imperialism in each issue of *Labour Monthly*, possibly the only intellectual journal read by working-class militants. *Labour Monthly* was required reading for all student activists and the analysis presented by Palme Dutt could always be assured of serious discussion – and criticism. One of the accepted assumptions of our student discussions was a critical approach to political questions of all kinds. We bandied around a phrase about 'Bolshevik self-criticism' which was only used in a half-joking way but we were serious about a discriminatory evaluation of given political situations; within, of course, a generally accepted set of values. At this time no other group or party emphasised the central importance of internationalism as did the Communist Party and we all read the radical literature from the rest of the world. These would include the writings of Mulk Raj Anand, the contemporary Russian and American authors, and the translations of Silone, especially *Fontamara*. In my case I would add Malraux's *La Condition Humaine* which I had been given while still at school by the senior French master, and which I had to read again when I knew something of the historical background. We all knew the details of the case of the Scotsboro boys and we all went to see the revolutionary films of Eisenstein and Pudovkin.

I come back to Raphael Samuel and his long account of what membership of the Communist Party was supposed to entail. He was writing about the late '40s and early 1950s. Social life for Raphael and his comrades does seem to have been rather cheerless. They met in cafés rather than pubs ('there was quite a strong inhibition against drink'); ballroom dancing was apparently not regarded as proper activity for communists; he and his mates were 'suspicious' of 'trashy American music'; communists 'eschewed "foul" language – the "effing" and "blinding" of the politically illiterate'. It is not always easy in these three long articles to distinguish between Raphael's own practice and that expected of Communist Party members, but it adds up to a social life that sounds unbelievably dreary for a student generation. Certainly my decade before the outbreak of war was very different. My memory of life in the LSE student party was quite dissimilar for it was very lively, intellectually exciting, and fun. And this is emphatically not a matter of imprecise shapes and sounds sixty years ago. I loved dancing, and indeed the only thing I hope I ever had in common with Hugh Gaitskell was our common pleasure on the dance floor. Leonard Woolf entitled his volume of memoirs between the wars *Downhill all the Way* and he meant it in its pessimistic sense. On any rational assessment this was a reasonable description of an exceedingly unpleasant and grim period in world history. But we were young in the 1930s and youth has a resilience, a buoyancy and a spirit that shines through the darkening vistas of contemporary life. It was not that we were pharisaical in our denunciations of the evils of fascism, or the hypocrisy of our own politicians but we still had hope and there was a life before us. So alongside our serious academic study, our wholehearted support of Republican Spain, our deeply-felt emotions when the Spanish cause began to be overwhelmed, and our bitter denunciations of the appeasement of the fascist powers, we also led an active social life. It was the great period of French films with an outstanding generation of directors and actors. The films I remember most vividly – *Le Quai des Brumes, La Grande Illusion, Le Roi s'amuse, La Femme du Boulanger* and of course, after the war, Marcel Carné's *Les Enfants du Paradis* we saw at the Forum (with the trains running overhead) the Academy and the Everyman in Hampstead. And these cinemas also showed us the Marx brothers and the Three Stooges. The commercial circuits gave us American films, so much superior to English productions except, of course, for the brilliant documentaries of John Grierson and his colleagues. *Night Mail* with the script by Auden was especially memorable. And then we heard Paul Robeson sing at the great rallies for Spain and we saw him in *Plant In The Sun* at Unity Theatre. When Unity staged their wonderful pantomime *Babes in the Wood,* the University Labour Federation, a united body of socialists and communists, took the whole theatre for an evening. And in between we had lots of parties at which memory suggests we seemed to be singing most of the time. Certainly there was never any or much hard liquor, mainly because no one had much money. We saved for more interesting occasions. We fell in love and a week in Paris would cost no more than five pounds: a skilled worker's wage. We were young and learning about life was exciting.

My LSE bursary paid my fees and the County Major scholarship, which was more or less automatically awarded, covered most of my running costs during term. Christmas and Easter vacations I lived on the family, but I needed to earn as much as possible during the long summer vacation. Of my first summer of 1935 I have only vague memories of doing odd jobs round my home town; but for the next two summer vacations I struck the equivalent of student gold.

During the early weeks of the summer of 1936 James Jefferys asked me one day if I would care to walk with him down to Transport House in Smith Square, beyond the House of Commons and almost on the Embankment. He was going to confirm a job that had been offered him by the Workers Travel Association (WTA). It was a matter of a few weeks showing tourists round London, and as we walked he told me about the job and what was expected of him. It gradually occurred to me that as the WTA also operated abroad my quite reasonable French might help get a job on the Continent. So when we arrived I went up to see the overseas manager. His French was a good deal more anglicised than mine, and I came away with the promise of nearly three months in France and Switzerland. I was to be available from the last two weeks in June, and my starting salary would be three pounds and ten shillings, about the lower level of a skilled worker's wage.

My first instructions were to travel with a party from London to St. Malo in Brittany. I arrived at the terminus about 7.15 p.m. – the train was due to leave just after eight o'clock – and my group gradually assembled. There were twenty-nine on my list, all women, not a man among them. They were of mixed ages, mostly middle-aged or that is how they looked to their guide and mentor, aged twenty. I was, I suppose, somewhat surprised at the gender composition of my group, but my own family had always been an active social group and I never had inhibitions about talking with women of any age. Once we arrived in Brittany and settled into the five hotels scattered through St. Malo and Dinard my duties were hardly arduous. I visited the hotels in turn and accompanied the pre-arranged visits as interpreter and friend. It rained almost continuously the first week, but the hotels were reasonable and there were not many complaints. The weather turned into summer for the second week, and my services were less often required.

The permanent WTA representative at St. Malo, whose responsibilities seemed to be minimal, was an ex-British soldier from the First World War who had become an ardent pacifist. He had married a French woman and they lived in a house on the coast just outside the town. They were charming and hospitable; their names I have forgotten; and madame was a wonderful cook. This was my first experience of French domestic cooking and I spent more and more of my time with them, especially, of course, over dinner in the evening. I had also made friends with a working-class girl from Porthcawl in South Wales in whose arms I lay happily in the afternoons of the second week, when the sun shone and the beach was warm. Naturally I introduced her to the delights of Madame's cuisine.

I must have done enough of the right things during my inaugural fortnight because my salary was now increased to four pounds a week. I first acted as a courier on a couple of journeys to Basle, and then, from the latter part of July I was sent to Paris where I remained until late September, nearly nine weeks in all. I had missed the great Bastille Day demonstration of the Popular Front but this was the most exciting year of the interwar years. I read *L'Humanité* avidly and most days also *Le Populaire*, the paper of the French Socialist Party, and when I could I went to meetings and occasionally walked in demonstrations. What immensely heightened the political atmosphere was the beginning of the Spanish Civil War from the middle of July and the sharp tensions between the traditionalist pacifism of the Socialist Party and the demand from the Left for arms for Spain. I attended a Socialist Party meeting in early September – I think in the Luna Park – when Blum's defence of the non-intervention policy was not well received. The real enemy was, of course, the British government but the blackmail put upon the French government by the British Foreign Office was not to be revealed at this stage, and certainly not by the French Prime Minister. The disgraceful and infamous contribution made by the British government to Franco's victory is too seldom remembered.

I was the only WTA's representative for three fairly large hotels not far from Montmartre, which in those days was a fairly peaceful area and a main centre for tourists. My duties again, it will have been deduced, were not especially onerous. Work came in bursts, mainly when there were planned excursions to Versailles or to museums and general places of interest. My personal record was taking four separate groups round the Panthéon the same day.

There were other kinds of expeditions to be organised in the evenings for the men in my hotels, some of whom wanted to explore the fabled pleasures of the night life of Paris made notorious by Victoria's eldest son. 'I know an interesting place called Le Sphinx,' I would answer when I was sure that I had interpreted correctly their often stumbling requests. 'And you don't have to do more than drink.' Le Sphinx was becoming well-known in these years. At the end of the decade James Boswell, famous as one of *Left Review's* trio of cartoonists, made a series of large-scale sketches of the interior. It was a prix-fixe brothel with two medical inspections a week, and it was through the LSE soccer club that I had come to know of its existence. In the spring of 1936 the soccer club accepted a sporting arrangement with the Paris HEC (Hautes études Commerciales) whereby we would play one match each successive year in Paris and London, and offer the teams two or three days hospitality. We went to Paris first, and after dinner that night, from which I with others emerged somewhat drunk, we crowded into taxis and found ourselves in Le Sphinx, not knowing at first what it was. It was, evidently, well-known to our French hosts. The very large room we entered had mock furnishings such as an Egyptian palace might be conceived by someone whose knowledge was derived from popular magazines. There were present numbers of young women covered by short green skirts and nothing else. Some of the French students took off straight away and two of our own group finally walked away with their chosen women; but the rest of us sat around preparing for the next day's match by further drinking. We played early in the next afternoon in a large stadium as a curtain raiser to a professional match, and we actually won.

Le Sphinx was obviously the place to recommend to my enquirers; indeed

I knew of nowhere else. The alternative was to direct them to the streets. So I made contact with someone at Le Sphinx who turned out to be the main assistant to Madame. I explained my position as a representative of an English travel agency and I suggested that the customers I brought needed to be treated gently. I confined myself mostly to sitting with Madame's assistant or just at the bar and occasionally, if business was intermittent, with one or more of the 'workers'. I regret now that I was not more sociologically inquisitive about their own lives, but these were the days long before I ever heard of oral history. I ought to have been more questioning since I am sure that they would have talked; but surrounded by so many bosoms on such attractive young women, it is perhaps not surprising that my intellectual approach was less rigorous that it might have been.

I doubt whether I would ever have accepted the offers of free love that were occasionally made to me. To be determinate about one's emotions and personal reactions at a distance of sixty years is never easy, but I am reasonably certain because I had already met Adèle. During my first week in Paris I had gone with three of four of a hotel group into Montmartre for an evenings drinking and dancing; and Adèle had been sitting at the table next to mine. Adèle worked in a night club as a counter-girl taking in coats and doing a variety of jobs in the front of the house. I saw her at work one night when I took a group of tourists into her night club. By chance, because I did not know where she worked and it was on the recommendation of one of the hotels. She came from Normandy. She worked from 9 p.m. to about two or three in the morning with two nights off each week, and about once a fortnight she went home for one or two nights.

I got to know Paris well during these weeks. Life was bliss and Paris has remained for me the enchanted city. Sometime in mid-September Adèle announced she was leaving her job and going back to Normandy. She gave no reasons and as I was also leaving fairly soon we knew we had reached the end. I went with her to the Gare du Nord, or it might have been the Gare St. Lazare, and we said goodbye. She walked away, and I stood watching her, feeling my world was slipping away. Suddenly she dropped her bag, came running back and flung her arms about me: 'Wish me luck,' she said, 'I am getting married next month'.

I met her again some thirty years later. We had kept in desultory touch. I was camping in Normandy with friends and two of my children, and we arranged to meet for lunch in a small town about forty kilometres from her home town. She arrived in a *deux chevaux*; we greeted in French fashion, grinned hugely at each other and entered the small restaurant for a very good lunch, from which we emerged three hours later. She had married a solicitor, had brought forth three children and already there was one grandchild. The war in her part of Normandy had missed much of her local region, and as with most rural areas the food situation was reasonable. She was well-dressed and obviously enjoyed her life. We said goodbye to each other with affection at the discovery of our lives since the days in Montmartre, and agreed there was no point in maintaining further contact. A charming and a compassionate woman.

I arrived back in London in late September 1936 in time for the long advertised demonstration of Mosley's blackshirts through the East End of London. Sunday 4th October was to be an anniversary rally and march, with fascist groups from all over the country. There had been many protests and demands that the march should be banned but the Home Secretary, Sir John Simon, the equivalent in ob-noxious political attitudes to Michael Howard in John Major's administration of the 1990s, refused all requests. They came from a broad spectrum of opinion.

The plan of the march was that after an inspection by Mosley in Royal Mint Street the 'troops'(uniforms were not yet banned) would then march up Le-man street, past Gardners Corner and along Commercial Road, the heart of the East End. There was vigorous debate within the London Communist Party as to the proper tactics to be used. According to Joe Jacobs (*Out of the Ghetto*, 1978) whose version may be believed, there was at first a majority on the District Party Committee against straight physical force; but popular pressures were strong, and together with the ILP the London District of the Communist Party issued their call to all London workers to come out on the streets and prevent the fascists marching. The main places of rally were Gardners Corner and Cable Street.

The police, with every man and horse mobilised, finally cleared a way for the fascists to assemble in Royal Mint Street, and after further baton charges Leman Street and the Minories were also made ready for the fascists. But from then on it became an impossible job for the police although their officers did their very best. Gardners Corner was packed with people, as were all the streets around, and while there were baton attacks on different parts of the massed crowds no way through was possible. Our LSE group was in one part of Gardners Corner but we were not attacked. The only other way into the East End was through Cable Street and the battles there have gone into legend. Mosley was stopped.

From my early days at LSE I had already been on a number of anti-Mosley demonstrations. James Jefferys always used to wear a cloth cap stuffed with paper, not as might be thought to protect himself against the hard men of the fascists, but as a buffer against police batons. I do not remember an anti-fascist meeting where the police did not think it their duty to defend the fascists against their protestors. It was widely accepted throughout the East End and by the Left in general that the Metropolitan Police, from Sir Philip Game, the Chief Com-missioner, right down the line, were more sympathetic to Mosley's fascists than to the political opposition, which, of course, in the East End, included many Jews. Studies of the Manchester police have suggested that in similar incidents they were somewhat more even-handed than the London Met.; but in spite of the excellent work that has been done over the years by scholars such as Colin

Holmes and Richard Thurlow there is still too much buried in the archives. Secrecy in public affairs is, of course, a British disease, more virulent than in most other advanced industrial societies, and we urgently need, among many other constitutional changes, a Freedom of Information Act.

The day of Cable Street was my last political activity until after my Finals examination although very occasionally I took a day off, as when the Hunger Marchers arrived in Hyde Park for one of the largest demonstrations of the decade. Communist students were expected to work hard for Finals and achieve the best possible results in their university examinations. The slogan 'communist students must be good students' has sometimes been misunderstood. My own perception at the time, and ever since, was that only students who became competent in their academic work would be capable of understanding, and refuting, bourgeois ideas and theories. It seemed to me sensible, and this of course was long before anyone had read Gramsci.

So I began working: for the first two terms a minimum of twelve hours a day, excluding intrusions such as meals and the platonic joys of getting to know my new girl friend. In the last three months I worked sixteen hours every day. I continued to play soccer during my first two terms but this would mean on Saturdays only the equivalent of half a day's work. In my second year I had almost completely missed all lectures, with Laski's weekly inspiration the only exception. I was the organiser for the LSE communist group, and that inevitably took most of my time; numbers were growing and political activity was lively.

During my second year James Jefferys was working for Finals and he refused to talk politics of any kind, national or local. We had supper together almost every evening and we would spend a couple of hours discussing his work. Although our special subjects were different we had five papers out of eight in common (the ninth was the general essay paper). For some of the many questions we could not answer or were unsure about I would accept the job of reading the relevant literature and reporting back. These sessions with James were enormously stimulating although it was only in my own third year that I realised how important they had been for me.

My third year did not repeat this particular intellectual debate but talking so much with James had made me realise, among many other perceptions, the importance of constant discussion of intellectual problems. I missed the keen intelligence of James to stimulate me but there were a number of specialist economists I could talk with, including Erwin Rothbart, and this was always very helpful and provoking. Towards the end of my second year, in anticipation of things to come, I went through every examination paper for the previous three years, to try and delineate main areas of interest in the particular subject of the paper. I picked out eight or nine such areas for which I prepared as extensive a bibliography as I could compile. Each paper required four questions to be answered and provided I had not chosen my areas of interest too narrowly it would be unlikely, or unlucky, if at least two or perhaps three questions would not fall within the broad areas I had decided upon.

I had help in political history, one of my two optional courses. L. G. Robinson, who had been at the School since 1921, and who was Dean of Graduate Studies, presumably an increasingly onerous job, lectured for this paper in the second year. I went to two or three lectures and enjoyed them, but then politics took my time and I listened no more. During the first term of my third year a friend who was now a post-graduate student, offered me a complete set of notes from Robinson's lectures. I was never clear whether these had been re-written, but I would think so, without adding much, if any, additional material. Robinson was obviously a marvellously effective lecturer with a well-planned summary of the subject. These lecture notes were not only extremely useful to help put my own reading into order but they also began to alter my off-hand approach to lectures as such (Laski being always excluded from such comment). It was a lesson I hope I continued to learn and think about in my later academic career.

I took my Finals examination at the end of May 1937. I was expected by contemporaries to obtain a First, and I think that I myself assumed I would. In the event I obtained either six or seven alphas out of nine papers, five being required for a First. Lance Beales, the social historian, with whom I was to become friendly, told me I had six alphas, but a young lecturer whom I knew quite well said that he had been informed I had seven. Beales I think would be the more reliable source.

The results of Finals would not be out before August, and by then I would be half way through my second stint with the Workers Travel Association. I began in the second half of June and did not finish until the end of the second week in September. Before I started travelling I wrote my research scholarship application which Lance Beales edited for me. The proposed subject was a study of international capital movements from the UK between 1870 and 1914 and like all my friends I assumed that it would come to me as it had to James. In the meantime there was a whole summer in Europe.

The WTA offered me the job of courier between London and Basle, and this I did for the whole period of my employment that summer. I would leave London on Saturday evening on one of several trains which left for Dover, and there might be a couple of hundred WTA tourists, sometimes indeed enough to fill one whole train. From Dover there was a four hour ferry service to Ostend, arriving around two o'clock in the early morning. We would then board the long distance train to Basle, which kept always on the side of the Belgium-French border and arrive in Basle at about 3 p.m. on Sunday afternoon. At Basle, once I had handed over the various parties to the guides or hotel representatives who would take them to their final destinations, my duties were over; and the week was my own until the following Friday evening when I would join the train to

Ostend, and so to London by Saturday afternoon. I would have time for a bath at the station, a change of clothes, sometimes a very quick dash into central London and then back for the eight o'clock journey again to Basle. It was naturally tiring work from Friday evening until Sunday afternoon since there was little time to sleep with all the changes from train to boat and back again; and there would always be some problem to be sorted out, in addition to seeing that your passengers got their breakfast in reasonable time: an organisational matter that had its fraught moments. The train always stopped on the French side of the station at Basle and we would be met by the WTA permanent official and also by the various hotel representatives.

Gustav, who was the head waiter at the hotel in the Black Forest I usually stayed at during this summer always met each train from London. He was a good-looking thirty year old and he always met his group at Basle dressed in Black Forest costume and hose. He had excellent English. Not to put too fine a point on his personal history, he exercised a remarkable fascination upon many of his hotel guests. 'Never believe, John,' he once said to me, 'the stories you may hear about the frigidity of English women'.

The Black Forest was a favourite tourist region for the British. There was never any sign of fascist brutality and it apparently did not occur to these tourists that they were supporting a barbarous and bloodthirsty regime.

I myself on this first journey was advised by the WTA representative to go on to Interlaken in Switzerland where the WTA always occupied a large hotel. It was run by a Madame Burki, a widow of about fifty years of age with two daughters who worked with her. Madame Burki accepted me as one of the family and I stayed with them on several occasions. I had free board and could join any expedition that was planned.

There were, however, reasons for going into Germany. Jack Cohen had become the full-time Party organiser for the British student movement in 1936. His parents were Jewish immigrants from Lithuania, and Jack, born in 1905 in what was a very poor family, joined the Young Communist League at the age of sixteen and thenceforth remained active in the communist movement. In 1925 he became a full-time organiser and remained in official positions until his retirement in 1975. He was an extremely nice man and married an Oxford student from my home town. Margaret Gay was head girl of the local High School in the same year that I was head boy at mine. I must have told Jack about my summer job and that I was planning to go into Germany, for King Street, the CP headquarters, asked me to come in. I forget whom I saw, but they said they wanted someone to carry letters into Germany for the illegal German Communist Party. Assuming that I got through Customs unchecked all I had to do was to buy stamps in Germany and post them in named places. At the time it did not occur to me that the letters I was carrying might have been from the Soviet secret service, but although it would have made no difference it was obviously sensible to give me the story they did.

The most unusual, unexpected and exceedingly unpleasant experience I had during these summer months was a shipwreck in the English Channel. It was sometime in mid-August. We left Dover around 11 p.m. on Saturday night in a Belgian boat called the *Marie-José*. There were about 800 passengers on board and half a dozen couriers from different travel agencies with the man from Thomas Cook the only full-time professional. By this time we all knew each other quite well, and around one o'clock in the morning we were talking together on an upper deck. It was a beautifully clear night, the sea calm and we could see the lights on the French coast. There was about one hour before we docked at Ostend and we decided to go down for our usual meal. In the saloon I ordered an omelette as a starting course – our next food would probably be around midday – and my fork was poised to take my first bite when there was a quite extraordinary explosive noise from just above the few steps that led down into the saloon. The scene remains vividly in my mind today, some sixty years later. The room was immediately filled with pieces of flying debris, and smoke. We rushed up the steps and onto the middle deck. There were screams and shouting with the Belgian crew rushing around in varying degrees of panic. In general throughout they behaved rather badly. We could feel the boat slowly subsiding and then it settled. A couple of hours later I went down as far as I could and the saloon in which we were going to have a meal was now three-quarters full of water.

What had happened was that a British coal-carrier had smashed its way into the *Marie-José* somewhere around midships. After the collision the Belgian captain had run on to a sandbank and thereby had more or less stabilised our boat. We were about three miles off Dunkirk.

The ship which had burst its way into our boat had gone right through the lounge reserved for women, and there were at least a dozen serious casualties. I do not recall any medical officer on board; there was one doctor among the tourists and there were volunteers. With the Cook's agent as our No 1, the couriers set about doing what little could be done. We checked our own groups during the first hour and there were no casualities among the 200 or so WTA tourists. The women's lounge, where most of us worked, was a gruesome and bloody business, and it must have been at least two hours before boats came alongside with doctors and hospital orderlies and took off those seriously injured. We were told that other boats would be coming from Dunkirk.

The boats that came for us were quite small and we had to take our groups down into the ship to meet the line of the sea. When the tourists had been evacuated the couriers got into a boat all together and we were astonished to see the very large hole in the side of the *Marie-José* and just as appalled at the number of pieces of luggage that were floating around. When we reached the shore the coaches were waiting to take us to Ostend. All the train schedules were wholly chaotic and what worried us even more than the Ostend trains were the connections from Basle and these we knew would not wait. I managed to get through by phone to our emergency service in London with the information that none of our WTA people were among the injured, and I also spoke to our representative in Basle.

It was, inevitably, a ruined holiday for many. I spoke to some of our people on their return journeys, and heard their stories. I had stayed in Basle for a couple of days in order to help sort out problems, and I then went to my usual small hotel in Freiburg in order mainly to sleep. I have rarely in my life remembered my dreams, but for two or three nights that week I had nightmares. I finished my tour of duty with the Workers' Travel Association at the end of the second week in September, and during the next week I had the interview for the post-graduate award. I was not successful. Three days earlier I had turned down a job with an international company selling cosmetics. They interviewed me in a suite at the Savoy. So now I was unemployed, and I returned home to live with my parents.

I was always called Stama at school, and Stam at LSE, the latter my remaining friends still use. As does my wife. I had been christened in a Lincolnshire village church with the name of Orestes Stamatopoulos. My father was an upper-class Greek, my mother an English working-class young woman from the village of Morton, near Gainsborough in Lincolnshire. My parents had met in Lincoln where my mother had gone to work in a hospital at the outbreak of war in August 1914 and my father, who had arrived before hostilities began, was attached to one of the big engineering firms in the city. He had studied science and engineering at Athens and Heidelberg and had come to England for practical experience. My parents were married about a year before I was born on 2 April 1916 by which time my father had been called back to Greece for Army service, and within a year he was killed. It must have been a marriage much disapproved of by both families. My Greek family were well-to-do, royalist in politics and no doubt with the usual snobbery.

When the war ended a friend of my fathers, who always remained in contact with my mother and behaved decently throughout, conveyed the information that my Greek family were willing to take me to their condescending bosoms but not my mother; and this, not surprisingly, she declined. As far as I know further contact was never made, and for my part I have never felt any interest in my Greek relations. My mother would rarely talk about her life with my father, and I accepted what I thought was an understandable reticence on her part.

The marriage must also have caused a good deal of consternation on the English side although again I learned little of the various reactions. My mother had a sister – another daughter had died before she was twenty – and my aunt Lily had become a teacher. She had left home when she qualified and went to live and work in the south. Most of her life she lived in and around Hertfordshire. My aunt, who was quite an attractive woman, never married because, among other reasons, that would have meant losing her job in the teaching profession.

When I was a few months old my mother went to London in search of employment. I always assume from this that my father made little or no financial provision for her before he went back to Greece. She first had various jobs in the Isle of Dogs but her living conditions were appalling; and then she was accepted in one of the new occupations open to women in wartime, that of bus conductress and she moved to Streatham to be near her home garage. She found lodgings with a congenial working-class family with whom she and I remained on friendly terms for many years.

I had been left in Lincolnshire when my mother went to London, with a working-class woman who had been helping to look after me since I was born. She was one of those women sometimes revealed in biographies or oral testimony. She was midwife to the street, the support of all the women round her, and the door of her house was always open. She was gentle but tough-minded, immensely competent, and a good cook within the range of her husband's wage – when in work he was a boilermaker's labourer. She gave me all that children need: love and affection and the sense of being loved. I called her 'Mammy' and until my teens referred to her as my 'Gainsborough Mammy'. 41 Waterworks Street, where I spent my infant years, still exists. Our side of the street was one long row of houses each with a small front garden. The back of the houses looked on to a yard which served four houses, with low brick walls dividing each group of four. Across the yard serving each house was a lavatory, still an earth-closet until the late 1920s, and a small coal-house which also held the mangle and wash-tub. Water was drawn from an outside tap which served two houses. Cooking was done in an oven or on the open fire, and not until the mid-thirties did the Allisons have a gas ring installed.

When I was just passed my fourth birthday my mother took me away from Gainsborough and I went to live with my aunt in the south. After the war ended my mother had taken jobs as housekeeper within the London area but was not able to have me. She was not heedless of what my removal meant to Mrs Allison and I always spent time each year in Gainsborough, and I remained in contact until she died in the last year of the forties. What the break at the age of four meant for me it is not wholly possible to assess. Everyone has told me that I was a happy child and this is my own memory, but the separation must have left some mark on my personality. For Mrs Allison there was always sadness.

My maiden aunt was nearly thirty when I joined her in the village of Ayot St. Lawrence. She taught in the local school and lodged in a large sixteenth century house. My aunt was a lively, auburn-haired woman, active in the life of every village in which she taught, and usually president of the local Women's Institute: the most important social unit for working-class women in rural areas. At one time she was president of three village institutes in the Chilterns where she remained all her life, and she would cycle many miles after school to take her seat as president. She was a good teacher, much respected and fondly remembered by her former pupils, and while not over-demonstrative she gave me what must have been a sense of security and affection. I look back on my days with her with gratitude, since the change from Gainsborough must have been marked. Ayot St. Lawrence was where Bernard Shaw and Charlotte had decided to live. My aunt later told me of the talk he gave, at her invitation, to the local Women's Institute, in which he explained how he came to pick upon this particular village. The story was published in her memories of Shaw by Blanche Patch, housekeeper to the Shaws, but my aunt had told it to me many years earlier. Charlotte and Shaw were looking around the area for somewhere to move to, not too far from London, and when they came to Ayot they walked around the church and graveyard; and they came across a tombstone which read: 'Jane Eversley. Born 1815. Died 1895. Her time was short'. 'This was the place for me,' Shaw told the village women.

After I had been with my aunt for nearly a year, attending the local school, my mother found a position in London's East Ham where the man for whom she was to become housekeeper had agreed to let me join her. Then, in the spring of 1922, my mother answered another advertisement for a housekeeper with child and we met a man called Saville at Liverpool Street station, a meeting I can still recall. He lived in Romford, then a small country town with a cattle market each week, about twenty miles from the centre of London and on the line from Liverpool Street to Chelmsford and Southend.

We moved very soon to 96 Willow Street, Romford, and this became my home for many years. I was six years old, and Mr Saville, a widower, had a daughter, Eileen, some fifteen months older than myself. My mother quickly established a pleasant family atmosphere in the house. She was a highly competent woman, physically very strong, a good cook and generally a woman of sense and sensibility. In today's world she would have made her way. Soon after my tenth birthday my mother married Alfred Saville, and we celebrated by going on holiday in North Molton, a village on the edge of Exmoor, the first of many annual holidays in Devon.

My stepfather was a master tailor who worked in some sort of executive position in a small factory in Brentwood, about six miles down the line from Romford. I don't know what he earned, but in the 1930s his income was probably between five and six hundred pounds a year. In addition to his regular salary he worked at home on private commission. He was a good tailor, and quite a number of his Masonic friends had their suits made by him. We lived a comfortable and interesting life. Eileen and I easily fell into the roles of sister and brother. We went to the local elementary schools, and my mother, who was an active Anglican, sent us to Sunday School each week. When I was eight years old I joined the local church choir, made up in those days of only men and boys, and so on Sundays I was required at matins and evensong. Our house was a semi-detached, built in the late 1890s with an outside lavatory attached to the back of the house but with a bathroom that was not connected for hot water until the late twenties. Until then our nightly baths were in a tin bath in the kitchen. A telephone was installed in the thirties but we never had a car. My mother, Eileen and I rode bicycles. We had a good family life, well-ordered and pleasant. Until I was about ten years old my mother read to us most evenings, and when I was nine she began to include extracts from the humorous writings of Charles Dickens. I joined the Cubs and Eileen the Brownies and later we moved up to the Scouts and the Guides. My step-father was an efficient handyman. In the late twenties he built several wireless sets and he was a keen gardener, with a small greenhouse in which he grew salad foods. In the thirties, of course, the wireless, as for most families, was an important part of our lives. My mother had taught me to swim soon after we came to Romford and in our early teens we began playing tennis every Saturday with the Church club. The Church was an important part of our lives until I went to University. It offered a very lively social life and there were parties and outings, especially for teenagers. I was never seriously committed to a religious faith, and by fourteen, the year I was confirmed – which meant that I could take Holy Communion – I had become consciously an atheist but there was no point at all in removing myself from what was becoming an increasingly interesting social life.

There were two grammar schools in the area, both single sexed. The Royal Liberty School, so named after the Royal manor of Havering-Atte-Bower, was about two miles from Romford in the village of Gidea Park: a largely commuter district of mostly lower to middle class. The school had been founded just after the end of the war and in the 1920s took in fee-paying pupils with a quite large quota of scholarship boys, whose group I joined. The 'Liberty', as it was always referred to, was a lively school with a notable absence of snobbery towards the 'scholarship boys'. Most of my own personal friends were fee-paying and lived in houses more middle-class than mine. During my years from 1927 to 1934 a new teaching block, large gymnasium and open-air swimming pool were added to the original buildings, the last being financed mainly by the Parents Association. It stood in its own large grounds. When I left in 1934 there must have been about six hundred boys on the registers.

The teaching was well organised and adequate to very good. Most pupils left at sixteen or after one year in the sixth, and went into business or the executive grade of the Civil Service or banks or solicitors' offices. The sixth form provided the school prefects and the Head Boy, but it was always quite a small group, especially in its second year. The number of university entrants was no more than two or three each year. Until I was about thirteen I read voraciously, mostly the usual schoolboy reading of Henty et al but encouraged by my mother I also read a number of the novels of Dickens. With the approach of puberty I began to explore the mysteries of life with the help of girls from the convent at Brentwood, to which the more snobbish of the local petty-bourgeois sent their daughters rather than to the High School in the town. All this was within the social life of the Church. I was continuing to attend Church and after I was confirmed I became a server, an assistant to the priest in the Anglican Church: naturally much to my mother's pleasure. While I now had no interest at all in the religious observances, I greatly enjoyed the singing and later in life was grateful for the knowledge I acquired of the Old and New Testaments, not yet, praise be, in their modern translations. Our parents were wholly unaware of the private lives we lived and as far as I remember – and certainly this was true of myself – there was no open youthful rebellion. Life in the home went on as always.

Until the age of sixteen, when I took the equivalent of O levels, I was uninterested in academic work, much to the dismay of my mother. I was becoming increasingly competent at most sports, except cricket, and very active in my Scout troop. We had four troops in the School. We camped every Whitsun and each summer there were two fortnightly camps arranged in Europe to choose from: France, Holland, Belgium or Switzerland. I always went with my own troop's arrangements. A fortnight's camping and travel normally cost five pounds. No one was allowed more than one pound sterling for pocket money. On two summers I went for eighteen days to the south of France for the enhanced rate of six pounds. We often camped just outside La Ciotat, between Marseille and Toulon. On several days when we were at La Ciotat we walked along the cliffs to Cassis, unaware, of course, that we might have seen one or more of the Bloomsbury group whose favourite village it seems to have been.

We engaged for several years in a rather special kind of vandalism. On the long distance trains there were always plaques which exhorted the passengers not to lean out of the windows or not to use the toilets in stations; and since the trains went across national boundaries these plaques, which were of enamel and screwed into the doors or walls, always described their message in more than one language. It was not difficult to unscrew the enamel plates but the central endeavour, which involved walking through the train and into every vacant toilet, was to find plaques in three or even four languages. My own personal triumph was a 'do not use the toilet in a station' in four languages: French, English, German and Italian. When I was fifteen my mother found my now large collection in a drawer in my bedroom and she was horrified; and all my beautiful plaques were tipped in the dustbin.

I took ten O levels and passed in five only, but fortunately with the right kind of combination, so I was allowed to enter the sixth form and take the London Intermediate examination after two years. For reasons which I cannot explain I now began to enjoy working seriously and for long hours. No doubt it was connected with the excellent teaching in all the five subjects in the social science syllabus. I still played a range of sports and in my last year I was Captain of the school, and captain of association football, swimming and athletics. In all three I represented my County. I took five subjects in the London Intermediate and obtained distinctions in three; but not in French although I was evidently on the borderline. But French was my joy and my French master was the famous Whitmarsh who began writing textbooks for schools which became widely used on both sides of the Atlantic wherever French was taught from an English background. He made a great deal of money. He was charming, extremely well-read in general and up-to-date in contemporary literature. He gave me Céline's *Voyage au bout de la nuit* but did suggest I might find it somewhat difficult. It was indeed more or less incomprehensible to me at the age of seventeen, but I managed to make more sense of Malraux's *La Condition Humaine* although I had to wait until my historical understanding was a good deal more sophisticated before I really appreciated what he was saying. Whitmarsh was wonderful, and he gave me a feeling for France and the French language which has remained. The other outstanding teacher in my fields of study was Bill Spedding, a somewhat irascible, strict disciplinarian who taught history and economics. History was his main subject. He was also sports master and we remained friends for many years. My schooldays were happy and enjoyable. It was later, in my last year at LSE, that I changed my surname to that of my stepfather and added the forename of 'John'.

The rejection of my research scholarship application left me with no immediate possibility of a future academic career. My mother and stepfather were understandably not at all happy to have me unemployed and living at home, but there developed a family crisis which concentrated their minds on other matters. My step-sister Eileen, with whom our amiable relationship had continued through our teens, had begun an affair with François Lafitte. François was the younger of the two sons of Francise Delisle, the companion of Havelock Ellis for the last thirty years or so of his life. François himself had been an original member of the Oxford October Club in the early thirties, and after graduation had worked in various political organisations. Then in 1937 he joined the staff of PEP (Political and Economic Planning) a liberal research group which had been established in the early thirties and which quickly developed an excellent reputation. Eileen and he were madly in love with each other. My parents discovered the relationship and after a series of volcanic rows Eileen left home to live with François in south London near his mother and Havelock who gave them their moral support. Back in Romford it was an exceedingly unhappy time. There was a reluctant conciliation after eighteen months and Eileen and François were married from our house in the year the Second World War began.

I had been able to escape much of the family trauma. After a few weeks I had been offered voluntary work, with travelling expenses paid, by Dorothy Woodman of the Union of Democratic Control, an organisation now largely forgotten except by historians. It had been founded in the very early days of the First

World War by a group of radical liberals. E. D. Morel, who had become known for his campaigning abilities against the Belgian atrocities in the Congo, was secretary, and the new organisation attracted a number of influential intellectuals and politicians. It was a radical rather than a socialist body. Morel died in 1924 and three years later Dorothy Woodman became secretary, to dominate its politics and policies for the next quarter of a century.

Dorothy Woodman was born in 1902, the daughter of a Wiltshire farmer. Politically she seems always to have been a left-wing member of the Labour Party, and in the early thirties she became close to Kingsley Martin, already editor of the *New Statesman*, and they took house together in 1935 at 16 James Street, in the Bloomsbury area of central London.

Throughout the 1930s, and during the years of war that were to follow, Dorothy Woodman and the UDC were at the centre of the anti-fascist and anti- colonial struggles. Just before I finally came back to England from my tourist agency work in mid-September 1937 Dorothy had organised the China Campaign Committee following the outbreak of large-scale war by the Japanese against China in July 1937. It was an exciting privilege to be accepted as a voluntary worker at the offices in Victoria Street. A stream of highly interesting people came through the office to talk with Dorothy or to interview her or to take her out to lunch. Claud Cockburn's *The Week* occupied a small room on the top floor of the building, and although Claud was rarely to be found there he was sometimes to be seen, usually rushing out of a taxi or frantically trying to get one. On one, for me historic, occasion Dorothy took me out to lunch with Kingsley Martin and Claud, and I met the latter a couple of times in a local pub with some foreign journalist and he always included me in his conversation. I was worked hard in the office under the efficient direction of Hilda White, Dorothy's secretary and I also became used as an outside speaker. The UDC were constantly being asked for lecturers and increasingly my subject was China and the Japanese aggression. Political support for China at this time has been somewhat overlooked by historians of the period, mainly, of course, because of the dominating issue of the Spanish Civil War and the growing menace of fascism in Europe; but there were activities in most of the big cities in support of the boycott of Japanese goods. The China Campaign Committee took the Queen's Hall in early November 1937 when Paul Robeson sang to a packed audience. My own small audiences for the China Campaign Committee were mostly Left Book Club groups of middle-class and professional people.

I was still living at home during my months with the UDC and my parents, my mother in particular, were becoming increasingly restless at my continued failure to achieve full-time employment; and through the father of one of my former grammar schoolmasters I was reluctantly seconded as a supply teacher to a Church of England primary school in my home town. I proved hopelessly incompetent as a teacher of nine- and ten-year-old children and quite inadequate

in maintaining discipline. Fortunately it only lasted five weeks. My flow of letters for jobs increased dramatically and one actually brought an interview. I was
accepted as personal assistant to the secretary of the Dictaphone Company at a
salary of three pounds and ten shillings a week. I was to work in offices in Oxford
Street not far from Oxford Circus.

My first decision after accepting this job was to inform my parents that I was
proposing to live in London during the week and come home at weekends. My
mother was upset, not least I would guess, because she knew that I would be
sharing a flat or house with my girlfriend. I had met Constance Saunders three
days after the academic session began in early October 1936, very soon after I
had returned from my two months in Paris with the WTA. Half way through
the Fresher's dance I saw a young woman, obviously one of the new generation,
sitting with two others. She was wearing a green dress and I went over before
the next dance and asked her to join me, but she explained she could not dance.
She later told me that she was somewhat embarrassed for her two companions
because she had already been asked two or three times, while the two young
women she was with had not been approached by anyone. She was beautiful,
with a wonderful complexion, and a great plait of hair round her head. I must already have started to become bewitched because I continued to stand in front of
her and pleaded to be allowed to push her round the floor. She was right about
her lack of dancing skills; evidently her family life had not included many social
occasions. This, however, was the beginning, and as I write these words sixty
years later, unless she is in the garden using her skilful green fingers, she will be
in the room below my study, at the front of the house which faces south: and
she will be reading, or listening to music, or practising her considerable abilities
as an embroideress. Among her other enduring qualities, she possessed what
Jane Austen's Captain Wentworth said he wanted in the woman he married: 'A
strong mind, with sweetness of manner'.

We found a flat at 47 Lambs Conduit Street. off Theobalds Road, a few minutes
walk from Holborn Tube station and within ten minutes of LSE. It was a top flat
with a rent of thirty shillings a week. We were next door to a funeral parlour. The
flat had a kitchen, bathroom, one large room and a small bedroom. The large
room was all-purpose and for a time in the small room we had Bert Turner and
his girlfriend as lodgers (Bert being the H. A. Turner who in due course became
Professor of Industrial Relations at the University of Cambridge.) We had lots
of parties at Lambs Conduit Street, mostly non-alcoholic, as I have explained,
and very noisy with talk and singing. All left student groups had a considerable
repertoire of songs, French and American as well as from our own traditions.
Unity Theatre had added many, quite a number getting themselves on to Topic
Records. Our parties were marvellously enjoyable.

The job with the Dictaphone Company was quite uninteresting. Fortunately
the work was not arduous; my boss was often away at the main office in King-

sway, and I had a fair amount of time for political activity during office hours. The most interesting contacts I had at this time – that is, through most of 1938 – were with the leaders of the London district of the National Unemployed Workers' Movement. The London secretary was Don Renton who had fought in Spain in the newly formed British Battalion commanded by Tom Wintringham. Renton had been quite seriously wounded and then captured by the Spanish Foreign Legion. He remained in prison, under harsh conditions, until he was exchanged in the early summer of 1938; and he stayed in London until the outbreak of war in September 1939.

The unemployed marches and agitation of the NUWM have been largely written out of public memory. The exception is the Jarrow March of October-November 1936 which arrived in London a week before the NUWM contingents. When the BBC produced a documentary on the 1930s, as they did in 1996, Jarrow was the only unemployed demonstration noticed. Yet the Jarrow March was of a quite different order. In the first place it had the support of the whole of Jarrow Town Council which included quite a large group of Tory councillors. The Labour Party had not long been in a majority and Ellen Wilkinson, who was Labour MP for the Jarrow constituency, estimated that about thirty per cent of Jarrow workers still voted Tory. The Jarrow March, from its outset, was always to be a non-political affair; and to underline the fact, ahead of the marchers went the two election agents for the division: Councillor Suddick, a Tory councillor and the Labour agent. The Jarrow marchers received a good deal of newspaper publicity but their arrival in London exhibited their lack of organisational skills. There was no mass demonstration in Hyde Park and their welcome at Westminster, when they presented their petition, was inadequately handled. This was in marked contrast with the NUWM reception. There had already been agreed some sort of understanding with the Parliamentary Labour Party, the London Labour Party and the London Trades Council, and not only did Attlee speak from one of the six platforms but two days later he moved in the House of Commons that the marchers should be allowed to appear at the Bar and state their grievances. After a debate of three hours his motion was defeated. There was a farewell rally in Trafalgar Square on the following Sunday and the next day all the marchers returned home, their railway fares coming from collections.

I was myself present at the great demonstration in Hyde Park which greeted the arrival of the various contingents of marchers from different parts of Britain. It rained almost the whole day and I listened at the platform from which Nye Bevan spoke. Estimates of the size of working-class demonstrations by the police, the press and other observers have always been widely different. On this occasion the *Daily Herald*, always vigorously anti-communist and therefore never favourably disposed towards the NUWM, offered the figure of 250,000 that had gathered in the Park. I cannot claim to have counted a quarter of a million but the Park was full, that I can testify. The police estimate was 12,000, a figure which some historians have been foolish enough to accept. The *Daily Worker* reported 100,000.

Hannington was an organiser of great ability and he was supported by some remarkable militants who included Harry MacShane and Will Paynter. Hannington had a lively sense of humour and was full of good stories. In the years between the wars he was jailed on five occasions and on one of his many arrests Bernard Shaw stood bail for him. Hannington loved re-telling the occasion. After the magistrate had gone through the normal procedures of identification and having fixed the bail at £100 he then asked Shaw the usual question: 'Are you worth £100?' 'Well, your Honour,' replied Shaw, 'That is a very interesting question. You see, I have £100, but I really don't know whether I am worth it.'

The work of the NUWM, which has been neglected by later commentators even more than their national demonstrations, included their daily help to unemployed workers where they had representatives or branches in the matter of the regulations for various kinds of benefit. The legal branch of the NUWM was always overworked and Hannington himself was probably the most competently qualified in the intricacies of unemployment benefits and support of anyone in the labour movement. Except for the 1936 March the NUWM marchers were always very roughly treated by the police, especially in the London area. The formation of the National Council for Civil Liberties was a direct response to the fears of mishandling by the police of the national marchers in early 1934.

To return to Don Renton, he came back to England at a time when national hunger marches were no longer a practicable way of encouraging attention to the problems of the unemployed. 1937 was the peak year of economic growth in the 1930s, although there were still one million unemployed, and the threatened downturn in 1938 only began to be offset by the expansion of the rearmament programme. What rekindled the possibilities of new activity was the introduction by the government in August 1938 of special regulations which permitted the Unemployment Assistance Board to give extra allowances to the unemployed during the winter months. The new regulations came into operation from 4 November and the NUWM soon discovered that the great majority of claimants were being refused extra money. Hannington recognised that here was the basis for a new agitation but appreciated that it would have to be of a new kind. 'Starvation was not news in Fleet Street ' he wrote at this time and he began serious discussions with Renton and others as to what could be done. He laid down certain conditions which must be met in future demonstrations: surprise, physical practicability, immediate relevance and all within the general context of activity which must encourage, and not alienate, public sympathy.

Their first demonstration was a lie-down in Oxford Circus by about two hundred men. Don Renton knew that I worked in Oxford Street and he asked me to observe how things developed and what problems might have to be avoided in the future. I agreed, of course, and suggested I might help in a minor way by telephoning police stations for a mile or so round the Circus offering false information about various communist disturbances likely to take place in locations well away from Oxford Circus. We mapped out all the police stations to be phoned and the various locations to be suggested. The lie-down was due to take place at Oxford Circus at 3.15 p.m. on the 20th December, and I was to telephone the selected police stations from a few minutes after three o'clock We had arranged a public phone box near my office to be occupied by two members of the NUWM so that I should not be delayed. I went out with my list of telephone numbers, and phoned them in turn. 'This is the *Daily Mail* press room,' I said, 'and we have information that the unemployed are staging a big demonstration at Westminster Bridge,' and then I put the phone down and went on to my next call. At 3.15 p.m. when the lights on their crossing turned red the unemployed lay down on their particular part of the road. The traffic continued to stop when the lights turned against them and soon there were men lying down right round the Circus, and the hold-up of traffic extended through Oxford Street and in all the other streets leading to the Circus. Naturally the London evening papers and the national papers on the day following wrote the headlines.

Two days later Don Renton led a hundred unemployed workers into the Ritz Grill Room and asked to be served with tea. Each man had two pence for the service. Renton explained to the waiters why the unemployed were there and after making sure that the press had got the story the workers got up and filed out. There were some equally successful demonstrations which filled the newspapers. On Christmas Day 150 carol singers met outside the house of Lord Rushcliffe who was chairman of the Unemployment Assistance Board, in Ashley Gardens, Victoria. They sang, of course, their own versions of traditional carols. The demonstrations continued in the New Year, and were now especially centred upon the famous Black Coffin which first appeared at a mock funeral on New Year's Eve which started from Trafalgar Square and ended at St. Pauls. The coffin was made of plywood and was the work of an ecclesiastical carver who belonged to the Stepney branch. It was used in a number of demonstrations in the New Year, nearly always the object of a struggle between the police and the unemployed for possession. On the outside of the coffin were painted different slogans: 'He did not get winter relief' was one. The whole story of the demonstrations of this winter was told by Hannington in a Fact booklet entitled *Black Coffins and the Unemployed* published in May 1939. The Fact booklets were monthly publications of around 100 pages edited by Raymond Postgate, and some still provide useful documentation. I myself took part in a small lie-down in Piccadilly Circus but the police must have been forewarned for we were soon overwhelmed.

I had continued to apply for jobs during my time with the Dictaphone Company and not long into the New Year of 1939 I was accepted as a research economist by the British Home Stores. The salary was five pounds a week, a considerable advance on my existing wage Britain. Among the top management the most intelligent was a Jewish Central European immigrant called, I think, Rubinski. I remember him as a man of the sharpest intellect and insight and it was he who suggested to the board that training an economist might be sensible. 'But you mustn't become over-theoretical' he said to me at our first meeting, 'and the first requirement is that you must learn something about how things work'. His standards for BHS were set by Marks and Spencer, which he estimated as the best chain-store in Europe, and all the store managers I met had fully imbibed the gospel preached from Head Office. To ensure that I did not become too theoretical Rubinski planned a nine-month course out in the stores. I was to start at the bottom and be given experience at different kinds of stores and at different levels of management. I began with a fortnight's stint as porter at Kingston-upon-Thames. I staggered back each night to Lambs Conduit Street exhausted and consoled myself the following morning that it was only going to last a fortnight. Thereafter working life was always quite hard but endurable. I went round the country, a month or so at a time, and I ended my last two months, which took me to Christmas 1939, as deputy manager of a newly opened store in Sunderland. The reports on me, with one exception, were satisfactory and I moved into Head Office in Baker Street at the beginning of 1940.

The 1930s came to an end for me between the late summer of 1939 and my call up for the Army in the spring of 1940. The growing political sympathy towards the Soviet Union was one of the most striking features of the British Labour movement in the 1930s. It was the coincidence in time between the beginnings of the world economic crisis at the end of 1929 and the launching of the First Five Year Plan that brought about a much deeper interest in contemporary Russia. Her industrialisation seemed to offer the sharpest contrast with the collapse of output and the rapid rise of unemployment levels in the capitalist world. As the dole queues lengthened, and families became grimly familiar with the problems of subsistence without the wages of work, it was understandable that increasing numbers of working people, and intellectuals, should begin to look upon Soviet Russia with a new appreciation. The Webbs, so long the expositors of the reformist and moderate Fabian tradition, mirrored these changes in their writings.

It is a serious defect of much political and historical commentary upon this period that it fails to understand the points of view from which Russia was mainly judged during the decade of the 1930s. For the mass of people in Britain, unemployment and job insecurity were the biggest facts of their lives. Economic historians have rightly emphasised the improvement in real incomes during the 1930s, but what mattered most for working people was a job or the regular nature of the job. Unemployment in Britain was always above the one million level, even in 1937, the most prosperous year of the decade, and the widely accepted claim that the Soviet Union was growing so rapidly that there was a labour shortage, especially of skilled workers, had a very considerable appeal. The literature favourable to the Soviet Union was quite remarkable in its volume, and much of it emanated from non-communist sources. Most important of all was the Webb's *Soviet Communism. A New Civilisation?* published in 1935. The question mark was removed for the edition of 1937. Sir Bernard Pares in *Moscow Admits a Critic(1936)* was especially notable as the views of an eminent Russian scholar who had altered his position from hostility to one of general sympathy with the Soviet regime.

One of the more important aspects of the pro-Soviet attitudes of the 1930s was the image that became accepted of Joseph Stalin. Citrine, for example, while highly sceptical of the processes of democracy in the Soviet Union, gave a not unflattering account of the man himself. Western countries' politicians and diplomats had little personal contact upon which to build an appraisal, and Stalin gave few interviews but from those reported he seems to have made upon the West the general impression of a highly controlled, intelligent leader. His conversations with Howard, the American publisher, and with H. G. Wells, were widely read and commented on. The Stalin- Wells talk was published in the *New Statesman* (27 October 1934) and led to a famous exchange between Wells and Bernard Shaw. Typical of the liberal attitude, and one that must appear astonishing to later generations, was the assessment of Stalin in John Gunther's *Inside Europe.* It was a book that had a phenomenal sale in Britain and America. It was first published in January 1936 and by October the British edition had gone through fourteen impressions, and a second revised edition came out in the same month. Gunther gave a blistering account of Mussolini and Hitler and their regimes, but while he did not slur over the harsh facts of the 'Iron Age', his approach to the Soviet Union was immeasurably more understanding and sympathetic. The commentary on Stalin which follows is taken from the first edition:

> Let no one think that Stalin is a thug. It would be idle to pretend that he could take a chair in fine arts at Harvard; nevertheless his learning is both broad and deep, especially in philosophy and history. One is instinctively tempted to consider this reticent Georgian as a roughneck, a man of instincts and muscle, not of brains. But his speeches quote Plato, Don Quixote, Daudet; he knew all about the monkey trial at Dayton and the composition of Lloyd George's shadow cabinet and the unionisation of workers in America; in his talk with Wells he showed as much knowledge of Cromwell and the Chartists as Wells himself ... Nor are his manners bad. He sees visitors only rarely, but one and all they report his soberness, his respectful attention to their questions, his attempt to put them at their ease ... is the only dictator who is serene.

And so on. The new Soviet Constitution of 1936, often referred to as the Stalin Constitution, underlined for much of the outside world the move away from the

'Iron Age' towards a more democratic way of life. By 1937 the overriding factor in the general assessment of the Soviet Union was her foreign policy in relation to the growing threat of war from the fascist countries. The Soviet Union, for the greater part of the labour movement, and for many outside, stood in sharply defined contrast to the appeasement policies of the propertied classes in Western Europe, with Neville Chamberlain as their leading figure. Appeasement meant not only the encouragement of the hope that Hitler would look to the East for territory but it also immediately involved the destruction of Republican Spain.

This was the background against which there took place the debates on any scale among the Left concerning the nature of Soviet society. The purge trials of 1936 to 1938 were seriously discussed although the rapidly worsening international situation considerably restricted – indeed often inhibited – the range and depth of the discussion. For many decades it has been accepted that the trials were without question a gigantic confidence trick; a frame-up of quite extraordinary ingenuity and invention.

The trials were intensely debated in my student circles and we read all the transcripts that were available. There were some American research students who were consistently critical but for myself, and most of my friends, it was Alec Nove who provided the anti-Stalinist arguments. He was at this time still using his family name of Novakovsky and while never a member of the student Communist Party it was with us that he mostly discussed his politics. Constance knew his mother quite well, and liked her very much. They were a Menshevik family and were, of course, very well-informed. Naturally, given the general appreciation of the Soviet Union it was going to take a great deal of evidence and persuasion to encourage scepticism, and there were matters which it was not at all easy for those who understood the trials to make their case.

The trials were open, dozens of Western journalists and diplomats were present. The defendants were almost all with long records of revolutionary activity. There were no signs of physical torture. Radek joked with the court, and Bukharin argued with, and rejected, a number of the accusations put to him by Vishinsky the Prosecutor. But no one – except Krestinsky in the last trial and he retracted the following day – spoke a word which suggested the evidence was faked. There was a volume of testimony which insisted on the correctness of the judicial procedures. The newspapers reporting the trials were world wide and the pamphlet and book literature was considerable, with the overwhelming conclusions in favour of the genuineness of the trials.

The range and degree of scepticism on the Left, even in Britain, was, however, greater than is sometimes recognised. The most remarkable analysis by a contemporary British observer was published in *Unto Caesar* by F. A. Voigt, the *Manchester Guardian*'s diplomatic correspondent. Voigt, a liberal-minded and intelligent Conservative, put his main commentary on the trials, rather oddly, in a six-page footnote at the end of the volume, but his careful analysis of the verbatim records of the trials offered serious questions that never reached the mainstream of the Left of the labour movement. His paper, the *Manchester Guardian*, of all the liberal and radical prints, was the most cogent and compelling in the information it offered for its own scepticism. Its correspondence columns would be worth serious evaluation. Included were letters from Russian émigrés, many from Menshevik groupings, mostly with Paris addresses, as well as members of Continental Social-Democracy. Nearer to the Labour movement was the *New Statesman* which for the most part articulated clearly the problems and dilemmas of the situation. H. N. Brailsford, the outstanding socialist journalist of the inter-war years, consistently regretted and sharply criticised the trials. The most persistent sceptic was Emrys Hughes, editor of the Scottish *Forward*, who flatly refused to believe that the confessions were genuine, and who throughout the period of the trials was constantly attacking the court procedures and asking his readers to disbelieve the 'fantastic' stories that were being told by the defendants. *Plebs*, the organ of the National Council of Labour Colleges, was also hostile, but it was a monthly with a fairly limited circulation. The right-wing of the labour movement, not unnaturally, was always sceptical and questioning.

There are a number of problems for British historians. One is why the responses within the British Left were less critical than those in either France or the United States. There was, as I have suggested, more doubt and scepticism than is often recognised but it was not of the same order of magnitude in either of the countries mentioned. At the time of the trials it seems to me now that there were two major reasons, in addition to those lesser factors briefly touched upon, why the political implications of the Stalinist terror exercised so little influence upon my generation. The first was that no defendant was prepared to use the open court to deny what was being alleged against them. The question: 'Why did no one stand up as Georgi Dimitrov had done in the Reichstag trial and denounce the Court' was the most telling argument from those who were defending Soviet justice; and it was a question and an argument which went far beyond Communist Party circles. Isaac Deutscher put exactly the same question into the mind of Trotsky's son, Leon Sedov, who was living in Paris during the period of the trials. Perhaps the most important factor affecting the attitudes taken towards the trials was the international situation. My generation was inevitably dominated by the rapidly growing threat of fascism and war. Bukharin was shot on 15 March 1938, three days after the Germans marched into Austria. The events of the years leading up to 1939 underlined the arguments of the Soviet Foreign Minister, Litvinov, that only the firm and steadfast opposition of the Western bourgeois democracies and the Soviet Union could withstand fascist aggression. Spain was the touchstone.

I find myself also in broad agreement with those who argued for a general support with one crucial addition which was not present at the time but painfully developed over the succeeding years. What we were witnessing were the early years of the destruction of the socialist commonwealth in Soviet Russia and the increasing degeneration of socialist ideas. It was the years of the Second World War after the Nazi attack on Russia and the extraordinary heroism of the ordinary Russian people that further held back the appreciation of what Stalinism involved. Inevitably there was weakened the understanding of what Ernest Mandel once described as 'the hideously distorted socialism' which in 1917 had been the hopes of so many. I make these as historical judgements, not in any way as apologetics, for the progress of humanity through the centuries has been, and will no doubt continue to be, for the majority of peoples, in the words of Thomas Hobbes, 'nasty, brutish and short'.

Part 2: **The War Years**

I was called up around the middle of April 1940, and for some reason – presumably because I had a university degree – I was first given an interview by a not very bright colonel. When he learned that I was working for British Home Stores he became a good deal more distant and begun mumbling about their share market record in the past by which I assumed he had lost on his investments. His memory was correct for there had been a severe drop in an earlier period. Whether he had the authority to recommend me for an Officer's Training Course I do not know, but it may be assumed. It may also be understood that I did not impress him, since I next found myself on the way to an anti-aircraft training barracks at Arborfield, in Berkshire. The nearest town was Wokingham.

At Arborfield I found myself in a Nissen hut with around two dozen other recruits. They were all working class except for one Jewish middle-class young man, Laurie Lipson by name, a public school boy who happened to be allocated to the bed next to mine. Beyond him was a dark-featured rather unhealthy but shrewd-looking character who later, several weeks later, told that he had been chauffeur to Oswald Mosley. By this time we three had become friendly in the way that one often, in the early weeks of a new situation takes those nearest to you among a group of strangers. 'Butch', Mosley used to call him, but he did not speak much about his days with the fascists, in part at least because it must have become clear immediately that we were not wholly sympathetic to jew-baiters. There may, however, have been more judicious reasons, although I must add that I always had doubts about the truthfulness of his stories. He had been among the fascists without doubt although the degree of his commitment was never clear, but whatever it was this was not the time to parade his beliefs.

Most of the recruits in our hut were from the East End of London. They had not qualified for the infantry largely because of physical weaknesses rather than weak eyesight. I recall how shocked I was to see young men of my age with what looked like varicose veins, and in general many with poor physique. My personal relations with most of them took some weeks to grow into friendly patterns, and this I had the sense to understand. They were not political in any obvious sense, but wary, distrustful, uneasy with those not of their class. The 'them against us' was not a very clearly defined sentiment but it formed part of their social consciousness in a diffuse, generalised way. I could, and did, modify my accent to some extent but it was quite obvious that I came from a different world, and there was a coolness towards me during the first weeks. As one of the Jewish boys said to me later when he was in my gun crew on the Liverpool docks: 'We thought you were a snotty bastard.'

It was interesting how apolitical they were. I don't think any had been in a trade union and I doubt whether any had been on the streets against the fascists. There was no jingoism and they took remarkably little interest in what was going on outside the barrack room. Inevitably the first weeks of elementary training, designed to toughen up our bodies, left us all feeling battered and physically exhausted at the end of each day, and all we could think about was getting ready for the next day. Quite a number who were married wrote to their wives every day, usually with the familiar SWALK on the back of the envelope (sealed with a loving kiss). The greeting new to me was BURMA, used when there was notice in the letter of a weekend leave (Be upstairs ready, my angel).

There are a few incidents from these very early days that remain in my memory. Standing in line for our first vaccination, for example, and watching quite a goodly proportion drop to the floor before the man with the needle was reached: a group which included Mosley's chauffeur. The most memorable was in the gym one day when a not very large sergeant – the physical training instructor – was bouncing up and down on his toes explaining the horrors to which we were to be subjected to toughen us. He called out one of our squad to stand on the mat facing him. 'Come on,' he evidently said, 'attack me: do what you like'. What the rest of us saw was our bloke take a step forward, spit straight into the sergeant's eye, and then put him on his back. Watching, having now been in the army a few weeks, we just about stopped ourselves from howling with laughter. The sergeant was furious, of course, but I cannot remember what happened next. After the session was over the victim said to me: 'But Johnny, he told me to do what I liked, and so I did what we always try to do at the beginning of a fight'. He worked on the docks in East London, very stockily built, almost as broad as he was tall. It was a demonstration of a technique I never forgot and once, years later, it came in useful.

'Johnny' was what I was always called in the Army: the English working-class habit of either shortening or lengthening your forename or substituting a sobriquet which fitted your occupation, looks or background. The habit, of course, was not confined to working people. The upper classes from the days of their prep schools – an experience which they never seem to forget – often had nicknames attached which went through their lives, not least, it would seem, if they had an Army career. The Times in August 1977 published a clutch of letters explaining why Second World War Generals had such childish names as 'Boy', 'Jumbo', 'Squeaker', 'Bubbles', 'Poppy' and 'Fairy'.

Our basic training finished after about six or seven weeks. It had included basic practice on the rifle ranges and in general it was quite sensibly put together. There was now a notable difference in the physical abilities of almost everyone. We were fortunate in our hut in having a reasonable sergeant who worked us as hard as everyone else but without the bullying that existed with some other training NCOs. We now moved into our newly formed Battery and began artillery training. Our guns were 3.7 heavy AA and at the centre of each section was the command post, with its predictors and height finders. The Major and Adjutant were in overall command, usually to be found on one of the gun sites. When the allocation of duties was made at the end of our training period I found myself on the command post: 'among the pips' our sergeant called it. This was also the first occasion when I was called before one of the local permanent staff about an application for an Officers Training Course.

It was the Communist Party's line that those eligible for a commission should accept. Applied to the Army it seemed to me at the time that for any socialist or communist the principle was wrong. Should there be any trouble – and in the summer of 1940 I had no idea at all what 'trouble' could be – it would be more sensible to be among the rude and licentious soldiery in the NAAFI than in the officers' mess. I argued this with senior comrades in King Street. I was not convinced by their arguments and I refused on two further occasions. The person who suffered from my decision in the long run was Constance who, after we married and had our first child, had to live in the later years of the war on a fairly meagre allowance. It has not been any solace to be able to reassure myself that I failed to appreciate the problem at the time and only realised it when I returned home from India at the end of the war.

We finished our artillery training towards the end of July 1940 and then went to firing camp at Bude in North Cornwall. By this time I was on friendly relations with my comrades and in social terms it was an interesting experience. These East Enders were very different from the young working men I knew in the engineering town of Gainsborough. Most were unskilled factory workers or in one of the many trades serving the docks. Their weekly pay, when in work was low, but any ideas the LSE economists had suggested about levels and trends of working-class income were soon overlaid by the facts of life to which I now listened. The Londoners I talked with almost all seemed to have some additional form of 'benefit' outside their weekly pay, whether they were in work or unemployed. One of my friends from Islington – decades before it was gentrified – specialised in removing lead from the roofs of churches. Two others, with whom I became very close, worked in the same factory, which produced the lightweight mangle which in the thirties was replacing the very heavy roller type still used by Mrs Allison and which you will occasionally see today in rural museums. One of my friends worked in the loading bay and the other drove a van; they would always at intervals add an extra machine to their official lists which they would then flog round their neighbourhoods for about thirty shillings, the cheapest commercial type costing around three pounds and ten shillings. It may, of course, be acknowledged that London, because of its size and great variety of commercial and industrial enterprises, offered many opportunities for this kind of entrepreneurial activity. A mining village had the pit and nothing else but in many places there were evidently always opportunities. We had in my section a more or less professional poacher from somewhere in the Midlands. He was a rather withdrawn character whom I was once, in our early training days, able to save from being charged with something or other by just gabbling away, in my normal accent, at our hut sergeant: an example, I thought at the time, of the deference that was shown to 'accent'. I was reminded of him years later when I read a comment made by Jim Connell, the author of *The Red Flag*, that there was no good reason why anyone should go without a meal when the estates of the wealthy were stocked with a great variety of game and birds waiting to be trapped or shot.

The summer of 1940 was full of sunshine and our firing camp at Bude offered a holiday which very few could have afforded in civilian life. Life was easy. Most of the country was concerned with the constant threats and possibilities of invasion, but little of this serious concern reached our firing camp. We could have completed our artillery firing in ten days had we worked seriously through the day and evenings and we could have been instructed in elementary infantry tactics. After all, this is what the newly formed Home Guard were doing. Instead, we worked a few hours a day and for the rest lounged about or went swimming and in the evening filled the camp cinema and watched live shows and moving pictures. Sometimes we walked into Bude and enjoyed its simple pleasures. Crisis, what crisis?

We left Bude towards the end of August and travelled to Liverpool, and life immediately became different. My section of guns was first allocated part of the defence system around Speke aerodrome, outside the city. Daylight raids from German bombers had already begun from about 25,000 to 30,000 feet. The 3.7 heavy anti-aircraft gun was an excellent weapon but the directional equipment we used, predictors and height finders, were still at a primitive stage, and were quite inadequate for the purposes for which they were intended. These were the days before we had radar on gun sites, and for the coming year or so we were dependent upon manual operation of the command post equipment. The guns' elevation and traverse were transmitted electrically from the command post, the command post then calculated a fuse number, and this was shouted to the guns. The number was set manually on the fuse in the nose of the shell which was then loaded into the breech. The breech block was closed and the order to fire was shouted from the command post when the appropriate calculations had been made. During daylight hours, below 30,000 feet, firing was often useful in breaking up enemy formations although direct hits were rare. At night the Ack-Ack firing during the year of the Blitz could first be regarded as a reassuring volume of noise for the civilian population. There was an important qualification, however, concerning the inaccuracy of anti-aircraft fire. If there was a significant concentration of guns round a particular objective – a group of docks or factories or important military centre – there would be sufficient 'flak' to damage seriously the attacking aircraft. All airmen testified to the dangers of flying through a great hail of shell fragments and while direct hits were always rare, a great deal of damage could be inflicted.

I had been made a gun sergeant before we began regular night firing towards the end of September 1940, and most of my gun crew – fifteen in all – had been in the same training section as myself in Arborfield, so we all knew each other well. We would begin to stand by between nine and ten in the evening, and firing would mostly continue until around three o'clock in the morning. We then went to bed and were up not later than 8.30 a.m. to begin a very heavy day's work: replenishing the ammunition bays (and each case contained two shells weighed half a hundredweight); cleaning the gun and, when firing had been heavy, the lining of each gun had to be changed every three days or so. Or it should have been, but there was a serious shortage of new linings in the early days. The linings were ribbed so that the shell was given a very high velocity of twist when it left the gun. Heavy firing over a few days smoothed down the ribbing inside the liner and the shells fired would lose a considerable acceleration, and therefore height. Changing a liner was always a troublesome business. We only had one fitter on each gun site, and much of the labouring work had to be done by the gun crews. It was very hard work not least because so often there were technical problems before the liner was properly in place.

I had a somewhat unpleasant experience in my very early days as a gun sergeant. The shell we fired was a single piece with the brass case containing the cordite joined to the shell itself. There was a primer in the centre of the base of the brass case. At automatic when the breech block swung across to close the breech the firing pin would then strike the primer which in turn would ignite the cordite and thus blow the shell along the riffled barrel of the gun into the air at a very high velocity. At the same time the brass case would be ejected from the breech at the rear of the barrel. Now in those days the primer and also the fuse in the nose of the shell both used gunpowder as the means of ignition, and it was always possible for the gunpowder to become damp, and therefore fail to ignite. If the fuse in the nose of the shell was damp the shell's mechanism would not work and the shell would come down, in one piece, until it reached the ground as a bomb. If the powder in the primer failed to ignite because the gunpowder was damp nothing would happen and there would be a misfire. The drill for misfires was quite straightforward. If a misfire occurred the gun sergeant would order No. 5 – the gunner on the firing platform – to set the breech to manual and then pull the firing handle. If again nothing happened the sergeant would then shout 'misfire' to the command post. The gun would be elevated to 45 degrees and pointed in the most neutral direction away from the other guns. After one minute had elapsed the sergeant would order 'unload'. No. 5 would then very slowly open the breech block with the sergeant standing directly to the rear of the gun ready to catch the shell when it was released by the breech block. The sergeant having caught the shell in his arms would then take it some fifty yards beyond the gun emplacement and lay the shell on the ground with the nose pointing away from the guns.

There was a mythology surrounding this particular operation. It was widely believed that there had been occasions when damp powder in the primer only very slowly ignited and that this would be further encouraged by the face of the breech block sliding across the base of the shell as it was being manually un-loaded. The resultant explosion would blow the breech block out through the body of No. 5 on the firing platform and the blast from the half opened breech would envelop and destroy the sergeant standing at the rear.

No one I ever met had ever been present at an accident of this kind but it was common gossip. Misfires with damp primers were not uncommon although the five I had that first night within two hours was unusual and somewhat unsettling for one as inexperienced as I was. For reasons, however, that I cannot rationally explain, I felt no excessive stress or fear on that first occasion. Partly I suppose it was my newly acquired rank that I had to justify but my general experience of fear, especially in my Army years, was that it varied much between individuals but also within the same individual. I always found being machine-gunned from the air terrifying, whatever shelter I was in, and on a more general level I have always been petrified by snakes, including those not venomous.

That winter of 1940-1941 we were firing almost every night, and it was very tiring and wearing work. We had a ten day break sometime in the New Year of 1941. The winter had been a particularly hard one and Oakengates, in Shrop-shire, where we went, was deep in snow. We had a wonderful time. We made a long toboggan slope; drank mulled beer with the local miners; slept half the day as well as long nights and forgave AA Command many of its stupidities.

The return to Liverpool found us still on the docks but now on the south side. Our daily and nightly routines were unchanged. Liverpool was almost continu-ally bombed during the first year of the blitz. We stayed until the last major as-sault on the port. For ten days in early May the city was blasted and had the ac-tion continued a few days later the docks might have been out of action for some time. Water and sewerage pipes were being destroyed over large areas and there was a stench which went round the city from the numbers of dead and wounded not yet collected or taken into care. People were leaving every night in increasing numbers. It was a grim and miserable time for the people of Liverpool but after that last ten days bombing the city never again suffered the tribulations and sor-rows of that first year of devastation.

Our Battery moved out during the second half of May and went to various sites in the Midlands, and since there was no firing we began to experience the equivalent of some of the idiocies of peacetime military life. We were stationed on one site where the officer commanding the district – probably no less than a Brigadier-General – insisted on dustbins being cleaned inside and out with the studs on the bottom of the bins being polished. Some parts of every day went into polishing boots and making equipment as shining as possible. It was in this period after Liverpool that I began to recover my political wits. Constance had always sent me literature each week and now I had time to read it and to start discussions. These were the days before the establishment of the Army Bureau of Current Affairs (ABCA) which was not set up before the Nazi attack on the Soviet Union on 22 June 1941. ABCA was introduced in August 1941. It was a much trumpeted affair and it was compulsory, or so it was announced. Junior officers were to conduct weekly discussions using the booklets produced by ABCA, some of which were of a reasonable standard. The problem for ABCA was the intellectual calibre of the junior officers which in my somewhat limited experience over six Army years was low grade. I had little contact with Regular Army officers but the young officers I encountered, a mixture of Territorials and increasingly former civilians, were intellectually ignorant of public affairs and minimal in their teaching abilities. Most were of the social class in my own grammar school who had left school either at the end of their fifth year or after one year in the Sixth and had gone into the lower end of the professions or business.

After the Nazi attack on Russia, in December 1941 the Japanese attacked Pearl Harbour, and Hitler, with remarkable stupidity, declared war on the United States before the end of the year. There had already been rumours that our Battery was to be sent abroad and it seemed to become certain in the New Year. It could only be the Middle East because Japan so rapidly overran Singapore and Malaya. In the Middle East the early successes in North Africa in 1940 had been thrown away by Churchill's decision, much influenced by an over-optimistic appraisal by Anthony Eden and accepted by Wavell, to divert troops from North Africa to the defence of Greece against the Nazi invasion: a disastrous judgement which prolonged the war in North Africa by two years. However, just at the time the rumours of our move abroad were becoming substantial, in the early spring of 1942, my personal situation changed dramatically.

New Anti-Aircraft Batteries were usually formed out of 'cadres' recruited from an existing regiment, consisting of three Batteries. A Major, several officers, a Battery sergeant-major and several NCOs would be taken from the old regiment, each Battery being allocated a quota. The cadre system was sensible in theory and indeed it was the most practicable way of expanding the much needed AA defences. It had one inevitable, central defect. To ask Battery commanders to supply cadres for a new unit meant that here was a splendid opportunity to get rid of the incompetent or the difficult, and since for the officers at least it would normally mean promotion, there would be little or no opposition. The racket was well-known throughout AA Command but inevitably it took time before the War Office moved to action and issued strict instructions concerning the quality of those transferred. How effective these new orders were is impossible to say, not least because there was now a new factor in the situation: the introduction of women onto gun sites to be responsible for the command post operations and other areas of work outside the guns themselves. All gun crews remained male and it was clearly understood that mixed Batteries would not be sent abroad (some were in the last stages of the war).

The first mixed Battery was deployed in late August 1941 and some six months later I was called into the Major's office and told that I was to be promoted to sergeant-major in a newly formed mixed Battery which was to be formed in the new future. He made the usual noises of regret about leaving his Battery but explained the strict instructions from the War Office concerning selection procedures. I told him that as far as I knew Army regulations I could always refuse promotion and I reminded him of the occasions when I had refused an OCTU. I went on to insist that I thought the introduction of women in a combatant unit was sensible but that I would never get abroad and we all knew that our present Battery was almost on the move. The chances of another blitz of the 1940-41 intensity were becoming unlikely and I found the prospect of the near equivalent of peacetime soldiering impossibly dreary. I would therefore ask the Major to convey my refusal to the Colonel. The Major, who was a reasonable man, suggested gently that I might run into trouble but that he would do what he could for me.

Within a few days I was called to regimental headquarters to be met by the Regimental Sergeant-Major. We knew each other from the days when he had been Battery Sergeant-Major to my own Battery. He was a red-faced, big man who would have provided an admirable model for the music hall caricature of the Army's sergeant-majors. He was also fairly stupid but to me he had always been agreeable. Before he marched me into the Colonel's office he whispered through his moustache 'Watch it, Johnny' and then swept me in to stand to attention before the Colonel who was seated behind a large desk. The Colonel first asked me why I always refused the opportunity of an officer's training course, and this I always found very difficult to answer. 'Well,' said the colonel, 'I can't of course insist on your getting a commission, but what about this present business?'; and he proceeded to tell me again the same story of War Office instructions about the usefulness of new cadres to the new units. I then repeated my own arguments about wanting to move into active service, and not sit around. We argued for a few minutes and then suddenly the Colonel got up from his chair, came round to the front of the desk and stood before me. 'I gather, Saville, that you are something of a Red. So am I.' Not surprisingly, I found this difficult to comment on. What does one say in response to this kind of absurdity? We went on exchanging arguments for only a few more minutes when suddenly the Colonel went red in the face, and rushed out of the room shouting over his shoulder 'I can't argue with you any more, Saville'. A minute later the RSM came in – he had probably been listening all the time – and told me to get back to my unit. The words he actually used were to bugger off and hope that I wasn't in too much trouble.

When I got back to the gates of the Battery the sentry on duty told me I had to report immediately to the Major. When I entered his office he said to me: 'Whatever have you been doing to the Colonel?' I explained that as far as I knew I had only refused the promotion, and that there wasn't anything else. 'Well', said the Major 'I have a message for you from the Colonel. Either you take this promotion or he will personally see to it that you are posted to Iceland, and I am especially to emphasise that the tour of duty for gunners in Iceland is two years'. And then the Major sat back in his chair and grinned at me. 'I am afraid', he said, 'that you have no choice in this matter'. It was a point I understood.

My new unit was to be formed at Blandford, in Dorset, a pleasant town with two quite good restaurants, by wartime standards, and with the proprietors of one I became very friendly. Constance came down and stayed with them during our period of training and we kept in touch with them after the Battery left Blandford. My new Major was a Territorial, a solicitor in civilian life, and although a heavy drinker and not very efficient, was a civilised person with whom I developed amicable relations. I had an interview with him and the new Adjutant (a nice man with whom I became friendly) and explained my position. I told them that I thought I was a competent soldier and that I would do all I could to make the Battery an efficient one. I then went on to explain my own position and that once we had been through firing camp and settled in our first site I should apply for a posting to a mobile unit – the term that was commonly used for one that was expected to go outside the United Kingdom. The Major offered no objections and my stay in this Battery for the next four months was uneventful and on the whole a pleasant and interesting experience. All the senior NCOs were Territorials – not a category of soldier, as I have already suggested, for whom I had much respect – but I only had to get rid of one sergeant and two junior NCOs, with unmistakable effects, I should add, upon those who remained.

The young women who took over the Command Post were mostly lower middle class in social background and better educated than the men in my old Battery. They learned quickly. We went to firing camp on the southern coast of Scotland for three weeks. It was now the middle of 1942, a year of serious military reverses for Britain until the second battle of Alamein. This camp, however, was like that at Bude, a pleasant refuge for the permanent staff with no pressures on the visiting Batteries. There were two other mixed Batteries at the firing camp, and with all the women around there was dancing almost every night and the odd film to keep our interest in the world beyond our narrow horizons. The world beyond did not include any discussion of the progress of the war. The Battery came out of its firing trials reasonably well and we moved to the south of England for our first site. It was just outside the village of Borstall which had given its name to the prison for young offenders. Our first indication of the remand prison was two days after we had settled in when the women's quarters were systematically burgled. This naturally encouraged the usual meetings of the top layers of the local command, but I thought we could also be helpful. So I took a small delegation to see the Chief Warden or whatever he was called, having picked two of the toughest looking sergeants to go with me, with instructions to keep their mouths shut (an harangue between the six of us would not have been helpful). We had an interview with three of their own senior Wardens, and I explained that while we sympathised with their problems with some of their own young bastards we would not expect it to happen again. If it did we should allow our people to take what action they felt necessary when they encountered any of the inmates. I then went on to suggest that some mixing might help. So we fixed up a series of football matches which became a regular feature of our week, and as far as I know there were no further practice runs at our expense.

I was not to remain long with the Battery. I had put in for a transfer to a mobile unit as soon as we arrived at Borstall and to my surprise it came through quite quickly. I had enjoyed my time, and the women had proved as efficient as any men, and they could have quite easily been moved into the gunpits. I got my mobile posting in mid July 1942 and I went mobile for three days: to Aberdeen where my new Battery was about to embark for the Shetlands. It was with some irritation that I went on board for the sixteen-hour journey to Lerwick, on the main island of Zetland. Our headquarters were in the south of the island where about half the Battery was deployed in the hills overlooking the aerodrome at Sumburgh Head, with another section left in Lerwick, the only town and port. Lerwick was an important centre for communication with Norway and Europe in general throughout the war years.

The Battery I had joined was about the average quality of Home Batteries but it had a particularly shifty commanding officer. The Major looked like a wide boy from London's East End. He was away from headquarters for considerable periods of time, in Lerwick and the Orkneys, and was quite uninterested in helping to train a more efficient unit. The rest of the officers were the usual mixture, and no one except myself and one other among the senior NCOs had come from the call-up of civilians. The exception was the sergeant in charge of the radar equipment which by now had replaced the primitive equipment of the first year of the blitz, although it would have been little use to us since our guns were first world war three inch. We were unable to find out when they last fired and we ourselves were certainly not inclined to use them unless there was an enemy attack. With old guns like these there was always the danger of a blow out.

The first thing perhaps one remembers about the Shetlands is the weather. Summer was for a short time almost nightless, while there were less than six hours daylight during the middle of winter. It was stormy for many months with very high winds, and although there were supposed to be two or three trees in very sheltered places, I never saw one. But Shetland was wonderful: superb scenery, beautiful walking country, and the long nights often having dazzling displays of the *aurora borealis*. It was the people, however, who remain in the memory. They were charming and courteous, generous with their hospitality, and I left after nearly a year conscious of a hard-working, civilised society whose integrity and sense of fairness was to be greatly respected.

Life for the ranks below sergeant, however, was certainly not wonderful and for many the Shetlands would have dismal memories. It must have been better for those deployed near Lerwick for although the island was 'dry' with no pubs, there were clubs to which access was not difficult and where there were the usual bars. And at least there were streets one could walk up and down and it was not difficult to get into the hospitable Shetland houses. Most of the Battery however, was in the south round Sumburgh Head, and those at HQ, where a gun section was also stationed, had no facilities outside the encampment. The ordinary gunner lived and slept at least five a side in a Nissan hut with only a very small NAAFI offering beer and whisky and the usual bits and pieces There was no cinema and within the first nine months there were two ENSA travelling shows (ENSA: Entertainments National Service Association – sometimes known as 'Every Night Something Awful'). The weekly ABCA sessions on most evenings attracted the greater part of the site population and in addition I organised a version of the very popular radio show, the 'Brains Trust'. It had been introduced during 1941 and very soon became an extremely popular, entertaining and educative programme, with a very large national listening public. My own officers' mess were not very helpful for our own version but I soon had a list of contacts with neighbouring units. The most intelligent of all the outside speakers was a Polish Major whose services I used whenever he was available. The audience could submit written questions as well as extempore from the floor. One of the most useful things I achieved in this important matter of relieving boredom was constructing an assault course. Within a couple of weeks I started digging. At the outset I did all the digging myself – not the normal occupation of the Battery Sergeant-Major – but I was not going to be the victim of the usual Army complaints about the poor bloody footsloggers while those from the sergeants' mess and the officers' mess shouted their orders: complaints, let me add, which were not seldom justified. By early October 1942 the ramps and the walkway and the various ups and downs of an assault course were completed. I was the first to go over the completed course, and then I set up competitive teams of six men in each group. As I hoped would happen, the competition between groups became an obsession and there would be practice runs every day. We opened the competition to groups from other parts of the Battery. In the HQ section I made everyone do at least one weekly run, and they included the cooks and batmen.

There was not much other training, for the Major was uninterested. I am not sure where he had been during the blitz but he organised nothing in the Shetlands and the officers' mess must have been dull and boring throughout the whole period of their time on the island. This was not true of the sergeants' mess and it provided the most enjoyable time in all my Army years before I went to India. For one thing we had the best Army cook I encountered in my six years in the Army, and the rations of food and drink were both plentiful and excellent. The lamb in the spring of 1943 was the most succulent I have ever eaten. The sergeant's mess over which I presided became a very lively affair. We had a whole Nissan hut for the mess, where we had a well-stocked bar, and we soon developed a range of social activities which suited our simple tastes during the long winter months. Exactly how it came about I cannot remember, but we developed reciprocal relations with the RAF officers mess on the airfield below us. Mostly they came to us, and although as with our gun crews they were officially on call there never seemed to be any problem for the mostly younger officers who joined us for an evenings social activity. Our own officers' mess were never invited. We always recited or sang at our guest nights, the contributions naturally varying according to the audience. *Hitler has only got one Ball* was hardly a song for mixed audiences, and there were a number of items much limited from the original: such items as 'They call me Venal Vira/I'm a lovely from Gezira'.

My own contributions on our stag nights were two poems. The first had been published in a *New Statesman* competition in the mid-thirties and I had learned it by heart. The first verse of 'Lady Chatterley's lover' began:

> His Lordship returned from Flanders
> Apparently intact
> For the social eye does not normally see
> What his Lordship really lacked

There were six verses in all and I have to say, with due modesty of course, that my many renditions, in the Shetlands and elsewhere, were well received. My favourite offering, however, was alleged to have been written by A.P. Herbert and it was also said that there were replies or commentaries by G.B. Shaw and others. I thought it had disappeared; no one who had been in the Army seemed to have heard it, and then in 1996 Fritz Spiegl published his erudite and highly amusing *Sick Notes*. It will be found under the heading 'Pudenda'. Here it is in my version which differs only slightly from that in Spiegl :

> The portions of a woman which appeal to man's depravity
> Are constructed with considerable care,
> And what at first appears to be a simple little cavity
> Is really a most elaborate affair.

Now doctors who've examined the abdomena
Of various experimental dames
Have made a list of interesting phenomena
And given them delightful Latin names

There's the vulva, the vagina and the good old perineum,
And the hymen, in the case of certain brides,
And lots of little gadgets that you'd love if you could see 'em
The clitoris, and lots of things besides

Now isn't a pity when you common people chatter
Of the mysteries to which I have referred
That for such a delicate and complicated matter
You use a vulgar, unattractive, little word

On some evenings we played the army games which went back at least to John Company's army before the Mutiny: crawling round the walls of the mess without touching the floor, and for us the more common hicockalorum. One team forms a sort of rugby scrum but in a straight line, each head between the legs of the one in front, and then the other team, in turn, take a flying jump on their backs. When all are landed they bounce up and down to the accompaniment of a tribal chorus in the hope that they can collapse the scrum. But the most successful of my own ventures to enliven the long winter nights were the evenings of dancing. On site, of course, there were no women, but for miles around there were crofts, of varying sizes, empty of men except the very young or the very old. The women had normally tilled the ground while their men were away working the fishing, and now the Navy or commercial shipping had claimed them for the years of war. On a motor bike or occasionally in a truck I toured the crofts within about a ten-mile radius, and with some families I became very friendly. After careful explanation, and usually with a greeting from another family, I persuaded the older women to allow their grown up daughters or younger sisters to come to our dances with, of course, a chaperon. We would pick them up and return them home by station wagon.

It worked well. The chaperons sat round the walls of the mess and we fed and watered them (sandwiches and whisky) while we galloped around with their younger sisterhood. The RAF came in strength. There were never any 'incidents'. I had called a meeting of the whole mess before our first dance, and made it clear that any drunkenness or wandering off with one of the women would be dealt with as a disciplinary offence. Wandering about in a Shetland night was an unlikely enjoyment, for the wind never stopped blowing and it always seemed to be raining or snowing; but given the ingenuity of the male in these situations, the duty sergeant was always instructed to keep his eyes alert. There never were any happenings and they were always pleasant occasions to become a regular date during our months, with what soon became known as the 'passion wagon' functioning efficiently on its tour of the crofts.

Sixteen to eighteen hours of darkness had to be filled and social life in the mess took only a part of the day. So I read. For reading at my table I had a couple of effective storm lamps, and I discovered to my surprise and joy that the Army educational service in this region was extremely efficient in providing the books I asked for. So I read or re-read all of Jane Austen and a good selection of the obvious nineteenth century writers. The book service even provided the two volumes of Langer's *Diplomacy of Imperialism* which I had read at LSE but now found more time to think about. Constance continued to send me communist literature but it would not have been sensible to pass it round as I had done in my first unit, and indeed during my whole period on the Shetlands I found no one with whom I could talk politics except the Polish Major I have previously mentioned. I have always been, throughout my life, a poor linguist – except in French – and although I learned some German at LSE for my first year language examination, I had forgotten most of it, so I restarted teaching myself.

There were always infantry battalions on the island and one was usually en-camped near us. During the early spring of 1943 I applied to join a training course for NCOs and junior sergeants. The battalion belonged to the Argyll and Sutherland Highlanders. The infantry course lasted one month: each day from 9 a.m. to noon with a whole weekend's manoeuvres to round things off. The sen-ior sergeants of the Argylls obviously thought I was somewhat mad, but I made the point that gunners would be fighting alongside the infantry – as the North African campaign had shown – and it would be useful to know even a small something about infantry work and thinking.

Except that there was very little thinking. The course naturally concentrated on infantry weapons – the rifle and the Bren gun but no mortars – and we spent many hours both on the firing ranges and in taking our weapons down for cleaning and quick assembly. The strenuous part was the assault course exercise which for many of the instructors seemed to be the most important part of the month's training. There was some instruction on how to instruct but what was remarkable was the absence of any discussion of the German army, and how it worked or was supposed to work. There was no mention at all of German guns and small arms weapons; no explanation of what sort of tactical operations the Germans might employ. The enemy we were in the war to fight did not exist; nor did the other arms of the British army. Most important of all, I do not recall a single mention of the role of tanks and the necessary coordination of the infan-try with tanks. The North African campaign was already finished and while the terrain in Europe was different the crucial importance of the close cooperation of the various arms of the Army and the RAF had been abundantly demon-strated. But not apparently for the Argylls.

I had applied for a transfer soon after I arrived in the Shetlands. This time I knew there was no point in asking again for a transfer to a mobile unit; after all I might still find myself on the mobile way to Iceland. There were two possibilities if I still refused a commission. There was first Intelligence which, with my French, was a reasonable possibility. The serious obstacle was my politics. Internal security within the Army was pervasive but haphazard and arbitrary in its impact. Communists who were known always had a file which went with them, and I already knew of two CP members whose files followed them around to the point where promotion was deliberately slowed down and their postings were in somewhat remote areas. On the other hand there were many communists whose career patterns were normal. I had little doubt that there was a file on myself but whether it had caught up with me in the Shetlands I could not tell. I decided that I could not risk an application for the Intelligence services. The other possibility was to apply to become a gunnery instructor, an elite group within the Artillery. It was generally recognised to be a very tough course. My application was duly processed and I had two long and hard interviews in the Orkneys. I was finally accepted and in late July I went to Manorbier, near Tenby in South Wales: the central AA gunnery school in the British Isles. The course would last between three and four months.

There is a further comment to be made on the Shetlands. An AA Battery has a total of about 450 men, each eating more food per day than the average civilian whose rations had steadily diminished since the first year of the war. And the 450 gunners had done nothing for their food. There were no air raids or air raid warnings and at this point in the war it was highly unlikely that there would be any. The aerodrome at Sumburgh Head could not have been seriously defended by the equipment we had, for the 3 inch gun could not fire higher than 12000 feet and a couple of Bofors guns would have been sufficient if there was any chance of a low flying attack. Lerwick was certainly an important centre but again the Bofors gun would have been more useful than our 3.7 guns. In short, there was no military argument for our presence in the Shetlands. The Normandy campaign and after was to expose the severe shortages of manpower in the British Army, and my own limited experience was sufficient to be aware of how many soldiers were simply wasting their time, a generalisation which includes all ranks. I was later to learn something of the rest home for many officers that Delhi provided, and in the years since the war ended there has been an abundant literature on the Army bureaucracy that enjoyed the pleasures of Cairo and similar centres, although there was evidently no city that quite matched Cairo.

I left the Shetlands with regret for there were still parts of the islands I would like to have explored. I had managed to visit the Pictish broch on the island of Moosa and I had seen the Pictish stones on Unst in the far North. It would, however, not be sensible to stay with this unit whose future was uncertain and I might well have found myself stuck in some out of the way sector for the rest of the war.

During the summer months of 1943 I was pursuing, with great energy and application, the gunnery course at Manorbier. It was well-organised, the syllabus covering all types of anti-aircraft weapons of all the belligerent countries, except the Japanese. The Major in charge of our course, a regular army officer, was extremely knowledgeable and an excellent tutor and lecturer. He was assisted by a SMIG, warrant officer class 1, also a regular and competent without reaching the very high standard of his Major. The instruction films that went alongside the lectures were very well made and I have always assumed that the techniques of the Grierson documentaries, which had so delighted my generation of the thirties, had been carried over into these army videos, although that was not a term yet in use. They were especially useful for me on the radar side, which I found the most difficult part of the whole course, having been a woeful failure at O level physics in my schooldays.

There was one rather surprising weakness in that there were no training manuals for the guns we were most concerned with. The standard gun in British AA was of course the 3.7 and for this there was no instruction book or booklet. What was available was a large handbook, written in undiluted technical language, for the use of the fitters and engineers who serviced the guns. This, for many evenings, we sweated through. We began to appreciate how backward our own people were when we started work on American weapons for which there were extremely well-produced instruction booklets. For the machine guns and the smaller calibre guns it would have been possible to understand their workings without formal teaching.

We went to firing camp for our own weaponry, and to Larkhill, the field gunnery centre on Salisbury plain, for instruction in the use of the 3.7 in its ground role. Most of our time was spent on the possibilities of the 3.7 as a field gun and rather fewer sessions on its use as an anti-tank weapon. Yet it had already been established, from relatively few examples in North Africa, it must be admitted, that the 3.7 could be as effective in an anti-tank role as the German 88 mm. This was understood in our sessions at Larkhill, yet the failure to accept the double role of this excellent gun is inexplicable, not least with the growing superiority of the RAF in the last year or so of the war and therefore the declining need for large concentrations of heavy AA guns.

There were about twenty on the Manorbier course, all sergeants except myself. There was automatic promotion to warrant officer class 2 if candidates passed the whole course. Towards the end of our time our ability to instruct was put to several tests, and as part of our final examination we had to speak extempore on a subject given to us when we reached the podium. This, as can be understood, greatly troubled some of my comrades for whom I gave some practice runs. My subject when I reached the platform and stood before the class – which also included several Manorbier officers – was 'Women in the Army'. After I had finished and returned to my seat there was a brief silence and then our Major instructor said: 'Sergeant-Major Saville. I have a pair of old boots I would like you to flog around the houses tomorrow'.

We all passed save one disconsolate character but it was a fair assessment, and after leave we reported to Woolwich, in south London, the central sorting house for all gunners waiting for their posting. There had always been stories about Woolwich ever since I entered the Army, but none did justice to the Dickensian flavour of the place. It was a home for a large permanent staff of bureaucrats, of high to low status, who were enjoying the pleasures of a quiet, well-fed war. Once in Woolwich it was not possible to leave during the day, and those below the rank of Warrant Officer were always expected to be given some duties. All my group from Manorbier, except myself, were in this position, for their promotion to WO 2 would take time before it was ratified through the War Office. To be confined to these ghastly barracks supervising the scrubbing of kitchen tables or digging trenches or whatever, was a frighteningly boring future. So it fell to me to do something. I went to see the RSM in charge of morning parades and explained that we were all Gunnery Instructors and promotion would soon follow. I told him that I had been to see the commanding officer of the nearest gun site who would welcome our expertise in training programmes and that he would inform his District command that we were available. It was all lies, but I found it easy to assume that these idle bureaucrats would not check up on my story. I then asked if the RSM at morning parades would call out all the Gunnery Instructors and I would then march them down to the first gun site and distribute them from there. And this is what happened. There were always a large number of working parties to be called out, and the next morning the RSM bellowed that all Gunnery Instructors should fall out. They formed into two ranks, took my advice to come to attention and turn left, and we quick marched out of the gate. We went down the hill swinging our arms and in good step, and after about half a mile or so I would march them into a side street; we then broke up, each to his own purposes. Most went back into barracks for the evening meal for only a few lived near enough to Woolwich to visit their families.

We now had a baby, born while I was in the Shetlands, and I was able to get passes from Woolwich every weekend to spend a couple of days in West Norwood where we occupied the flat at the top of Constance's family's house. With the New Year, however, all the gunnery instructors got their postings. Some went abroad immediately but I had a number of different jobs at home. These included a couple of firing camps; a fortnight with American AA units where the informality between officers and men was pleasantly refreshing. I had a month on the East Coast on light anti-aircraft sites as a sort of observer. There was a fairly constant strafing by German low-flying aircraft and once again I experienced the disagreeable exposure to machine-gunning from the air. The most useful period of work, or so I thought at the time, was my attachment on two occasions to an intensive course on German gunnery equipment, and most particularly on the 88 mm, the all purpose anti-tank and anti-aircraft gun which had such a successful history in North Africa and later France. We all knew, in a general way, about the preparations for a landing in France – this was the very early spring of 1944 – and it was assumed that a number of gunnery special- ists would be helpful when enemy equipment was captured. The War Office, however, mixed up its files, as was too often its habit, and six weeks or so after D-day I found myself on the dockside at Liverpool, there to board a 30,000 tons troopship whose destination was Bombay, the main port for all personnel going to the Far East.

I was about to begin a quite different life. My Army years in Britain had been a mixture of liveliness and boredom, with limited periods of danger. What I know now of these years has come from reading and there are only two mat- ters of which I have any serious recollection. The first was the growing demand throughout 1943 for a second front in Western Europe to relieve the enormous pressures on the Russian front. Popular attitudes towards the Soviet Union had changed dramatically and it was an issue for serious discussion. The other mat- ter on which I have quite vivid memories – since it came when I had finished my gunnery course and there was time both to read and discuss, was the release of Oswald Mosley and his wife from prison in November 1943.

Mosley had inevitably been swept up under the order 18B in the early summer of 1940. There was quite a lot of pressure on the Home Office from members of the propertied classes – including Churchill – to ease the conditions of their imprisonment. In the autumn of 1943 there was serious discussion in the Home Office about Mosley's health, and whether he could be allowed to die in prison and no doubt become a martyr to his bigoted and thuggish followers. Herbert Morrison was Home Secretary and he decided that the Mosleys should be re- leased. He informed the Cabinet on the 17th November with Ernest Bevin the only vociferous opposition, and on the morning of 20 November the Mosleys were smuggled out of Holloway jail, to spend the rest of the war in comfort under what technically was called 'house arrest'. When the news became public the uproar throughout the nation was formidable. The standard biography of Morrison by Donoghue and Jones states that it was 'the biggest storm of Mor- rison's wartime career'. The National Council of Labour dissociated itself from the Government's action and asked its constituent parts to consider the ques- tion. The TUC discussion produced some very blunt speaking and was in total opposition, the National Executive Committee of the Labour Party regretted the decision and the Parliamentary Labour Party only defeated a critical amendment by 51 votes to 43. There was a whole day of Parliament given over to debate the question, and Morrison found himself in difficulties over the medical reports which, until 9 November, had found no reason to question Mosley's detention on grounds of health. Mosley, it needs to be remarked, died in December 1980, some thirty seven years after his release from what was said to be a very serious condition of phlebitis, and after a very active life in the post-war world.

Robert Skidelsky produced his sympathetic biography of Mosley in 1975 and has a typical approach to the episode of the release from prison. 'Protest was largely, though not exclusively', he wrote, 'organised by the Communist Party'. It would suit his case, of course, to suggest that it was only the extreme Left who were really active against the Mosleys, but it was not true. And when he further generalises that 'The opposition was, on the whole, a mean and squalid affair' he is seriously distorting the record, for the whole Labour movement as well as all liberal-minded people, were outraged. I was at Woolwich and can recall the support I got from all sorts and conditions of people for a general letter of protest to the Prime Minister. Skidelsky ends his account by suggesting that it was 'a storm in a tea-cup' that subsided quickly. What is true is that the National Council of Labour and its associated bodies decided just before Christmas to call off the campaign against Mosley's release. There were many more important questions to be concerned with, and these included the obvious preparations for the intense fighting in the year to come.

It is not likely that Skidelsky's apologetics for Mosley will remain serious reading except for professional historians, but one other matter is worth mentioning. Mosley was a very good speaker, at times a quite outstanding orator. I heard him speak on several occasions and inevitably Skidelsky makes much of his abilities on the platform. It is necessary to remember that Mosley's perorations were normally translated by his following in less elegant terms. There was a refrain I often heard on the streets of East London, and I have continued to hear it in my memory throughout my life: 'The Yids, the Yids, we've gotta get rid of the Yids'.

There were about a dozen gunnery instructors on board the troopship, some from the Field Artillery and all except one sergeant were warrant officers. The warrant officers were allocated the same two top decks as commissioned officers, the only difference being sleeping quarters. I have a much better record of this voyage and of all the months I was to spend in India, since the letters I wrote were kept by my wife and, while they inevitably did not discuss military matters, they contain a quite full account of my general way of life, including what turned out to be a surprisingly active political life.

The food was of a quality, and quantity, that belied the fifth year of the war. We were served by waiters. I gave Constance the menu for one day; not, I think, a very sensible thing to do given the meagreness of home rations (always worse in London than almost any other place in the country except for those with clubs or money for restaurants). My day's menu read: breakfast, porridge or flakes, a kipper or scrambled egg on fried bread or a meat rissole, with marmalade and toast and tea or coffee. Lunch was soup, grilled cod and sauce and a choice of either curried meat or cold corned beef and salad with semolina pudding to follow. A cup of tea at four o'clock and dinner at 6.30 which followed the usual pattern: soup, entrée, and a sweet, with an orange in addition every two or three days.

This was not, however, for our lone sergeant who, although he had passed his artillery course, was still awaiting formal recognition. Along with all troops of sergeant and below, living and sleeping accommodation were on the deck below ours. They ate at long tables nearly the width of the ship, men on both sides and very cramped, and they slept in a hammock above the table, or on the table, or on the floor beneath the table. Food was delivered in buckets and very large tureens to the top end of each table and then ladled out to be passed along to the far end until all were served. The atmosphere was fetid at all times but much worse during the period of seasickness as through the Bay of Biscay. We smuggled our sergeant onto our deck whenever we could and he told us the story, but it so happened that two years or so later, when the war was over, I was to travel back to England on a troopship where, because of overcrowding, only commissioned officers were on the top two decks with all the conveniences listed above. All warrant officers, including Regimental Sergeant Majors – I was now a SMIG, the equivalent – travelled on the troop decks.

On our travel to Bombay we on the officers' decks enjoyed the amenities of a pleasure cruise while the men on the mess deck lived in the aptly named pig-sty. The ship was dry but the bars for soft drinks were open all day and we walked round the decks, played deck games, and a lot of cards and slept in the hot afternoons. The most spectacular part of the whole voyage was sailing down the Red Sea and the astonishingly beautiful sunsets. I had taken as many books as I could cram into my kitbag but I had been told that Bombay had some excellent English bookshops; and so it proved. The only poetry I had apart from an anthology of English verse was a volume of Baudelaire's *Fleurs du Mal* – most of which I knew by heart. The book which made most impression on me during this voyage was a little-known classic of anti-colonialism: Clive Branson's *British Soldier in India*, published only a few months earlier. Branson went to Spain to join the International Brigades and after a few months in action he was captured by the Italians but released through an exchange after a fairly short time. He was called up early in 1941 and as a troop sergeant in the 25th Dragoons, Royal Armoured corps, he was killed in action on the Arakan Front in Burma in February 1944. His letters are full of indignation at British attitudes towards the Indian peoples and the record of a brave, honest and remarkable personality.

My copy of Branson's letters went the rounds. I had two especial friends on this voyage. One was a gunnery instructor in Field Artillery – Jacko we called him. A skilled worker in the printing trades, tough with a nice sense of humour and happy to read what I could offer. The other came from a different social background. Freddie was one of three brothers in an affluent middle-class family. Two were Mosleyites and one was leftish. Freddie was one of Mosley's former admirers. He was a good example of the petty-bourgeois who feel the injustices of modern society, desires in a vague way to do something about these evils but wholly isolated from any progressive movement. He was physically tough but unlike so many of his social group did not expend his energy on traditional sports. He first took up boxing, then ju-jitsu and became a member of an Anglo-Japanese wrestling club; and then Mosley. I doubt whether he was ever consciously fascist in the accepted sense of the term and he was beginning to move away from these ideas in the year before war broke out. He joined the Territorial Army – which his Mosleyite brother refused to do – and came out of France just before Dunkirk with pleurisy. I lent him Branson before I knew much about him, and when we talked about the book he put forward what may be termed the traditional *Daily Mail* arguments. Then I pushed Shelvankar's book on India and this continued to disturb him. He was a very pleasant man, reasonable in argument and if he couldn't answer a question he would say so. We spent many nights walking round the deck or hanging over the rail talking politics and it was a great pleasure.

The weather got steadily hotter. We looked down on Aden and the last stage of our journey across the Indian ocean had begun. By this time we were of course in tropical kit and extraordinary as it may seem we still carried topees which were no longer worn by troops in India, at least since the war began to be taken seriously. We steamed into Bombay harbour after about five weeks at sea and somehow the topees got lost or left behind. The life that was going to be different was about to begin.

Bombay was frightful and frightening. The buildings in the centre were I suppose what may be called classic colonial architecture and this was the area of large shops including salesrooms of very expensive cars. The contrast was striking and unpleasant between this administrative, residential and shopping district and what seemed to be the rest of Bombay – filthy, smelly, the streets full of rubbish with the native Indians looking half-starved. Beggars were everywhere. 'It eats like acid into the brain' a liberal contemporary wrote of the urban poverty of India. There were, according to a report of the City Engineer's office, about 200,000 sleeping in the streets of Bombay on any night.

It took me about two or three months before I stopped being conscious of Indian poverty to the point where it became just one more fact of life. And while this was understandable for almost everyone coming to India for the first time, what was notable was that while many who first saw poverty on this scale were conscious of British domination over this country of such abysmal misery, it did not take the average soldier long before it was the 'wogs' themselves who were responsible for the filth and squalor in which most of them lived . The racist attitudes that were so widespread among the armed forces were an exaggerated form of the attitudes that were all too common at home towards racial minorities. I shall not forget the card in the window of a working-class house in Slough: Lodgings. No Welsh – this, of course, during the thirties when the mass unemployment in the Welsh mining valleys was pushing men out to find work in the Birmingham-Oxford-London region.

On my first day in Bombay – we went back on board to sleep – I took a taxi to the Communist Party headquarters in order to deliver some letters from King Street and I was met at the entrance by Mohan Kumaramangalam whom I had known in his Cambridge days. Mohan belonged to a wealthy landowning family in Madras province. Both his parents were students at Oxford and all their four children were educated in England. Mohan himself went to Eton and then to King's College, Cambridge. He was to become the first Indian President of the Union and returned to India just before the beginning of the war to spend a couple of years in jail until the Comintern line changed with the Nazi attack on the Soviet Union. He was released in 1942 and was soon elected to the Central Committee of the Indian Party, becoming very close to P.C. Joshi, the general secretary. He spent most of his time at the Party commune in Bombay. There were dozens of activists in the commune each earning forty rupees a month of which thirty were taken for food. Mohan became a close friend; we corresponded regularly and in the months following the end of the war with Japan I spent over two months in Bombay and saw him almost every day. He ended his life as a Minister in Indira Gandhi's cabinet and was killed in an air crash in 1973 at the age of fifty-six.

After a few days in Bombay we moved to Deolali, not very far from Bombay and there we waited for our instructions to proceed to the central gunnery school in Karachi. Deolali was a very large transit depot with a bazaar of dozens of shops and restaurants. I had not realised how ubiquitous were the Chinese restaurants in India. They were in every town and offered large menus with English food on one side and Chinese on the other. There were no comparable Indian restaurants and no one ate in the small Indian food shops that opened out onto the streets. The large hotel restaurants which offered good Indian cooking, which were only to be found in the big cities, were often for officers only and would in any case have been too expensive for the ordinary soldier. But the Chinese restaurants were excellent and offered a variety of dishes that no one coming from Britain had seen since the war began.

We moved from Deolali to our gunnery centre in Karachi after a couple of weeks. The journey from Bombay took two or three days and I encountered once again the very different treatment of officers and (usually also warrant officers) from the rest of the army. India is a sub-continent with very long distances to travel from one centre to another. Its railway mileage is considerable and the railway service had been organised to meet the requirements of a white dominated country. There were three classes for travel: first, second and third. For Army travel officers went first class; warrant officers and sometimes very junior officers were in the second class and all the rest of the British army were in third. This is what might be expected but what was more striking was the difference in comfort between the first and second classes and the third. There wasn't much to choose between the first and second. Both were single compartments, with comfortable seats along the two long walls which at night could be turned up to make beds. Each of these two classes had a large ice-box for drinking water, and a lavatory of course, and once in your compartment you stayed until you reached your destination since there was no connecting passage with either the first class or the third (except of course for railway officials) The third class was very different. The carriages were like the British railway compartments, with seats across the train and a passage way along one side. The seats were wooden. There was no restaurant on any train I travelled on, but since journeys took many hours there were fairly frequent stops – every two or three hours – at stations along the way where the platforms were filled with every sort of hawker selling drinks and food. Travel even in the most comfortable seats was tiring, since the journeys were so long, but in the third class they could be quite appalling. Twenty-four hours on wooden seats with a carriage half filled with Indian peasants, wives and children and sometimes their animals was memorable. There was, however, another difference which made travel for the ordinary soldier so typical of the class structure of the British army. For every twenty-four hours travel, as a warrant officer, I was allowed travel expenses of ten (possibly twelve) rupees. I cannot remember exactly the rate we were allowed but it was not less than ten (a rupee was worth one shilling and sixpence). I always reckoned that on any journey I would spend on food and drinks about ten rupees. The rate for officers would, of course, be higher according to their rank. The rate for ordinary soldiers was four rupees every twenty-four hours with, I assume, increased rates above each rank up to sergeant. Travel, it must be remembered, was usually in sub-tropical or near tropical heat.

I left Deolali on Tuesday and arrived at the Central Gunnery School in Karachi on Friday evening, having had a full day in Bombay before taking the long-distance Continental to Karachi. Agatha Harrison in London had given me some addresses in Bombay and on this day I first went to Wilson College to meet Professor John Maclean. It was a Church of Scotland Missionary College and Maclean was professor of mathematics. He was busy but promised to send some addresses in Karachi and then passed me on to Professor J.J. Anjaria at the Bombay School of Economics. When we met we discovered we knew each ther from LSE. Anjaria was a liberal-minded nationalist and we remained in contact throughout my time in India. On this occasion he introduced me to C.N. Vakil, the Director of the School and on of India's best-known economists. They invited me to lunch and after a couple of hours' pleasant academic discussion I left with more Karachi addresses.

After lunch I went to the Communist Party headquarters to see Mohan Ku-maramangalam again and was introduced to P.C. Joshi, the General Secretary. Joshi, I wrote to Constance, 'is about 36 with a mass of black hair and tremen-dous energy and bounce. You feel it when you meet'. He was on his way to a meeting and we talked only for about ten minutes, and Mohan and I then con-tinued for about a couple of hours, mainly on British politics.

We had a very pleasant reception at the Gunnery School and as with most permanent Army camps and barracks everything for warrant officers and com-missioned ranks was comfortable and well organised. There was the usual com-plement of permanent residents for whom the war was far away, although the general atmosphere was not as self-satisfied and indolent as at Woolwich. We were told that we would be at the School for the next few months, partly to be-come familiar with the different units in the Indian Army, partly to learn Urdu, or the romanised Urdu adapted to gunnery life.

Life was easy. The dhobi-wallah washed and ironed our clothes, the mess of-fered excellent food, and sporting activities took up a considerable part of most days. The official working day was from 8 a.m. to 5 p.m. but this normally in-cluded games and sports: badminton, a lot of hockey – the Indian teams were always more skilful – and there were regular athletics competitions. For the first time since my schooldays I ran the 100 yards and the quarter-mile.

My most interesting life came outside Army quarters. The details I know be-cause in my many letters home I set down most of my political/social life. I be-gan to visit some of the addresses John Maclean had sent me. Karachi, I should add, was at this time a city of about a million people and probably the cleanest of the larger cities of India. For most of the year its climate was pleasant and only in the middle summer months did it become intolerably hot. In the mid winter months of my arrival we would wear jerseys in the cool evenings. Through Ma-clean and the addresses given me by the Bombay School of Economics people I met quite a large number of Karachi's leading citizens. They were almost all Muslims, most in the Muslim League and some very active. The most interest-ing personality of those early days was Hatim Alavi, the only politician in a large family of businessmen. Hatim had travelled much in Europe. He had been may-or of Karachi and after the establishment of Pakistan was to become a Governor of the Bank of Pakistan. He introduced me to what soon became a large number of acquaintances. We ate mostly in restaurants but occasionally Hatim took me home to his 'bungalow', the term for a large and luxurious house. It was quite near to the Karachi Zoo, Hatim being very knowledgeable about the natural world. He had a favourite zebra who would trot up to the fence when we ap-peared, open wide his very large mouth and allow me to throw in peanuts until he decided he had enough. He then closed his mouth with a loud snap, chewed away and when finished opened his mouth for more. One of Hatim's nephews was a postgraduate student called Hamza with whom, since we were politically much the same, I became very friendly. Hamza came to England soon after the war and for many years taught at the University of Manchester.

John Maclean had put the Mallik family at the top of his list and the first time I visited their house the parents were away and the older daughters received me most pleasantly. They knew the Macleans well. Kamla was twenty-three and there was a schoolgirl of about fifteen. Both spoke excellent English and I commented in a letter home that we used to remark in London that middle-class Indian women usually spoke better English than their male brothers or friends. There were always exceptions of course. Mohan spoke the most beautiful English but he came of a very wealthy and upper-class family, all of whose children were educated, like their parents, in English public schools and universities. One of Mohan's brothers became an Army General, and his father had reached greater heights by becoming president of the All-India Cricket Federation.

I had made contact soon after my arrival in Karachi with the secretary of Karachi's Communist Party. Bukhari – I have forgotten his forename – looked more like the pictures of Lenin than anyone I ever met. We became quite close friends and naturally he introduced me to other Party comrades. The CP in Karachi was quite small in numbers although its influence, as so often with communist parties, was a good deal greater than its numerical count would suggest. For the first two months or so of my period in India I had not discussed at any length the politics of the Indian Party. Naturally I was reading a great deal but at this time, and indeed for the whole time I was in India, I broadly accepted the general line of the CPI, and it was only in later years that I appreciated how ignorant I had been of the many twists and turns the Party had executed.

Bukhari put me in contact with the British communists in the region who had also made themselves known to him. They were mostly RAF from two very large aerodromes/workshops in the district quite near to the city. It was the group from the Drigh Road camp who were the largest in number and the most active. We would all meet on Saturday evenings for a Chinese meal and then have a sort of Party meeting, although I have now forgotten where at this time we held our discussions. The CPI had launched a two and a half lakh fighting fund – a lakh was 100,000 rupees and the rupee exchanged for one shilling and sixpence. We decided to contribute ten per cent of our pay for one month and by early April we had collected 800 rupees.

The Drigh Road group had established a discussion group, with the agreement of the camp's education officer, and sometime in March 1945 I went over to speak on British intervention in Greece. There were about sixty RAF present to hear me condemn in unequivocal language the attack against one of the biggest and most effective resistance movements in Europe. According to my letter to

Constance, which described the meeting, when a vote was taken only the education officer and an acknowledged former Tory candidate were against me.

I accumulated my political facts from the *New Statesman* which Constance sent me every week – it took about a month to reach me – the *People's War* and the various publications of the Army's educational centre. The most useful, however, was probably the *Statesman,* the Calcutta newspaper which reprinted long extracts from the London *Times* (which was critical of the Greek intervention) and the *Manchester Guardian.* Greece, and British intervention, were to remain for me in the immediate post-war years as important a cause for political action as Spain had been to 1939. When I was demobilised in the early summer of 1946 I immediately joined the various organisations which had established themselves to support the anti-fascist operations of the republican movement and I always accepted invitations to speak on the Greek situation. My intense political dislike of Winston Churchill went back to his opposition to the very moderate reforms proposed for India in the 1930s, to his support for Edward VIII and the dreadful woman Edward wanted to marry, and to his failure to recognise the importance of Republican Spain, in spite of his antagonism to Chamberlain and the appeasers. His private description of ELAS/EAM as 'banditti' was matched later by Macmillan in his memoirs. It was Ralph Miliband who forced me to accept the positive role that Churchill occupied in the reorganisation of the British government in May 1940 with the defeat of Chamberlain and Halifax. Later documentation has revealed that they were still prepared to encourage Germany to concentrate against the Soviet Union with some kind of neutrality agreement with the West. There is little else for which I would offer credit to Churchill. His military strategy has been shown to be a series of misjudgements by a man still dominated by the ideas which brought about Gallipoli. He was not alone, it can be accepted, in supporting the disastrous war in Italy; his hopes for Turkey's involvement were quite wrong-headed; and the British military leadership had his personal agreement in attempting to slow down the Second Front. Pogues' biography of Eisenhower has some remarkable stories of Churchill's personal interventions.

I was to remain at the Gunnery School until early April. I was told that I should be attached to an Indian Brigade and it was indicated that it would be operational. I went to Delhi for a two-day conference at which the gunnery requirements of the Burma-Malay campaign were discussed. Delhi was interesting although I had only two evenings to walk about the centre of the city. It was full of staff officers who entertained themselves at the many hotels reserved only for commissioned ranks. I used to think that Mountbatten moved his headquarters from Delhi to Kandy in Ceylon because of the enervating atmosphere of the capital city, and when I read Artemis Cooper's book on Cairo I began to understand what 'enervating' really meant. There are certainly some contemporary statements by Mountbatten which suggest that he wanted to get away from the bureaucratic air – if from nothing else – in Delhi but for the post war decades we have now had many descriptions of the grossly over-staffed luxury of South-East Asia Command in their new headquarters. The British upper classes always set such a good tone. Mountbatten's official biographer wrote that 'Kandy was an efficient headquarters, but it was also an expertly contrived theatrical entertainment'.

I left the Gunnery School in the second week of April, and thenceforth, until the end of the war in early August with the dropping of the two nuclear bombs, working life became very hard. The Indian Brigade I was part of was a unit within Operation Zipper which was expected to launch its first landings on the coast of Malaya at the end of July. This was then delayed until the end of August when, of course, as a military operation against the Japanese, it was no longer required. Our working days began at 8 a.m. and finished when it was getting dark. In most places drinking water came in containers on bullock carts, heavily dosed with chlorine. I celebrated VE day with a half bottle of beer; soon after I went down with a rather virulent attack of dysentery and much enjoyed my four days in hospital. I ought to have had at least a week but my Major IG, who was a nice man, presented me with a long list of duties on my third day which he hoped I would soon be able to cope with. I went blind – literally blind – for two days and with great difficulty obtained a pair of dark glasses which were not a normal issue to anyone on active service, at least not in the areas I was involved in. In the middle of a week's special training course for which I was the main instructor, I was hauled out and sent on a jungle training subsistence course. Living conditions were everywhere primitive and by the beginning of August I was beginning to feel the strain.

But I was physically very tough and I don't think I had been too dulled by the Army, something which happened to many. I managed in the four months to the end of the war to have two short weekends in Poona, and went straight to the Communist Party Commune. The Poona group was naturally smaller than headquarters in Bombay but it was an important regional centre for Maharastra. It was there that I met the Kamats, Anant and Kamala, with whom I became close friends. Anant was a lecturer in mathematics at the local College and Kamala was a full-time Party worker for the women's movement. They were both Brahmins in family origins, Anant being a fish-eating Brahmin and Kamal not, and it was Kamala who was more elevated in the hierarchy. It was a mild family joke for Kamala's family had violently objected to her marriage, although there was later a reconciliation. What was not a joke was their joint agreement about this shameful and disgusting relic of Indian medievalism.

They lived in a stone flat of two rooms. The kitchen had cold running water and the main room, sitting room and bedroom, was not much bigger. At night when I was staying they put up a biggish malaria netting for their double bed which was simply a stuffed rug of sorts on the floor, and then there would be a smaller version for me alongside. I once slept in the Party Commune without a malaria net and appeared next morning covered in bumps. But malaria, *Laus Deo*, was something I did not catch during my Indian months.

The Kamats were wonderfully hospitable and charming. When the war ended we moved to within about fifty miles of Poona and for about six weeks I spent every weekend with them and sometimes a night or two during the week. It was here that I began to get some understanding of Indian social life. The comrades in the Commune also kept me busy. I gave several talks, mainly about politics and political movements in Britain, which is what they mostly wanted. There was one very instructive occasion. I had been at the Kamats in the afternoon and after an evening meal I walked round to the Commune to pick up some old copies of *People's War* that a comrade had promised me. When I got there I found a Kisan (peasant) school for full-time workers in Maharastra in session. I went in and squatted beside Parulekar's wife, she being joint secretary with her husband of the Provincial Kisan Sabha. I knew both of them. After only a few minutes Parulekar introduced me and immediately the Kisan workers began asking questions about England and the British labour movement. Most of the questions were the ones commonly asked: why the British CP polled so few votes in elections; what was the political role of the trade unions; were there any differences between the immediate policy and programme of the Labour Party and the Communist Party; and so on There was one question that very often was asked: why could anyone just join the British Party by signing an application form whereas in India there was always a definite period of probation?

When I had time to look around I saw there were about thirty Kisan workers present, rather more than half of them peasants and the rest students or ex- students. The peasant group were sturdy, tough looking and they listened to the questions and answers, translated by Parulekar, with great attentiveness. There was one young man I was particularly interested in. Some weeks earlier the Party weekly had featured the story of the organisation of the Warli peasant aborigines. A young twenty-year-old student had gone to work among the Warlis about six months previously. Their working and living conditions were mediaeval, without qualification. They were subject to forced labour, rates of pay were one anna a day or nothing, and they were subject to constant intimidation and beatings from the police and the landlords. When Dalvi – the young student – travelled in their areas he was always provided with a bodyguard. The Warlis were already coming together in organised opposition and in some districts wages had already increased to three annas. The Kisan Sabha was now preparing a concerted programme for a rise in wages to twelve annas. I talked at some length with comrade Dalvi, and I have not forgotten his grave, pleasant earnestness or the cause for which he was sacrificing so much.

Before I left Poona I had what turned out to be a mild example of the violence which was not uncommon in many parts of India. On some nights, in the weeks after the end of the war, I went to Poona for an evening with my friends but I would cycle back to town because the lorry that would take me to camp left quite early the next morning. Renting a cycle was always common in army cantonments. One evening – it was dark but with a moon – I was walking back – I had a puncture – and a child came screaming out of an alley and there were more screams from within the alley. I walked my bike a few yards into the alley and the moonshine was bright enough for me to see two men holding a woman, and it was she who was screaming. When I appeared they let go of the woman and ran about three steps to me. I realised, of course, that I had been set up. I threw the bike at one of the men and turned to the other, grabbed both his arms just above the elbow, spat straight into one eye, lifted myself up and ran both my boots down his legs ending upon his bare feet. And then let go and ran, and ran. For about a quarter of a mile, I should think. When I stopped, breathing very heavily, I knew what fear was. There was a somewhat bizarre ending to this tale. The next morning I stayed in town and persuaded a sergeant in the Military Police to take a van out and have a look at the scene of the attempted mugging. It was, I should add, in a part of Poona that was out of bounds to troops because it was a red-light district but I think my sergeant believed me when I explained about my friend at the College. When we arrived at the entrance to the alleyway there was my bike, somewhat bent but with everything else in place!

I was in constant communication with Karachi about my leave, now long overdue. I had asked for a month which had been agreed and it was now only the normal bureaucratic procedures that were delaying my departure. I finally left for Bombay in the middle of September. I had been writing to Army friends in Bombay about accommodation but nothing so far had been offered. Then Professor Maclean invited me to stay at the Mission. I had been in desultory correspondence with him during the previous months, but his invitation was a surprise and most welcome. So far I had not met Agnes Maclean, who was a Quaker, and, as I was soon to discover, widely known in Bombay with many friends in the Indian and Parsee communities.

Their large house was in a spacious compound, surrounded by trees. It was not in an especially fashionable part of the city, and the Party Commune was only about ten minutes walk. I had a large, pleasant room, with bathroom attached. Breakfast was at 9.30 a.m. and dinner at 8 p.m. In between it was expected I would be out, but lunch was available if I wanted it and tea was always around. The house was a Mission building belonging to the Church of Scotland and there were sometimes other people staying, often only for the odd night or two. The Macleans were extraordinarily kind and helpful. I soon began to accompany Agnes on her visits, both to the slums and to the rich. She was a woman of quiet determination, wholly dedicated to the welfare and wellbeing of the people in whose country she lived. She seemed to know almost all the Congress leaders, and Sarojini Naidu and Bhulabhai Desai (leader of the Congress Assembly Party) lived quite near. I had obviously been exceedingly fortunate, and I stayed with the Macleans – almost a member of the family – for the next two and a half months.

As soon as I was settled in I began to make a case for an additional month on leave in the form of a secondment to the Bombay School of Economics. I had discussed this possibility with Professor Anjaria and his Director and they were very willing to write references on my behalf. The argument with my headquarters was that I expected to return to academic life when I was demobilised – to take up again my Ph.D. at LSE for which I had already registered on a part-time basis – and I cited the early release of those whose university careers had been interrupted by war service, a practice which seems to have been accepted in most parts of the armed forces. This extra month I was to be granted but before that I already had ten days added to my original leave. How I managed this I have quite forgotten but it meant that I was to be in Bombay until the end of November. It was understood that my demobilisation number would not be affected. My pay I drew once a fortnight from an army depot in the city.

It was always my intention to offer my services to the Indian Party, and although my social life was much more wide-ranging than I could ever have anticipated, I very soon renewed contact. For the next two months or so I worked several days each week at the Party Commune on a variety of jobs. I wrote at least two pamphlets – one on British working-class history which was published under the name of J. Stammers – and I was given quite a lot of editorial work of different kinds, some for the *People's War* which did not immediately change its name with the coming of peace. I gave a number of lectures to the different schools the Commune organised, talked a good deal with the British communists who visited the headquarters, and naturally had much discussion with members of the Commune itself, including some of their leading personalities: G.M. Adhikari, Arun Bose and B. T. Ranadive. I saw a great deal of Mohan for we often ate together and I was to have at least two quite long sessions with P.C. Joshi. The reason he found time to talk with me – and there were always others present – was because of the differences between the Indian Party line on the national question and that accepted by the Colonial Bureau in the UK; and that, of course, meant Rajni Palme Dutt. What I had become conscious of by the late summer of 1945 was the hostility of Congress to Indian communists. The first speech made by Nehru after his release from detention in mid-1945 was a vigorous attack upon the Communist support for the war after the German invasion of Russia. Until my period of leave in Bombay I had met mostly Muslim Leaguers in Karachi or Party comrades round the country. In Bombay, however, it was Congress people with whom I mostly talked and their general attitudes were very different everywhere.

There were other parts to my life in Bombay. I went to seminars at the

Bombay School of Economics and tried to bring myself more or less up to date on the holdings of periodical literature in the College library. And I began to accompany Agnes Maclean on her many visits to the widely different social groups with whom she maintained regular contacts. So I saw the slum buildings from the inside where Agnes talked with families whom she had obviously known for some time, and on another day we would go to the luxurious houses on the Malabar Hills. The most interesting social occasion I was present at among the rich was a twenty-five-year marriage celebration when once again the magnificent saris provided a remarkable and quite stunning extravaganza high up against the background of the city of Bombay.

Then, towards the end of November, the Army caught up with me and I was instructed to attach myself to a Brigade, once again quite close to Poona. My demobilisation number was 27 and that should be coming up quite soon in the New Year. I was, therefore, anxious to get back to Karachi in order to make certain – as far as one could ever be certain in a bureaucratic world – that my personal and army details were in proper order. I had been temporarily promoted to Warrant Officer Class 1, which made me a SMIG, but it was unlikely to be a substantive rank so I assumed I would be discharged as a Warrant Officer Class 2. Karachi could, perhaps would, sort out matters like these and the sooner I was there the more relaxed I would be. What I really meant was that I would be among friends for the final weeks in India.

On the day after I arrived at Brigade headquarters I was walking across the parade ground when I was greeted by a Captain I G. 'Ah', he said, after we had introduced ourselves, 'I am glad you have arrived. We have a great deal to do and it will not be easy to persuade people to start training again'. 'But the war is over,' I replied and now I took a good look at him. He was about my height but somewhat thinner, and his knees were white, always a mark of identification that one looked for. White meant either a bureaucrat or, more likely, a new arrival. He explained once again that there was much to do. I looked round to see if there was anyone in hearing distance, and as he was continuing to list my training duties, I interrupted him. 'My war is over,' I said, 'and you can go and fuck yourself'. And I turned about and walked away.

It was a foolish comment. This was my sixth year in the army and it was not unreasonable to assume that I knew most of the ways of the army world, or at least I thought I did. What I ought to have said was that I was naturally happy to help but that my demob. number would be coming up soon, and already I had asked to see the Brigadier about returning to the Central Gunnery School to get certain matters sorted out. I had made the request the day before on my arrival. But in the meantime … and nothing would have happened for a few days by which time I would expect to be on my way again.

The interview with the Brigadier came in a couple of days, and I assumed that he would have been briefed by my Captain IG. It would not be unfair to describe it as cold to freezing, but to my amazement I was informed later in the day – by some ordinary office-wallah – that my travel documents would be ready within forty-eight hours. I went by truck to Poona, spent a night with the Kamats, said goodbye to the comrades in the Party Commune, and then took the train to Bombay where I had half a day with John and Agnes and next morning, with Agnes coming to see me off, I boarded my second class compartment for two nights and three days. I thought I was almost home.

My return to headquarters at Karachi was a dismal affair. Everyone I knew a year earlier had gone and the new senior officers were exceedingly unfriendly. I was immediately called in to see the CO and the Adjutant who were clearly incensed at my additional sabbatical leave from the Army, although there was no work at all being done by anyone in the Gunnery School. They were also in receipt of a report from the Brigadier of a week earlier. I argued vigorously that I had always been an efficient soldier; that I had worked well and hard during the preparations for Operation Zipper (which they hadn't heard of) and that my record would show there were no complaints. My secondment to the Bombay School of Economics and my additional leave in general had been endorsed by the Gunnery School. They were not all happy with my position but there was nothing they could do except make my life as difficult as was in their power. And that was minimal. While I could still use the sergeants' mess I was sent to the mainland to look after one of their former training camps which was now occupied by a Parachute unit but which still had quite a lot of our gunnery equipment lying around. They were not to know that the move was much welcomed. It meant that I was nearer the city and close to my Muslim friends and the various Communist Party contacts whom I soon met again. Christmas was celebrated at headquarters with excellent food, but for me with a minimum of drink, since I had decided that returning to civilian life required a normal sober existence. And then, in the middle of January, there occurred an unforeseen event at the RAF Drigh Road aerodrome that was to involve me in a period of intense political activity both in India and especially back home.

The communist group in Drigh Road was as lively as when I first met them. We continued to meet in town every Saturday for a meal and then a discussion. The numbers were somewhat larger than the year previous and on a few occasions there were some Americans present. On Thursday 17th January 1946 Station Orders at Drigh Road RAF informed everyone that on the following Saturday there would be a parade in best blue uniform and this would be followed by a kit inspection. 'Best blue' meant clothing issued in Britain and quite unsuitable for the much higher temperatures of India, including the relatively cooler Karachi; and kit inspection could only mean the beginning of a return to peacetime conditions. There were particular reasons why the wartime RAF were becoming discontented with their lives. It was increasingly rumoured that the RAF were to be subject to a slower rate of demobilisation, and this was in fact correct. Living conditions in most of the large camps were inadequate to grim for the ordinary aircraftmen and Drigh Road was not an exception. There were some interesting social differences between the RAF and the Army. The RAF were usually in large numbers at any one particular camp and their civilian background, working class like the Army, was often of a more skilled kind with membership of a trade union a good deal more common than the average infantryman or gunner. Collective action, if sufficiently provoked, and not least now that the war was over, could therefore be more likely among the RAF, a statement which does not exclude possible activity of the same kind in the other two branches of the armed forces, of which there were, of course, examples.

In the late afternoon and early evening of this Thursday at Drigh Road rumours began to circulate of a meeting on the football pitch at 7.30 p.m. when it would be already dark. About eight or nine hundred men assembled – a broad guess and if correct would be about half the total on the camp. There was no one in command and the meeting could easily have broken up in angry disorder but Arthur Attwood, one of our comrades, intervened and took over the chair. The Party group had not called the meeting nor does it seem that there was any prior discussion but it was obvious that some direction was required. Arthur had been active all his working life in the Electrical Trades Union – he was now thirty one – and in the weeks to come he was to show remarkable powers of leadership. On this first night he controlled matters so that only one person spoke at a time and it was finally agreed that on the Saturday morning they would all parade in khaki drill, not best blue, and they would not prepare for a kit inspection. It was also agreed that anyone who had the chance to talk with their officers would explain their very strong grievances and that it would be hoped there would be no punishments for what was being done. When Saturday morning came all the men appeared on the parade ground but not one was in best blue. There was apparently a good deal of confusion among the officers present, to whom it must have been clear that no official parade could take place, and when the CO arrived he appeared flustered and harassed. He talked with several groups and promised a senior officer would come and discuss their grievances and he specifically said there would be no punishments. And that was all.

We met in the usual way on the Saturday evening when those of us outside Drigh Road first heard their story. There had been some talk of a strike but Arthur Attwood was against it and so was I, but I was also clear that only the Party group could offer the kind of sensible, well thought out political leadership that the situation demanded. It could easily go very wrong for those who were publicly involved and I was wholly sceptical of any promises that might be made by the top brass in the RAF, or the top brass in any of the Services. It was therefore important that a practical list of demands should be put before the Senior Officer who was supposed to be coming to talk with the men at Drigh

Road. There were some eight members of the communist group at Drigh Road and they were all helpful, but the two outstanding members, alongside Arthur Attwood, were David Duncan and Ernie Margetts. Duncan was a wireless mechanic who began to re-train within the Education Corps when the war ended, and Ernie Margetts was an armourer who in civilian life would, like Duncan, become a teacher.

I must add here that I was deeply conscious of what could be involved for our comrades. My status as an Instructor in Gunnery meant that I never became part of any particular unit, and I had therefore a good deal of independence. I took orders from a Captain or Major IG but I was not subject to the daily routine of the ordinary unit. Outside my duties as an instructor – and these as I have made clear could be onerous – I was very much on my own. And this was true of all Gunnery Instructors, in Ack-Ack or Field Artillery. I was able to talk with a lot of different people from different units and I already knew at least the broad outlines, if not always the detail, of a number of 'incidents' somewhat comparable to what was happening at Drigh Road. In the event the Drigh Road group worked out a very reasonable list of points to be put before the senior officer who would be visiting them, and they included the central issue of demobilisation and eight other points relating to their grievances concerning food and living conditions as well as permission for a petition to be circulated and sent to the Prime Minister at Westminster. When the senior officer did come to Drigh Road it was one with the rank of Air Commodore – a superior being whom almost no one had ever seen before – and a delegation of twenty was elected to meet him. Arthur was in the chair for the delegation and it was Duncan who went through their list of requests/demands. The Air Commodore had obviously come in conciliatory mood – discontent elsewhere in India was already showing itself – and the Drigh Road delegation were given eight out of their nine demands. The Commanding Officer at the first meeting had already stated that there would be no punishment, and following the visit of the Air Commodore living and working conditions improved almost the next day. It was a remarkable victory for plain good sense, or so we all thought; and it was with these thoughts that within the next few days I left Karachi on my final stage on the way home.

The assembly point for all gunners was the camp at Deolali, the camp in which we all had made our first acquaintance with India. One could never gauge when your name would be called for the boat home, so once again the educational facilities were explored. And now there was a Forces Parliament on the lines of the original Cairo Parliament, and it was at my first meeting that I met members of the communist group. There were some interesting personalities, among them Bert Ramelson and Mervyn Jones. Ramelson was a Canadian Jew who had fought in Spain, and in the British Army in North Africa he was in a tank regiment. Bert was taken prisoner and was in an Italian prisoner of war camp on the mainland of Italy when Italy pulled out of the war. The British command in Italy issued instructions to all prisoners of war that they should remain in their camps until liberated by the Allies: just one more mistake in the long catalogue of errors in this wholly miserably managed campaign. Bert told me that the camp's senior officer had announced the Army's decision but that within a few days he noticed that units of the German army were moving south, not north. In other words the Germans were intending to continue their defence of southern Italy and for him the obvious thing to do was to leave as soon as possible and find the way to the Allied lines. And this he did with a few of his mates and they walked four hundred miles before contact was made, assisted, as most British soldiers were, by the Italian peasant communities. The majority who remained in his camp, like those in other camps, ended in Germany and stayed there until the war ended.

When I met Bert he was a captain in the legal branch at Deolali (he had qualified as a lawyer) and he lived a comfortable life in a very pleasant bungalow. It was being shared by Mervyn Jones, a lieutenant originally in an anti-tank regiment who was now awaiting a posting. He was to become well-known in the post-war world as a journalist and novelist, and it was his experiences in Bombay which provoked a passionate debate in the Forces Parliament.

India was by now in considerable political ferment. With the end of the war with Japan and the release of the Congress leadership the politics of independence inevitably provided the background for debate and discussion over the whole sub-continent. There was one political issue that for most was unexpected, at least in terms of the fervour, often amounting to frenzy, that was generated. This was the Indian National Army (INA) which had been formed by Subhas Chandra Bose to fight alongside the Japanese in their attack upon India. It is an interesting story that has been well documented, although it is difficult to evaluate what emotional or political support the INA had in India during the war itself. The end of the war with the Japanese meant of course the collapse of the INA and its soldiers were brought back into India as prisoners of war. And then the British made a monumental mistake which might perhaps be assumed given their many examples of stupidity in the last years of the Raj. It was decided by Auchinleck, the Commander in Chief and agreed to by Wavell, the Viceroy, to make an example of three of the senior officers of the INA by putting them on trial, charged, among other wrong-doing, with 'waging war against the king'. During the years of war the Congress Party, inside jail and outside, had been divided in their attitudes toward the INA but now, with the war ended, political attitudes were to change. In September 1945 the All-India Congress Committee had passed a resolution on the INA calling for their release. But it was decided that the trial must go ahead. The court martial would be held in the historic Red Fort in Delhi. The country was aroused; the accused were found guilty and sentenced to transportation for life. This was in November 1945 and the turmoil was such that Auchinleck cashiered the three officers and released them. It was finally decided that only those soldiers of the INA who could be proved to have committed brutality or murder against their fellow countrymen would be tried, and these trials during 1946 continued to create new outbursts of public feeling. The INA episode has not been fully appreciated in some accounts of the background history that led to independence but it was a public and popular protest of quite remarkable proportions. Subhas Bose (who was killed in an air crash three days after the war with Japan ended) remained a subject for mass adulation in the decades that followed. The popular sentiment during the autumn and winter of 1945-6 was so strong that the CPI, already highly conscious of their isolation from the national movement because of their wartime policy, gradually moved from a position of at best neutrality to one of more general support for the wartime soldiers of the INA.

The INA story was part of the growing tensions that were increasingly evident within India in the months that followed August 1945. On 16 February 1946 sections of the Indian Navy mutinied in Bombay. It lasted for six days and there was some support from certain groups of technicians in the Army. Bombay mill workers proclaimed a general strike and it was only the intervention of Congress in the first instance that brought peace to what was potentially a very dangerous situation for the British administration. It was Mervyn Jones' witness of one day's events that led to the debate in the Forces Parliament at Deolali.

Mervyn went into Bombay on the second day of the mutiny and he went to the mill district. He walked down the Suparibaug Road, which appeared to be quite normal although quite crowded when suddenly an Army truck came round a corner into the main street. Two machine guns opened fire from the back of the truck and then, with dead and wounded lying around the street, disappeared again as fast as it had come.

Mervyn returned that evening to Deolali and we held an emergency meeting of the communist group in Ramelson's bungalow. We decided at the next meeting of the Forces Parliament that we should move an adjournment and Mervyn would present a report on his experience in the Suparibaug Road. We should then each make the most vigorous protest at the atrocities that the British Army had inflicted upon the peaceful citizens of Bombay. Our intentions were made public in order to obtain the greatest possible number in attendance, and we were informed by the camp's Education Officer that if we proceeded with our protest the Forces Parliament would in future be closed down. The individual members of the group scattered themselves at different points of the hall, and after Mervyn had spoken everyone made an individual contribution. We were not alone, of course, and there were some dissenting voices, but we carried the protest by a very large majority. The next morning, early, I left for Bombay and went straight on board the troopship for home. The Forces Parliament was closed down.

Part 3: **1946-1956**

There was an unpleasant surprise at the top of the gangway of the large troop-ship that was to take us home to post-war Britain. The pleasure cruise of the outward journey was not to be repeated. All non-commissioned ranks, including warrant officers, were to travel on the troop decks. The ship, inevitably, given the pressures of demobilisation, was seriously over-crowded. Accommodation on the troop decks was at the long tables I mentioned earlier, the atmosphere was always foul even before we reached the vomiting zone and as often as possible I slept *a la belle étoile*. There was no point at all in making complaints. I decided that to keep myself more or less normal it might be interesting to reflect on the last six years, an experience I assumed I would not have to accept again. So I found myself an out of the way corner and began writing. Most of the notes I made then I still have.

I began with what I could remember of a long letter I wrote to Constance when I was in hospital with dysentery, in the summer of 1945. I had just finished reading Wilfred Macartney's *Walls Have Mouths*. It had been published by the Left Book Club in the later thirties and I read it then, but now I thought I was able to appreciate how related prison discipline was to the traditional regular army of pre-war days. The object of prison discipline, as explained by Macartney, and he was in a British prison for ten years from the later nineteen twenties, was to crush the convicted into subservience by a process of deprivation of all comforts and cultural amenities, and by a harsh discipline. The social origins of crime were not appreciated to any serious degree. Discipline in all armies is a central part of the soldiers' training. The question is how the discipline is enforced and through which centres of power. To have any degree of effect, other than sheer terror, it ought to be conducted in ways that were understood to be legitimate and fair. The Prison Commissioners and the Army Council, however, never recognised the convict or the soldier as a citizen in society, and too often they were disciplined in ways that were arbitrary and unjust. The result was a cynicism that became deep-rooted and anti-social. There were many ex-officers in the higher ranks of the prison officials and Macartney reckoned that about a quarter of the wardens were army pensioners or ex-members of one or other of the services. The transition from army life to a position of control in prison, however lowly the position, was not at all difficult.

The Army and the Prison authorities were agreed in their attitudes towards things of the mind. The soldier, however, was not a convict and given the necessity of engaging in some occupation outside straight military duties, sport of some kind was the obvious activity. Any kind of intellectual discussion was apparently never seriously considered. It took nearly two years into the Second World War before it was accepted that some understanding of the war in progress might be a sensible idea, but it is interesting that ABCA discussions were for the ordinary soldiers and were not evidently considered for commissioned officers. Officers' mess at meals was never the place for any conversation about politics or matters relating to the conduct of the war; indeed discussion of such affairs was regarded as a breach of manners

One of the many problems of the British Army, as far as my own experience went, was that relations between different ranks, and especially between officers and those below them, were not of a kind to encourage a sympathetic appreciation of problems likely to be confronted. Throughout my army career I had been continually made aware of the sharp differences between the living standards of the officers and those of sergeants and below. While my own personal experience soon became more or less equivalent to the life styles of junior officers, I saw enough of ordinary soldiers' existence to remain highly conscious of these material differences. In countries like India and those of the Middle East they contributed, in part at least, to the racist attitudes that were regrettably common. I thought the Army a somewhat stupid organisation with India Command being a good deal more backward than that in Western Europe. Operation Zipper, for example, which was largely the responsibility of India Command, would have been a disastrous affair had the war not ended. I had met in Bombay during my October leave a British sergeant with whom I had worked in a Sikh regiment to which I had been attached. Apparently when Operation Zipper was cancelled it was decided to carry on with a dress rehearsal after the event. The sergeant was in the back half of the first wave and he said that it was horrendous. His landing craft had hit a reef that had not been identified from the air, the beaches were incapable of taking most vehicles, the Japanese covering defence of his beach was a good deal more extensive than had been assumed. The publication of the official history of the Far East campaigns (Volume 5, in 1969) confirmed the story I had been told in unpleasant detail. The situation on the beaches, if the war had not ended, would have been catastrophic. India Command could not possibly have tested the beaches in the way that was done for the Normandy landings and the various war diaries of those involved offer quite extraordinary accounts of these 'peaceful' landings.

In the last month of the war I was somewhere in the wilderness waiting for the move to the port of embarkation, and working very hard in terrible heat and the most primitive conditions. One day in early July 1945 a tank regiment parked quite close and after a couple of days I walked through their lines and read the Orders of the Day. They began: 6.30 a.m. STABLES. I found that they had been motorised from a cavalry unit within the first year of the war and they had fought in North Africa. There were always stories circulating about the poor quality of British-made tanks and as was common knowledge most of the tanks at the second battle of Alamein, which Montgomery won, were American Shermans. There were also stories about the difficulties that developed with close infantry cooperation, with suggestions that some tank units behaved like Uxbridge's heavy cavalry at the battle of Waterloo. There is, of course, the particular attraction of the horse for the ruling classes of most countries, but it is not usual to find a navy having strong nostalgic feelings for the sailing ship as a ship of war or the air force for the bi-plane of the First World War.

Musings on the ship taking me home roamed over the previous years but increasingly, and naturally, I was thinking about the future. I had several possibilities for employment. My brother-in-law, François Lafitte, who was now a leader writer on *The Times*, had written about a job in the research section of the Ministry of Works. James Jefferys, who was a senior research worker at the National Institute of Economic and Social Affairs, was also suggesting that there might be the possibility of a job in his section. The most attractive option had come from John Maclean who wanted me to apply for a teaching position at Wilson College, Bombay and, full of India as I was, this certainly was the one I would most enjoy, or at least that was what I was thinking. There was a problem: I was an atheist not a Christian, and the Church of Scotland in Edinburgh might not be as enthusiastic as John Maclean. And indeed, they were not.

As the ship got nearer to Britain we were able to hear the BBC and I began to put my ideas together. What was so distressing was that Labour's foreign policy and especially her imperial policy, was no different from that which a Tory government would have pursued. There were three parts of the world which especially concerned me. The first, which was almost never discussed in Britain, was French Indo-China or Vietnam, which was its correct name. It had been taken over by the Japanese and when the war ended the resistance movement – the Vietminh – took control in both parts of the country, that is, in Hanoi and Saigon. In the second week of September British forces landed with the stated objective of liberating and arranging for the passage home of Allied prisoners of war and other internees of the Japanese, and of course for the disarmament of the Japanese military machine. According to the Indian papers, of different political complexion, this was not how things were working out, and by Christmas 1945 the French were back in control of the southern half of the country, whose capital was Saigon. When I got back to civilian life in England I found that this British intervention on behalf of the French – including using Japanese troops against the Vietminh – had stirred no ripples on political life in Britain. The intervention on behalf of the Dutch in Indonesia, with British forces also being used, received much more publicity, with strikes by Australian dockers against the supply of arms to the imperialist forces.

The second country was Greece, and here the Labour Government followed Churchill and the wartime Coalition; and the third was Spain. Almost all in the British labour movement, and those elsewhere in the world, assumed that the conclusion of the war would bring the downfall of Franco. During the war Franco had sent the Blue Division to Russia, and had opened Spanish ports to German submarines. To allow this butcher of so many thousands of his own people to remain in power in the post-war world, with fascism in Germany and Italy overturned, was for me a confirmation of the conservative iniquities of British labourism. The modest improvements in social welfare, with the National Health Service the most advanced, were the least that could be expected to be introduced and full employment, common to all the advanced industrial countries, was the most significant part of the general increase of living standards. Far too many of the conservative structures of our society were left untouched and the six years of Labour rule were followed easily and without any spectacular changes by thirteen years of Conservative governments. What they did was steadily but without publicity move various social structures and policies back into the range of the market.

We docked at Southampton and after demobilisation I met Constance one evening at Waterloo Station, and was shocked and upset at her appearance. She had suffered a very rough war, being bombed three times, and in London food for its ordinary citizens was less plentiful than elsewhere in the country. Items on the ration books were, of course, the same but almost everywhere else, and naturally especially in the rural areas, there were always additional foods to be obtained. If you were working in London there was usually a canteen meal at midday; if you could afford it there were always restaurants, and there was the black market. Constance was a lone mother with a baby, in south London. Her friends were elsewhere and her allowance as the wife of a warrant officer was nothing like as generous as it would have been had I taken a commission.

Three days after I got home in early April 1946 I received a telegram from Karachi : 'Arthur arrested. Please help. Dunc.' What had happened was that the Special Investigation Branch (SIB) of the RAF had moved into the Drigh Road camp during the last ten days of March and had begun investigating the events of January, which we had so innocently believed had been condoned and forgotten about. The SIB were exceedingly unpleasant in their interviews. One of our comrades was asked if his wife had a private income, and how would she manage for ten years while he was in jail? Everyone knew about Norris Cymbalist, who was already in jail for ten years for political activity of the kind that had taken place at Drigh Road, and his case was already quoted throughout the Far East. Arthur Attwood himself was still at Drigh Road, and was interviewed but allowed to proceed on his demobilisation journey. It was in the assembly camp, from which airmen left to join their ship, that he was arrested and began his months of imprisonment that ended only in early July. The story of those days has now been written and published by David Duncan, in a well-written pamphlet entitled *Mutiny in the RAF.*

There were to be a large number of people involved in the Attwood Defence campaign which I helped to initiate, but without Arthur Attwood's steadfastness and courage, and David Duncan's constant flow of information from India the efforts of the Defence Committee in Britain would have failed. It was Duncan who organised an Indian legal team for the defence in the court martial. His telegram sent me to the headquarters of the Communist Party in King Street, Covent Garden, where I saw Michael Carritt. Michael Carritt's own account of his Indian years is in *A Mole in the Crown* published at his own expense and it is a lively, interesting story that would certainly be worth re-publishing. He sent me to D.N. Pritt, the independent socialist MP for Hammersmith, whom I now regard as the greatest British civil liberties lawyer of the twentieth century. In Attwood's case I think that without Pritt we would probably not have won. There were many other people whose contribution to the Defence Committee was important and there are some, such as the Indian solicitors and lawyers who were employed as defence counsels, whose role was indispensable. Yet it was Pritt who kept the questions flowing in the House of Commons and who was never too busy to answer requests for help from myself and others. He was a great man, with a remarkable sense of humour and a collection of witty stories that he told with a fine sense of timing. He had been expelled from the Labour Party for his support of the Soviet Union in their war against Finland in 1940, but he easily kept his seat in the 1945 election, only to lose it in 1950. I met him several times in the fifties and both he and his wife came to meetings I organised. He was, as I have always explained to everyone, the exemplar of one of the major paradoxes of left politics in the twentieth century. He was, to the end of his days, a hard-line supporter of the Soviet Union, but his personal history, as a defender of justice in all matters that were brought to his attention and where he could judge the evidence, was quite unassailable. His three volumes of autobiography, especially part two, provide detailed accounts of some of his important political cases, including that of Arthur Attwood. His vehement defence of those subject to legal and political injustice included a superb support of Greek seamen during the Second World War and counsel for Jomo Kenyatta in the 'fifties.

Arthur Attwood was finally released. There had been a large meeting in the Memorial Hall in the Farringdon Road, with widespread support from the London trade union movement. The pressures from within Parliament and from outside support, meant that the politicians had to overrule the reactionary blimps among the senior members of the RAF. One important consequence of the victory in the Attwood case was that other court-martial decisions were now reviewed, and a number were overturned. The one that perhaps received most publicity was the case of Norris Cymbalist who as noted above had received a sentence of ten years, which was reduced to five and after pressure from within Britain he was finally released after serving two and a half years.

I was now in the Economics section of the Chief Scientific Division of the Ministry of Works. Operational research had become what is today called a 'buzz word' during the years of war and the original idea was to establish a peacetime section using the techniques developed for various social projects. The head of my section was Marion Bowley, the daughter of the well-known statistician. She came from University College, London where she later occupied one of the chairs in economics. There were some interesting people around: Jacob Bronowski was head of the statistical section and there were others who later became well-known in the academic world. This was one of the problems. Too many, like myself, accepted the job as a standby as we looked around for a more permanent position. Our main activity within the Division was the analysis of the many problems of the housing situation and the work that was produced was not entirely unhelpful. We were not, however, approved of by the permanent civil servants nor did we expect to be, given that our status as travellers looking for new pastures was well understood.

I had applied for several research jobs, without success, but early in the New Year of 1947 I was given a serious opportunity. James Jefferys was at the National Institute as a senior research worker and among his colleagues was Ian Bowen, who had just been appointed to the chair of economics at the University College of Hull. Bowen was looking for an economic historian, his present lecturer having given notice of leaving at the end of the 1946-7 session.

I went for an interview at the University College of Hull on a Friday in May. There were a number of University Colleges in those days, most of them having been established during the years between the wars. Among others, besides Hull, were Reading, Leicester, Southampton and Exeter. They were universities in all respects except that they did not award their own degrees. All the University Colleges taught to the syllabus of the University of London, in all subjects (or nearly all subjects) and their students sat for the External Degree of the University of London.

The train journey from London to Hull in those days took about five hours but at least it was straight through. I came out of Paragon station and saw devastation around me. I could see from the station right through to the centre of the town; the large stores and buildings in between having been flattened. Hull was one of the worst bombed cities in Britain. German planes were guided by the broad expanse of the Humber – there were seven miles of docks in Hull – and it was then a straight line across country to another major port, Liverpool.

I took a taxi from the station to the University College which was towards the outskirts of the town. The journey from the station took no more than ten minutes and away from the centre the evidence of bombing became much less obvious. The College was in a pleasant tree-lined road and consisted of two large buildings fronting the road with a great deal of open space behind. My interview was before the Principal, the Registrar and three academics, but not Ian Bowen.

He came half way through our meeting, mumbling some excuse to the chair
– somewhat characteristic of him, as I was to discover later. The interview, I
thought at the time, was a rather lackadaisical affair. I had indicated that I didn't
think I could come for less than £700 a year, having mildly exaggerated the salary I was getting in the civil service. I was unaware that for each child an annual
supplement of £50 was always added to the salary.

After a perfunctory cross-examination of my abilities, as a scholar or a teacher,
the interview ended and I was sent on my way, with Bowen making no attempt
to see me before I took another taxi to the station. I got home very late, very tired
and quite certain that this was not the place for me. I knew a certain amount
about the University College before I went for my interview. Its numbers were
very small before the war, about 250 each year. The library had about 130,000
books and the annual grant was small. The academic staff, however, in pre-war
days had some remarkably interesting people. Eric Roll was professor of economics, Jacob Bronowski had come in the middle 'thirties, A.C. Hardy had left
in 1942 and there was a young assistant to Hardy who was to become very well-
known in the field of marine biology. The trouble was, as Bronowski was ready
to point out when he talked to me about Hull, almost all the bright intellects
had left during the war and there was a fairly unhelpful group of senior professors whose research output was very small. So next morning, a Saturday, I told
Constance that unfortunately I thought I should be in a backwater from which it
might be difficult to move. It was for this stage in my life that had I been Hazlitt
I would later have written 'The Importance of Being Dilatory'. I was busy that
weekend and I meant to write my letter of withdrawal on the Monday, but life in
some way or another got in the way, and no letter was written. On the Tuesday
morning a letter arrived from the Registrar of the University College offering me
a lectureship at the starting rate of £700, with the usual annual increase of £50
a year and, of course, the £50 for each child. 'Hull', all my friends said, 'where's
that?': the usual response of Londoners to anywhere north of Watford.

I spent all my free time in the next few months reading in the LSE library for
I had been away from academic life for many years and I would be teaching to
the syllabus of the London External degree. I was the only economic historian
so I would be giving the compulsory paper in the B. Sc.(Econ.) degree together
with two of the three papers for history specialists. The third, on the 16th and 17th
centuries was taken over by Conrad Gill, one of the more-enlightened survivors
from the pre-war years. In addition there was just being started a social studies
department and they would require a paper in social history. I decided that for
this first year I would have to be alone, and Constance and our first born would
stay in London, but at least there would be more money.

I found myself fairly awful working-class lodgings quite close to the College,
where I was installed in a Nissan hut, one of several to house the increased academic staff. Student numbers were increasing quite fast, mostly from ex-service

applicants and by 1949 the total was nearly one thousand. I worked every night until midnight and then gave the lectures I had been putting together the next day. For the first two terms I allowed myself no spare time activities. John Clapham's great three volume economic history of the nineteenth century was my basic text but naturally I read as widely as time would allow. I loved my life, lunching every day in the week at High Table with mostly younger lecturers who were intellectually lively and delighted, like myself, to be teaching. I saw a lot of Cyril Lucas, Hardy's former assistant, who used to invite me to supper at his house where his wife Sally cooked excellent meals, and I also lunched regularly with Lackman, a devout Hayekian and very bright. He was contemptuous of Bowen and within a couple of years had accepted a job in South Africa. It was members of the English department whom I found especially congenial, with a number of very lively young men and women who passed through on the way to better libraries and improved facilities in universities round the country. Barbara Hardy stayed for a year or two, and my closest friends in the English Department were Margaret 'Espinasse, whose husband was professor of zoology, and Rachel Trickett, who died while this section of my memoirs was being written. Rachel left Hull in 1954 for St Hughs and her obituary in *The Guardian* was presented by John Bayley with insight and affection.

The College library was somewhat more liberal in its range than I had feared. I developed rather bad relations with Agnes Cuming, the Librarian, and I later recognised that it was mainly my fault although she always seemed to me conservative in her organisation of the library. But the real problem was that the Library was starved of funds, the Principal found her unsympathetic and the senior members of the academic staff were quite uninterested.

This is where Bruce Truscott comes in, a name and a book (*Red Brick University*) that will not be known to many at the beginning of the new century. In the autumn of 1947, when I first arrived in Hull, it was being read by everyone. The first part had been published in 1943,the second in 1945 and a Penguin edition of 1951 included the whole of part one and most of part two. I quote below from the Preface to the Penguin edition, which sums up the purpose of a serious and well-documented critique:

The very heart and root of my criticisms is the deep conviction that in certain respects the modern universities are not pulling their weight, and that the responsibility for this lies at more doors than anyone has yet realised. The Treasury has starved Redbrick of money, making its grants so minute that it cannot do a tithe of the things of which it is capable. The schools have starved it of talent, sending all their brilliant pupils to Oxbridge and encouraging even the average ones to go there if they can. Professors and lecturers, though admittedly underpaid, have been content to spend only a modicum of time on research and to regard themselves as fulfilling their duty by doing a bare eight or ten hours a week of teaching. Laymen with little understanding of academic problems have done untold harm by their activities on University Councils. Undergraduates have pursued a narrow course of study, thought too little of the world beyond Redbrick's unlovely quadrangles, and rejected all kinds of opportunities of widening their vision.

Red Brick University was widely discussed. What its practical influence was is difficult to estimate but my experience at the University College of Hull provided too many examples of its analysis. The senior members, almost all carried over from pre-war days, were idle and were able to list only small items of research in the annual reports. Sherard Vines, Professor of English, who had been a radical in his day, would include 'Reviews in the *Listener*' as his only contribution to scholarship during the previous year. I have a particular memory of Sherard Vines. During 1952 he decided to resign, and the College advertised for a replacement. The external referee was a well-known Cambridge scholar whose responsibility was to confirm the short-list which, for reasons I cannot remember, was also discussed by Senate. I happened to be one of the two lecturing staff members on Senate and I had been asked by nearly all of the lecturing staff in the Department of English to argue the case strongly for the inclusion of William Empson. Now Empson's application was the result of the intervention of Francis Klingender. Francis, a well-known Marxist art historian, had become a member of the Sociology Department in 1948. This was my doing; at least I had persuaded a reluctant Klingender to apply for the job when it was being advertised. He had three distinguished references and as I had explained to him it was unlikely that anyone on the selection committee would have known about his Marxist reputation. Francis knew Empson, who was at this time teaching in Beijing and who wanted to come back to England. So Empson put in an application for the job in Hull and was not included in the short-list which came before Senate. Naturally, with the majority of the English department behind me, I argued at some length that Empson's reputation could not be repudiated in this way but it was clear that the Principal was firmly against him and it was also clear that most of Senate had never heard of Empson. Six months later the University of Sheffield appointed Empson to a chair. I must add that the man Hull did appoint was a good scholar and almost certainly was to prove a better head of a department than Empson would have made, but this does not in any way excuse Vines for what was a matter of grovelling to the Principal. There was also, of course, the fact that my politics were now well known and for the first two decades at Hull there were always some of the senior staff who never listened to any of my arguments but just voted me down.

Truscott's criticisms fitted so many of the internal workings of the University College. The Library was the obvious one to concentrate on since, theoretically at least, everyone beyond the professorial dead ground would be interested.

During my second year I was able to persuade a lawyer and a physicist to sign a one page memorandum which we then duplicated and circulated to the whole of the staff. Its main purpose was to draw attention to the many inadequacies of library provision which could only be remedied by an increase in the book and periodical grants. The most important consequence of this first initiative, which was well received by those of the academic staff who read books, was the establishment of a Lecturing Staff Association which soon became the Lecturing and Administrative Staff Association (LASA). Most staff, including myself, were members of the AUT, the official professional union to which the majority of academics belonged, at least in the provincial universities, but at Hull it was dominated by the old brigade and would never have undertaken the protest campaigns that LASA was to engage in.

The history of LASA is probably somewhat unusual in the post-war history of universities in Britain. What makes LASA interesting is not only that in its first decade especially it was an active campaigning body but also that it seems in some matters to have been recognised officially. In the first three visits by the University Grants Committee – in 1950, 1955 and 1960 – after the recognition of Hull as a grant-aided University College in 1946, the Lecturing Staff Association on each occasion was given an hour's slot in the agenda of the one-day UGC visitation. During our meetings with the UGC in 1950 and 1955 we talked almost entirely about the inadequate library provision and we undoubtedly made the library a central issue within the University College. We were to be greatly helped by two changes of personnel. Agnes Cuming retired in 1955 and the young Philip Larkin was appointed in her place. More important, in the short run at any rate, was the change of Vice-Chancellor. Brynmor Jones was elected in place of J. H. Nicholson and took up his new position for the 1956-7 session. It was an appointment which at the time I thought unfortunate. Brynmor Jones was professor of chemistry and he was building a lively department, but I regarded him as a sycophant toward the Chancellor (Lord Middleton) and the businessmen on the Council of the University. I don't think I was wrong at the time, but what I did not foresee was that Brynmor would grow with the job. It must be admitted that his period of office was the most interesting period of university history in the second half of the twentieth century but he handled most matters well and I suspect he was more liberal than many of his senior professors, but he was always very cautious. He had certainly taken full note of our agitation about the library.

To return to LASA. It was an organisation which was genuinely democratic and represented a majority of the lecturing staff. The most active member, alongside myself, was a liberal minded Unitarian in the Department of Chemistry who, also like myself, was to be among the first batch of senior lecturers to be appointed. But we did have an active group support from almost all departments and the only department not represented was Adult Education. Its absence was probably the influence of a somewhat dictatorial head, although there were throughout the decade of the fifties some interesting personalities in the department who could and should have taken their own decision to be included. They included Richard Hoggart.

While for the visits of the UGC there was a concentration on the library problem, we became increasingly concerned with the general ways in which the College was organised. During the first term of University status in 1955 LASA produced a quite detailed document which considered a large number of the problems the new University would confront. Among the matters emphasised was the very low ratio of senior grades among the academic staff. The memorandum, which was sent to all members of Senate, included one page of comparative statistics of senior staff ratios of all universities in England except Oxford and Cambridge. Senior staff included professors down to senior lecturers and the national average in relation to lecturing staff was 29.2. The Hull figure was less than half the national average at 14.1 and it was at the bottom of the table for the whole country.

This memorandum of 1956 was concerned broadly with the transition from College to University. Four years later LASA undertook an enquiry into the relations within departments between the lecturing staff and their seniors. All lecturing staff were circulated with a one page questionnaire and written replies were received from about 60 per cent. These replies were supplemented by verbal enquiries in some cases, especially to those in departments which were considered under-represented.

I was chair of LASA at the time of this particular exercise and the answers we received were of no surprise to anyone who had read Bruce Trustcott. There were some favourable comments but the majority of replies were intensely critical of the undemocratic character of their departmental lives. At the same time there did not appear to be a pronounced dissatisfaction with life in general at the University. There was one episode during the early 'fifties that should be mentioned, since it is unlikely ever to be repeated in later years, in such a dictatorial fashion at least, at Hull or anywhere else. In 1953 Dr Cheddi Jagan and his People's Progressive Party won a majority in the general election in British Guinea (Guyana). The Colonial Office in London, fully convinced that the Progressive Party was communist-inspired, suspended the constitution, removed all the Party's ministers from the Assembly and sent troops to ensure 'peace and tranquillity'. Later in the same year Jagan came to England, and the student's Labour Society at Hull invited him to speak. I found him accommodation with friends and Jagan's visit was duly advertised. Rather too well, apparently. Some lay members of the College Council were showing visitors round the Student Union and came across notices of the Jagan meeting. This was the time, it must be recalled, of the last phase of the Korean War, the worst period of British MacCarthyism in the post-war years. The Council members were, it would seem, much affronted by the threatened presence of this subversive character on the campus and obviously feared the violation of student innocence. So the Jagan meeting was cancelled by order of the Council, which presumably had to be specially convened for the purpose, but of these details I am not sure, except that the meeting was cancelled.

LASA wrote a polite but firm letter of protest to the Principal and received one in return. Our guess at the time was that the Principal regretted the decision but Trustcott's 'Laymen with little understanding of academic problems' were continuing their harmful interference. But some public protest had to be made. I invited Jagan to speak to the Senior Common Room and we got about thirty members of staff to listen to him. And at my first academic lecture of any size after the ban had been announced I spent the first twenty minutes listing some of the difficult campaigns of the past that had helped to establish freedom of speech – they included the great campaign of *The Poor Man's Guardian* during the first half of the 1830s against the taxes on knowledge – and I concluded with a short reading from John Stuart Mill's essay *On Liberty*.

I much enjoyed my teaching and the department attracted some very lively students. Among the ex-military group of my earliest years there were two whom I found especially interesting. Eric Precious was a working-class young man who came from Witherinsea, a village on the coast not far from Hull. He had left school at fourteen and before he was called up worked for a brewery company, mainly on horse-drawn delivery wagons. For reasons I never understood the Army picked him out for a very intensive two-year course to become a Japanese speaker. He finished his course the day the war ended and was sent to Singapore for some eighteen months, working as an interpreter in the examination of Japanese prisoners of war. He had entered the College in the autumn session of 1948 and was the best student I ever had in all my decades of teaching. Like all our students he took the London external degree in his Finals and obtained seven alphas out of nine papers. It was apparently the outstanding result of all candidates, internal and external, who specialised in economic history, and he was awarded the Gerstenberg scholarship, to be held at LSE. He started work on his Ph.D., lasted three months and came back to tell me that this was not the life for him. So he joined Shell, worked in various places round the world, but never in Japan, married a French woman and ended his career as European manager for Shell, working from Amsterdam. He retired in his early fifties and died soon after.

Mike Brown was a contemporary of Eric Precious and they remained friends in later life. Mike spent some years of his younger days in an orphanage in Hull, where he was born. The discipline was brutal but there was no sexual abuse as far as he knew. The Army made him into a light infantryman. He was a good, hard-working student and a very pleasant man but I had no appreciation that he was to become one of the outstanding teachers I was to know in my whole academic career. He began teaching in schools on the Hessle Road, which ran parallel to the docks, including the Fish Dock, and was the district where the greater part of the trawlermen lived. The schools were reckoned to be the most difficult within the town; the children were tough and often violent (they assumed at this time that their future was on the trawlers) and the turnover of teachers was always high. He left the Hessle Road to join the staff at the College of Commerce which provided a variety of courses, including the syllabuses for those who had failed O or A levels at school. It was with these groups that Mike was especially successful. He had a remarkable empathy with those who were struggling in one way or other and a notable ability to enthuse them to ride through their difficulties. I was able to persuade him to apply for a history lectureship at the University, to join my department, and he showed the same ability to encourage the downhearted and to uplift those who thought they were on the floor. There was no sentimentality in his approach and he was much liked by all levels of students – a teacher of the kind that all departments need. I tried very hard, at a time when I was a senior member of the academic staff, to get him promoted, but even in those days teaching abilities were very rarely sufficient to win a higher grade. Today, of course, I would guess it is almost impossible. I grant that it is a difficult matter for promotion committees, but universities in general have always paid too little heed to the crucial importance of good teachers whose work does not end when the lecture or academic tutorial is finished.

As I have already indicated I enjoyed my time in the Department of Economics in the 'fifties. While we continued to take the London external B.Sc. (Econ.) degree it meant that we had almost no teaching in the summer term. Students had to take an examination at the end of their first year and then Finals after three years, so our main teaching in the third term was almost entirely limited to second year students; *and* we had no examining. From Easter until the end of September most of our time was therefore free, for reading and research.

In 1950 I had been asked by Michael Young if I was interested in undertaking a historical/economic survey of a rural area of south Devon with the central focus on rural depopulation. Michael had been a contemporary at LSE and although we did not seen much of each other over these past decades, we remained friends and our own large circle of friends helped to maintain contact. He was a member of the Dartington Trust, having been educated at the progressive school there and he always had very close links with Dorothy and Leonard Elmhirst. Dorothy was a member of the Whitney Straight family and it was her money that allowed the purchase of Dartington Hall and its restoration. So I spent just over two months travelling around the South Hams, working in local libraries, talking to all kinds of people and coming back in the evenings to enjoy the company of the many visitors who were guests of the Elmhirst's hospitality. When I returned to Hull and produced my report, I suggested that this was a problem of national importance and that I would be happy to undertake a general survey of rural depopulation in England and Wales during the past hundred years. This was agreed and the book with that title was published in 1956. My survey covered 1851-1951. What I mostly needed for my basic research were the Parliamentary Censuses. The University Library had almost no Parliamentary Papers at that time, but to my astonishment and delight the town's main Library had a complete set of the Parliamentary Censuses from 1801.Ten minutes by bicycle from my house in the very pleasant Avenues, with their long rows of trees, and the Census data every ten years were there in front of me, the volumes deposited by a member of an always obliging library staff. But librarians everywhere, in all parts of the world where I have been, have always been helpful. I had already, before I left London, started working on Chartism and I published in 1952 extracts from the writings of Ernest Jones, the last major figure in the Chartist movement, with a longish introduction on his life and place in the movement. There were no technical ways of copying newspapers and articles in those days for ordinary readers and I spent many hours in the British Museum's Newspaper Library at Colindale, transcribing long extracts from the radical press. I should add that in recent years there have been important revisions of certain aspects of Jones' life.

My work on rural depopulation, which occupied the middle years of the fifties, went alongside continued research into the history of the early labour movement. Labour history was to be my central historical interest for the next two decades although I interpreted that interest reasonably widely. I had already helped James Jefferys with his collection of documents on the middle years of the nineteenth century before I left London (published as *Labour's Formative Years* 1849- 1879) and for me this was the beginning of my association with what became the Communist Party's Historians' Group.

There had been some coming together of Marxist historians before the war but it was after 1945 that a working collective got under way. Eric Hobsbawm wrote an excellent essay in 1978 on the organisation and composition of the communist historians' group between 1946 and 1956 – the decade of its greatest significance – and I want only to underline some of what to me are interesting questions. No one, for example, in 1939 would have expected the historians to be the liveliest intellectual group within the Communist Party in the immediate post-war decade. It was J.D. Bernal and J.B.S. Haldane who were among the most prominent intellectuals of the thirties, and it would not have been unreasonable to expect the left-wing/Marxist scientists to continue their leading role among intellectuals in general. Again one could have argued for the literary Arts to be well represented among the most radically minded of the post-war generations, and they were for some years. But by the end of the 'forties intellectual life in Britain had already undergone a marked political shift towards the Centre and the Centre-Right, and among the student populations there was a growing conservatism, often of an apolitical kind. Very few in 1945 would have anticipated such a rapid decline in the radical temperament of the nation. The general election of July 1945, it accepted, was a firm repudiation of the Tory policies of the inter-war years and the way was open for widespread changes. One of the central problems of these immediate post-war years was the failure of the Labour leadership to understand the class nature of the society in which they lived and worked, and the strength and tenacity in national affairs of the propertied classes. The Conservative Party, accustomed to controlling Parliament, was inevitably thrown off course with the overwhelming Labour victory of July 1945, but not for long, and they were soon providing a very sharp opposition to the Labour front bench. In the country at large, Conservatism, in its press and on platforms, developed an unrelenting criticism of Labour politics, with populist organisations such as the Housewives' League enunciating in increasingly shrill terms the feelings and sentiments of middle-class England. Food and petrol were severely rationed, domestic servants were now, with full employment, increasingly difficult to come by, and foreign travel allowances were sharply restricted. Need life be so difficult when it was widely believed that the workers, with full employment and improved social benefits, were doing so much better than ever before ? Too many of the middle classes thought they were bleeding.

Labour's response to an increasingly tough opposition by the Tories on the domestic front was weak and ineffective, and it was made more difficult by the agreement of Ernest Bevin with the Tories on matters of foreign policy. It was against this background of declining radicalism that the Marxist historians began their serious work on mainly British history. The relationships between the Party Centre and the Historians' group were always friendly and helpful. This point needs emphasis because it was not true of other specialist cultural groups, among them the scientists and those with literary and arts interests. And the main reason could only be the absence of a serious interest in British history from within any intellectual milieu in the Soviet Union. This, of course, had not always been the case for there were some famous names a decade or two earlier. There was nothing coming out of the Soviet Union against which the native British historians had to measure themselves. By contrast the scientists had to contend with the absurd Lysenko controversy, and then for the arts there was the Zhdanov emphasis upon socialist realism. But the British Historians' group was left to its own purposes and these were not of a dogmatic and sectarian kind – for several reasons. Both Marx and Engels had left a very considerable legacy of historical writing, and while not all could be agreed by later historians, it was abundantly clear, from their correspondence for example, that they had no problems in changing their analysis if they considered that new materials suggested the change. In this context I always quote Marx on the Irish question. Further, almost all the leading members of the Historians' group were in academic posts, and they were only too conscious of the intellectual hostility of many of their colleagues towards their Marxist positions. Their writings could be expected to be carefully scrutinised; sometimes, of course, damned out of hand. There was, it should be recorded, no historian in the group who specialised in Russian history. I found the meetings of the Historian's group exciting and very stimulating. We were divided into main periods, with the classicists and the 17th century being the strongest intellectually. We had almost no one who worked in the 18th century until George Rudé joined us, and in the 19th century group only Eric Hobsbawm and myself had academic positions, but there were many teachers. It was when the different sections met together than I appreciated the privilege of being associated with so many lively and interesting intellectuals. For our national discussions we usually met at Netherwood, a conference centre near Hastings, and in July 1954 we held an important week's conference which surveyed the history of capitalism in Britain, beginning with the early mediaeval period. In previous years different groups had worked through Maurice Dobb's *Studies in the Development of Capitalism*, published in 1946. It was the most important of our texts and occupied many sessions, especially on the problems of the transition from feudalism. These discussions came early in the nineteen fifties and the well-known Dobb-Sweezy controversy was followed by further commentaries from the Japanese Marxist Takahashi, Christopher Hill and Rodney Hilton. The nineteenth century group, which met usually twice a year, was especially concerned with the role and place of the working classes in a developing capitalist society and in particular with the struggles and conflicts to establish democratic liberties, viable trade unions and a political presence. The struggle of classes was still largely omitted in the general teaching of history and it was upon this history from below that our early discussions mostly centred. For me in general it was enormously stimulating and I must add to those mentioned the name of Victor Kiernan who in later years became a close friend: a man of wide-ranging erudition and always stimulating in discussion.

In 1954 I edited a collection of essays in honour of Dona Torr, who may properly be described as the mentor of most of the members of the Historian's group. She was born in 1883 of privileged parents, her father being a Canon of Chester Cathedral. The volume was somewhat sparsely reviewed with one reviewer noting that there was more Marxist scholarship around than was generally appreciated.

The Historian's Group had a considerable long-term influence upon most of its members. It was an interesting moment in time, this coming together of such a lively assembly of young intellectuals, and their influence upon the analysis of certain periods and subjects of British history was to be far-reaching. For me, it was a privilege I have always recognised and appreciated.

There were other benefits in addition to debating with lively minds. Our meetings, especially the national conferences, attracted a few older members of the Party, some of whom were historians such as Dona Torr and A.L. Morton, but there were others who joined us out of general interest. Dona became a close friend in the half dozen years before her death in 1957, and Leslie Morton I continued to know for a long time. His wife Vivien was to work for me in later years on the Labour Dictionary. Of the others George Hardy is the one who remains most vividly in my memory, partly I suppose because he was born in a village close to Hull, and after our first meeting at Netherwood George, who used to visit relatives, always came to see Constance and myself at our home.

George had a remarkable career. He was born into an agricultural family in the East Riding of Yorkshire and after a number of jobs he left England for Canada as an assisted emigrant. It was then that his political life began as an industrial militant who became a leading figure in the Industrial Workers of the World (IWW). He talked about his political and industrial experiences vividly, and at great length, and I was one among several who pressed him to set down in writing the history he talked about with such vigour. The book that came out was, however, a somewhat uneven affair. The first two thirds, the story of his union struggles in Canada and the States, was straightforward and interesting, although George certainly talked better than he wrote, but the published account of his years as a Comintern agent was much less informative than the accounts he gave me. Hardy's story is solid testimony to the implacable hostility of the owners of property in situations where they consider their position is being threatened. There are, as we know, different methods of meeting these threats, with the British Conservative control of Parliament through most of the twentieth century offering a notable demonstration of the ways in which cajolery, deceit and a timely use of the coercive power of the State can come together to offer the expected deference to the rich man in his castle.

George became a leading figure in the IWW in the immediate post-war years but he was already questioning seriously their refusal to understand the role of politics in the struggle between classes. His interview with Lenin in 1919, after over a year in jail in America, provided further arguments for moving beyond the IWW non-political attitudes. He was expelled in early 1922, after trying to build a minority movement within the IWW and he then became a full-time worker for the Comintern. He was in Hamburg in 1923, during the abortive rising by the German Communist Party, in Britain during the General Strike of 1926, in China for three years from 1927 and later in South Africa for underground work with the South African Communist Party. I was already deeply interested in Chinese revolutionary history and it was in 1927 that Chiang-Kai-Shek broke with the Communist Party and butchered many thousands. George went to China in that year as a business man, located in Hankow, and he worked with a number of leading communists in the underground, including Chou-en-lai, whose main headquarters at this time were in Shanghai.

George Hardy is an almost unremembered name these days, yet his history must be recorded if the repressive nature of capitalist society is to be fully appreciated. It was one of the central purposes of the Communist Historian's Group to make available the details of the struggles of the past, to give voice to those who fought against their exploitation, and to explain their victories and their defeats.

The world within two or three years of 1945 was rapidly becoming an uncomfortable place for those on the political Left who had traditionally supported the Soviet Union. Our attitudes were only in part carried over from the years before 1939. The Russian peoples had suffered the heaviest burden of death and destruction during their years of war, and without the Red Army it is likely that the Nazis would have been victorious. The toll of Russian deaths – military and civilian – and the range of physical devastation were on a scale beyond anything experienced in western Europe, including Germany. The terrible consequences of the war for the Soviet Union never became part of the history of the Second World War in the consciousness of the British people. We have the remarkable paradox that the country, and its doctrines, dedicated to the destruction of world capitalism, provided the instruments of its salvation. The rapid growth of anti-Sovietism inevitably blurred and distorted national memories, with MacCarthyism in America exercising a powerful influence throughout western Europe. It was a crucial shift in Anglo-American popular understanding that was regrettably encouraged by the incompetence and ineptness of Russian foreign policy. From the beginning of the days of peace Stalin did all in his considerable power to play down the extent of the destruction in eastern and central Russia, and he allowed Molotov to adopt an unyielding position on many issues of disagreement between the Soviet Union and the United States and Britain. The anti-Soviet position which the western powers made into their central assumption was certainly not imagined but it should be the purposes of diplomacy to neutralise as far as possible what begin as seemingly intractable problems. This was not the attitude of the British Foreign Office, and Ernest Bevin concurred. He was bitterly anti-Soviet and although Bevin in his early days was very careful in his public pronouncements, because of his own back-benchers, his attitudes were becoming clear to most by the end of 1947. Bevin's mind was closed to any new ideas by the time he reached the Foreign Office in late July 1945. He certainly had no idea of what a socialist foreign policy involved. He was an old-fashioned imperialist confirmed by the wartime discussions within the War Cabinet, and he emerged into the years of peace with ideas which were no different from those of the Tory Party. Anthony Eden on a number of occasions confirmed their general agreement. There were a number of ludicrously stupid decisions by the Soviet Union in the area of foreign relations which greatly damaged their reputation within western Europe. The case of the Soviet wives was the most obvious of the populist issues – the English women who had married Soviet citizens and were refused exit visas – but it was also the dogmatism of too many intellectual decisions inside the Soviet Union that greatly harmed their international standing. The Lysenko controversy was perhaps the best known. More important in the long term were the political developments within the countries of Eastern Europe once Communist rule had been assured. In the years immediately preceding the death of Stalin in 1953, and following upon the break with Tito, there were a series of events which it has now been accepted were the product of Stalin's growing anti-Semitism. The arrest of Rudolf Slansky, vice-premier of Czechoslovakia, in November 1951 and his execution a year later, together with the 'Doctors' Plot' within the Soviet Union, were not obviously helpful to those arguing for some kind of agreement between the major powers.

It is possible that if Stalin had not died when he did, in which case one can assume that the 'treason' trials would have continued, the defections from a pro-Soviet position might have increased rapidly. This, I think, would have been my position. I regretted the quite stupid decisions in the case of the Soviet wives, not least because it made clear that the leading Soviet foreign office representatives were contemptuous of the movements in popular opinion; I deplored the insistence upon Lysenko's conclusions since this was not the way scientific progress could be helped; and I became increasingly sceptical of the Soviet Union's arguments in their conflict with Tito. When the original break came in 1948 I remained more or less neutral, although my friend and colleague Francis Klingender was taking a very firm line and over the succeeding months eased himself out of the Communist Party with little fuss and no publicity. My own attitude was changed quite radically by the reading of James Klugman's *From Trotsky to Tito* published in 1950. I bought a copy at Collets in Charing Cross Road and read it almost completely through on the five hour journey from London to Hull. And I was much dismayed. I knew Klugman well. He had been a brilliant scholar at Cambridge, graduating around the middle 'thirties and had then lived in Paris working as secretary of the World Youth Congress. During the war he had gone into intelligence and ended serving the British SOE agents in the Balkans from headquarters in southern Italy. After the war he became head of the Communist Party's educational services with the former student organiser, Jack Cohen, as his assistant.

I liked Klugman. He was in personal terms a gentle man, always pleasant and interesting to talk with, and there is no doubt that he sacrificed a great deal when he left Cambridge for a political career. His book on Tito, however, was a thoroughly wretched piece of Jesuitical writing which greatly worried me. These were the times, however, when I was much more concerned with the iniquities of British foreign policy in general. It was already becoming accepted that Britain was primarily interested in the preservation of her colonial Empire, not least because in the immediate post-war years their contribution to the British dollar pool was of quite major importance. At the same time it was being recognised that British subservience to the United States was already a fact of world politics. It must immediately be noted that the overwhelming majority of the British people were not yet prepared to accept this fact, and certainly not its implications. And this is still true.

To return to my years in the late 1940s and early 1950s. There was already in the States a growing anti-Sovietism and anti-communism upon which Senator MacCarthy was to build such a powerful movement of opinion. It was the Korean war, which erupted on 25 June 1950, that vastly encouraged the hysteria in the United States and underlined the anti-communism of western Europe. I remember the period of the Korean war as unpleasant political years of my life. Hostility towards communists could be as common on the campus as in the streets, if you spoke on street corners as I did at times. The academic world in Britain did not, of course, follow the vulgar, frenzied abusiveness of the MacCarthy years in America. They achieved more or less the same results by typically British means, and there are a number of examples that could be documented of scholars who were not promoted or not appointed. Christopher Hill is on record that he applied for several chairs, but was never appointed. In 1957, after he had left the Communist Party, he was asked by the chairman of one selection committee if he would give an assurance that he would never write in the columns of the *Daily Worker*.

There were all sorts of games being played. In 1947 Victor Kiernan who at the time was a Research Fellow of Trinity College, Cambridge, applied for an academic position at Oxford. One of his referees was also a Fellow of his college and he wrote a blistering denunciation of Kiernan's politics. Kiernan later saw a copy. But when Kiernan applied soon after for a similar position at the University of Edinburgh in the department of History, the same man wrote a bland statement of Kiernan's virtues and the job was his. And there Victor remained during his long distinguished career until he retired in 1982.

It was the Korean War that once again confirmed the iniquities of the capitalist order, and it was the reporting of Alan Winnington in the *Daily Worker* from North Korea that made the war such an important part of my understanding. His remarkable story is told in *Breakfast With Mao* (1983). He and Wilfrid Burchett were the only western journalists reporting from North Korea. Most historians have accepted that it was intervention by North Korea, with one major exception who happens to be the outstanding scholar in the field. This is Bruce Cumings, professor of East Asian and International History at the University of Chicago and in his last two massive volumes he documented at enormous length the argument that the origins of the war were much more complex and indeed inevitable given the antithetical structures of society in the two halves of Korea. The reporting by Winnington and Burchett has rarely, if ever, been used by the historians of the Korean war yet it was the only documentation from the North. At the time it was ignored except when there was an incident of major importance. Such was the reporting of a large-scale massacre by the South of political prisoners. In August 1950 Winnington radioed a very long despatch to the *Daily Worker* describing the discovery of around five thousand bodies near a village which he called Rangwul. The number of the dead was later increased to seven thousand. They were all political opponents of Syngman Rhee, killed by Rhee's police and soldiers, with American advisers present. Winnington took photographs, collected American cartridge cases and Lucky Strike cigarette packets and talked to local villagers who had been forced to dig pits for the bodies. By the time the reports were published in the *Daily Worker,* and also in a pamphlet, this area of the South was again back in American hands and it might have been expected that some at least of the many journalists or the dozens of American military observers would have investigated the story. Winnington's reports had been described by the American Embassy in London as an 'atrocity fabrication' but no one – no one – from the United Nations normally called the UN Police Action felt it necessary to provide an independent investigation. Bruce Cumings, in volume 2 of his 1990 work, summed up: 'The American internal evidence suggests that the executions Winnington discovered did occur. although it might have been two to four thousand instead of seven thousand'.

There was to be another report after Winnington's which also, for a short time at least, became a national story. James Cameron was in Korea, in the UN sector, and reporting for *Picture Post* which at this time had attained an important place in weekly journalism in Britain. In the late summer of 1950 Cameron visited a military compound in Pusan and came across about seven hundred political prisoners of the Korean government. They were not prisoners of war but opponents of Syngman Rhee : 'They were skeletons … puppets of skin with sinews for strings – their faces were a terrible, translucent grey. They were manacled with chains or bound to each other with ropes'. And most, so Cameron was informed, were to be shot. In his autobiography he explained that his report to *Picture Post* was written 'with the best restraint and care of which I was capable'. His editor, Tom Hopkinson, was in agreement with his general approach, and recognised, as did Cameron, that although there had been accounts of atrocities in *The Times* and *Daily Telegraph* and other papers, this story with its accompanying photographs would be a sensation. So between them they wrote and re-wrote and in Cameron's later words : 'All things considered, it was a journalistic essay of elaborate moderation'. The feature was entitled: 'An Appeal to the United Nations'. The issue of *Picture Post* was going through the press when Edward Hulton, the proprietor, ordered Cameron's article to be withdrawn. The bitter row that inevitably ensued brought Tom Hopkinson's dismissal which was followed by Cameron's resignation and his move to the *News Chronicle.* There was a wave of outrage from the unions and *Picture Post* moved within a year or so to its closure.

The war in Korea more or less ended during the middle of 1951 when negotiations began but fighting, especially American bombing, continued. The Chinese, who had entered the war after many warnings to the Americans that they would do so if the 38th parallel was crossed, were anxious for peace, as were

the North Koreans. It was the Americans who again and again brought the negotiations to a temporary halt. It should be noted that although British troops
were on the ground there were no British representatives at the negotiations and
British press coverage was notably thin. Whether the Americans attempted to
use chemical weapons is still an open question, mainly because it is no longer
seriously discussed. There must be substantial evidence in American government files that requires further analysis and Joseph Needham, who was on the
unofficial commission of enquiry, was still insisting, a decade later, in a letter to
Hewlett Johnson, that he had not changed his mind about American guilt. This
was communicated to me by Diane Kirby, a former postgraduate student, who
was working on the Johnson papers at Canterbury.

   The Americans bombed large parts of North Korea to rubble and used na-
palm extensively. We thought at the time that the Americans behaved as they
did because of the hysterical waves of MacCarthyism that we were all reading
about, but it was not until a decade or so later that I really began to appreciate
that their anti-Sovietism was deeply embedded in the thinking of their senior
diplomats and officials. It was in the middle nineteen sixties that I began reading
the relevant document. National Security Council 68 (NSC 68) which President
Truman had ordered to be drafted. The shocks of 1949 – above all the victory of
the Communists in China and the acknowledgement of the Soviet atomic bomb
– had encouraged a comprehensive survey of the world situation. George Ken-
nan had resigned as Director of the Policy Planning Staff and Paul Nitze was in
his place. NSC 68 went further than any previous statement concerning the supposed aims and purposes of the Soviet Union in world affairs: 'The fundamental
design of those who control the Soviet Union and the international communist
movement is to retain and solidify their absolute power, first in the Soviet Union and second in the areas now under their control. In the minds of the Soviet
leaders, however, achievement of this design requires the dynamic extension of
their authority and the ultimate elimination of any effective opposition to their
authority'. NSC 68 was completed, and accepted, in the early months of 1950
and the outbreak of the Korean war became a positive endorsement of its basic
ideas. When Eisenhower became President in 1952 his Secretary of State was
John Foster Dulles. The general analysis of NSC 68, with only residual qualifications, now became the broad approach to the activities of the United States in
world affairs.

   It was through the opposition to the war in Korea that I met Sir John Pratt who
was in vigorous and voluble disapproval. John Pratt was a distinguished civil
servant who had spent most of his diplomatic career in the Far East. His father
had been in the Indian Salt Revenue Service and he himself, born in 1876, was
of course now retired. He had been called to the Bar after his schooldays at Dul-
wich College, became what was then described as a Student Interpreter in China
from 1898 and joined the Consular Service in the years before the First World

War. In 1925 he transferred to the Foreign Office and remained in various diplomatic positions, all in the Far East, until retirement in 1938. The outbreak of war brought him back into service and from 1939 to 1941 he was head of the Far East section of the Ministry of Information. He continued to occupy various administrative positions for the remainder of the war years.

This was the man who spoke and wrote with zest and wrath against the UN war in Korea. He wrote several pamphlets and spoke all round the country. I organised a meeting for him in Hull. Our former diplomat was a nice man, and I met him again on a further occasion in London where we shared a platform, with others: a broad front against the war. John Pratt's brother was Boris Karloff, born William Henry Pratt, the youngest son of the family. There will be many readers too young to remember that Boris Karloff in his day was the best-known actor in horror films and plays. He went to the Merchant Taylors' school in London and Uppingham and was diverted into the acting profession when he went to America a few years before the First World War. There was a slight facial resemblance between John Pratt and his brother, both handsome men, but only I would guess if you already knew the family relationship.

In the summer of 1952 I was recalled to the army on what was known as Z Reserve. The war in Korea was still continuing and the British government – now Tory, although it is unlikely that Labour would have acted differently – decided to call up for a fortnight's re-training various specialists among whom gunnery and radar instructors were included. I went to the central gunnery school which was still at Manorbier, near Tenby in South Wales. At Manorbier, the one man above all others I wanted to see again was on the platform at Tenby, having travelled in the same train as myself.

Norman Brenner, called Nat by all his friends except myself, had been at Manorbier while I was on my instructor's training course. At the time he was a sergeant instructor in Radar, and he was a marvellous companion: witty, well-read, my sort of politics and from within the theatre world. He had been involved with Unity Theatre before 1939 and after the war joined the Bristol Old Vic, becoming in time the head of their training school. I went to see him on a couple of occasions after the war. He made this re-training fortnight for me. We ate together and talked through most evenings and I have vivid memories of his lively personality.

The intervention in French Indo-China, Indonesia, Greece, the acceptance of Franco Spain, Korea, the beginnings of the troubles in Cyprus and Kenya, were among the issues which confirmed my general approach to British politics and which set me apart from the mainstream of Labour politics. Later reading and research extended the critique of the Attlee administrations but at the time it was these matters of foreign policy that mostly determined my general understanding. I was also a member of an historian's group that was beginning to dig into the history of the struggles of the ordinary people of Britain and I continued to

express publicly my political views without restraint or qualification. Intellectually and morally on the central political issues in the middle years of the nineteen
fifties I was more or less at peace with myself. But not for long.

I worked at the university a year before the family joined me. Constance came
up during the summer vacation of 1948 to help look for houses and we decided
– it was largely her sensible decision – to choose a fairly large house and garden,
together with two garages, in the Avenues district towards the outer reaches of
the town. I never understood how the house managed to have two garages at
the end of its longish garden and it was over a decade before we bought a car. In
the meantime we rented out one and kept our bicycles in the other. At that time
everyone rode bicycles because the town was almost everywhere flat and in any
case it was in those days, as now, a poor town by national standards. The street
we lived in was one of four long avenues of trees. The houses were mostly built,
like ours, during the building boom of the late 1890s and early twentieth century and it had buzzers in all the front rooms of the house by which the peasants
in the kitchen might be summoned. The Avenues, which were charming and
have hardly altered during the past sixty years, were still largely the residences
of the middle class – there were three or four university professors in our street
– and it was only in the following decade, with the increase in the number of
cars, that the middle classes began to move out into the further suburbs or the
very pleasant town of Beverley and the villages of the East Riding. The very well
to do and the landed classes were, of course, already there. It was to be one of
many pleasures of our move to the North to discover how interesting the rural
areas of the East and North Ridings were, not least their lovely churches. And
of course we were close to the coast. A family of close friends had a cottage in
the village of Easington – the last village before Spurn Point – and we ourselves
bought a former fisherman's cottage for £400 at the end of the fifties, before we
had a car.

I had by contemporary standards a not unreasonable salary for the middle
class; but our problem was that we had no capital savings. So after the first year
in Hull I began to work for the department of Adult Education in evening classes
and this was not only financially helpful but we also made a goodly number of
friends. Some years I worked three evenings a week – somewhat tiring. of course.
For the first decade at the University I continued to work steadily in the evenings
but then I began to earn additional income from writing although I kept contact
with Adult Education, largely because the students were almost always interesting.

I liked Hull. Some of its most interesting buildings and streets had been very
badly bombed but there was still enough left to make a ride round the town informative and enjoyable. Betjeman thought the Dock offices the most stylish of
all the nineteenth century buildings and there were some very good houses and
warehouses along the River Hull – in the middle of the Old Town – that were

handsome and attractive. The Wilberforce and other museums were among their occupants. We bought the local daily paper – a conservative journal – in order to inform ourselves of what was going on and there was one feature that I found intriguing. Whether it was available in the south I don't know because it was never my custom to read the local obituaries. But by chance I found myself one day reading the death columns and discovered a practice I had not known of. At the local undertakers or at the newspaper office the relatives could look through a long list of doggerel verse and include a piece in their obituary notice. Apparently this is still a fairly common practice. I learned later that the classic verse in this genre appeared in the *Liverpool Echo* and it went like this:

> The Golden Trumpet sounded
> Saint Peter shouted 'Come'
> The pearly gates flew open
> And in walked Mum

When Elvis Presley died expressions of sympathy, perhaps grief, overflowed into the obituary columns of Hull's local paper. *The Guardian* was interested and looked at about fifteen other local evening papers in the North but none apparently reached the Hull standard of fervent doggerel. Constance told me some years ago that when he was about sixteen my eldest son said to her: 'If you cut me open, you will find Blue Suede Shoes engraved on my heart'. Presley was, of course, a national phenomenon.

I joined the local Communist Party in Hull after my first year or so. Constance had ended her membership at the time of the Nazi-Soviet Pact of 1939, but she remained sympathetic and was soon to become a successful collector of money for the *Daily Worker*. We both within a couple of years took over a stall every Christmas period for the one day bazaar. For about half a dozen years, until 1956, I delivered a Saturday *Daily Worker* round the nearest housing estate, on my bicycle of course, and a couple of times a year I went up to Durham and Northumberland to take a miners' school for the North-East district of the Party. My most active local political work was organising a British-Soviet Friendship Society with monthly meetings for about nine months of the year. These were the years – the early nineteen fifties especially – when there were quite a large number of delegations, of varied social composition, who visited the Soviet Union and would usually publish their reports in pamphlet form.

The communist party in Hull had about two hundred members on the books with about twenty who were active, almost all of whom were working class. There were no dockers, or no dockers attended meetings. The strike of 1893 had ended with a major confrontation and an overwhelming defeat for the dockers; and from this time until the 1950s a large part of the docks remained unorganised. The beginnings of change came with a rank-and-file strike in 1954, supported by the London based 'Blue' union of the London stevedores.

In the following decade there was to be the emergence of a well-organised militant rank-and-file movement, hostile to the current Transport Union organisers, and I was to become on quite close terms with some of its leading personalities. But in 1954 I had very little contact except that I met for the first time Gerry Healy, one of the main Trotskyist figures at this time, with whom I was to have somewhat more contact before the end of the decade. I disliked him at our first meeting and my feelings were not to change.

Life is not all politics and in my lifetime there have been too many examples of single-minded individuals blighted by their intellectual narrowness and dominated by political sectarianism. We now had two more children – another boy and a girl – and we spent much of our holiday periods on the beaches at Easington, the last village before Spurn Point. Constance and I both took our bicycles for evening rides. The East Riding has a goodly share of interesting churches. In Hull itself we had a lively social life. The Left Book Club had been a very active organisation before the war and there were a number of families still interested in the Left in general, mostly not politically organised except for specific causes. There were about a dozen of us and we ate in each other's houses and went on excursions together. The most prominent couple were the Horsleys. Alec was chairman of Northern Dairies, later Northern Foods, and his wife Susan, like her husband, was a tennis player of county standard.

Harold Laski died in late March 1950. He has remained the most important influence in my own intellectual life. It was Harold who offered all who listened to his lectures the ineradicable insistence of debate and argument on moral and political questions. It was Harold who sent you in the library to begin to try to match his own remarkable erudition although you could never believe that could be achieved. But he insisted upon knowledge, and scepticism about everything. His own views were firm and vigorously argued, with the clear understanding that his role as a teacher was to encourage dissent and argument in the minds of his students. I am not suggesting that I, or others of his students, have been faithful to the rigour of these exhortations or indeed that Harold himself was always dependable in respect of his own statement of principles. What he communicated was a love of knowledge, an insistence upon a willingness to debate, and an openness to argument.

His last years had not been happy. He was increasingly concerned with the direction of Ernest Bevin's foreign policy and with the hostility that was being shown towards the Soviet Union so soon after the end of the war. Laski was never an apologist for Soviet misdeeds, whose extent were growing, but he was fully aware of the directing anti-Soviet influence of the United States in world politics and of the increasing intolerance within American politics. The failure of his libel action in 1947 greatly distressed him and his reception in the States on his last visit there before his death added greatly to his emotional and psychological unease. His insistence upon taking an active part in the British General Election in early 1950 contributed materially to the rapid worsening of his physical condition. He was ordered to take six months complete rest but it was too late. He was too weak for an operation and he died in hospital. Frida was with him.

I knew Laski only slightly on a personal level since I was not one of his special subject students. But Constance and I later became very friendly with Frida and she stayed with us in Hull on several occasions. I used also to visit her in London – an unhappy woman in her old age – and it was during her last decade that I persuaded her to allow me to deposit all the correspondence between Harold and herself in my own university archives. She was at one time seriously considering destroying all the letters between them. It was a large collection for when Harold was away he usually wrote to Frida every day.

This part of Laski's history needs further elaboration. When he died his death was recorded round the world and warm tributes came from his many former students. There must, however, have been very few former eminent scholars so widely recognised and appreciated during their lifetime and at the time of their death whose reputation fell away so dramatically and in such a short space of time. He died towards the end of March 1950, a few months before the beginning of the Korean war. These were the worst years in Britain of all the decades of the Cold War, and the climate of opinion in Britain and America was to encourage the rapid downsizing of Harold's intellectual position. The change in attitudes was now really quite remarkable. It was not until 1993 that there appeared two large scale biographies which provided serious scholarly interpretations of one of the great British scholars and teachers of the twentieth century.

Part 4: **1956**

The middle years of the 1950s, after the death of Stalin in the spring of 1953, were a period of cautious de-Stalinisation for the Soviet Union. Beria had been early eliminated in the usual way. In Yugoslavia, a useful yardstick at this time by which to measure changes in Soviet foreign policy, a trade agreement had been signed in October 1954, and about the same time Tito's speeches began to be factually reported in the Soviet press. During 1955 there was a continued improvement in diplomatic and political relations, with a visit from the Soviet leaders to Belgrade in May, in the course of which Khrushchev put all the blame for the bitter dispute between the two countries upon Beria. It was an accusation that was soon to be extended to cover most of the crimes of the later Stalin years. Inside the Soviet Union the principle of collective leadership was increasingly re-affirmed, and the cult of the individual was being steadily denounced. Stalin was not yet being named as being directly involved in the crimes that were being at least hinted at. However, the 20th Congress of the Soviet Communist Party which met towards the end of February 1956, was soon to define 'the Stalin question' in very certain terms.

All the world's communist parties naturally sent their leading comrades as fraternal delegates to the Russian Congress. From Britain these were Harry Pollitt, General Secretary, George Matthews, Assistant General Secretary, and R Palme Dutt, Vice-Chairman of the British Party and its most important theoretician. At the Congress the reports of both Khrushchev and Mikoyan both emphasised the 'negative' effects of the cult of the individual and the absence of collective leadership : 'for approximately twenty years,' said Mikoyan. In his speech Mikoyan further accepted responsibility for certain of the tensions in world politics, and Khrushchev denied the inevitability of war. The public speeches in general emphasised and underlined the policies involved in 'de-Stalinisation'. It was clear from what was being said from the platform that the 'mistakes and errors' of the Stalin years were responsible for the repressive acts which had outraged public opinion beyond the Soviet Union and for which the world communist movement had acted so long as apologists.

It was the speech of Khrushchev on the last day of the Congress in a secret session from which all the foreign delegates were excluded that provided the explosive material of 1956. The revelations of judicial murder, mass repression and complete denial of democratic procedures inevitably became known to the world outside Russia, although it was an uneven process. An edited version was circulated to most communist parties within a month to six weeks. What is plain is that the British Communist Party leadership was notably unwilling to encourage any discussion of the secret speech. For those who followed the international press, however, especially in the countries of the Soviet Eastern European bloc, the details were soon to be known. As early as 4 March the East German Vice-Premier Walter Ulbricht was reported in *Neues Deutschland* as saying in a speech that Stalin had done 'severe damage to the Soviet State and the Soviet Communist Party', and on 17 March he added that the 'myth' of Stalin as a military leader of genius had been developed by Stalin himself. One of the earliest published summaries of the secret speech seems to have been in an article by Jercy Morawski, one of the secretaries of the Polish Communist Party, on the 27 March. In the Soviet Union itself the attacks on Stalin developed by stages and it was not until the 28 March that *Pravda*, in the course of a sharp attack on earlier malpractices, mentioned him by name. During March and April there were announcements from the Eastern bloc countries of the 'rehabilitation' of a number of leading communists who had been executed following the so-called 'treason trials' of the post-war years. These included Rajk in Hungary and Kostov in Bulgaria, and on the 9 April Trofim Lysenko, a name well-known among the scientists of Western Europe and America, resigned as president of the Academy of Agricultural Sciences.

By the end of March, therefore, and for specialists in international politics, within the first fortnight after Khrushchev's speech, the main thrust of his indictment of the Stalin era was beginning to be understood. But not in Britain where the communist leadership was showing itself to be remarkably obtuse in encouraging every possible delay to an open discussion. In the days after the open speeches at the Russian Congress the London *Daily Worker* was receiving a stream of letters from its readers, some of which were published, and then, on the 12 March the editor, J.R. Campbell, announced the discussion closed, and he rounded it off with an article on the 15 March. There was already in train a national Party Congress to be held in the last days of March and the columns of the *Worker* were now filled with comments and letters on the Political Resolution and the Discussion Statement which had been first published on the 28 January. There was, however, one major article on the political significance of the Russian Congress. This was by George Matthews, the deputy secretary of the Party, and it was based on the published speeches of the Russian leaders. It appeared in the Party weekly journal *World News and Views* on 17 March and it was a typical product of the Stalinist years. There were, course, mistakes and errors but these had been fully recognised and now 'an exceptionally healthy situation exists within the Party, with the fullest operation of inner-Party democracy'. Moreover, the criticism of the cult of the individual and other mistakes must not obscure Stalin's 'positive services' to the cause of Socialism and especially to his role during the Second World War.

Whether Matthews knew the full content of the secret speech is not known, but it is unlikely for his article must have been written early in March. From inside the office of the *Daily Worker* we learn from Malcolm MacEwen and others that the main facts of the secret speech were beginning to be known to the journalists from about the middle of March. The pages of the *Worker* continued to be filled with material on the forthcoming Party Congress. The 24th National Congress took place at the end of March and subsequently, during April, the correspondence columns of the party press were devoted to extracts from the Congress discussions. None of these reports related to the new facts revealed by the secret speech and members of the British Party gained their information mainly from the national press and from foreign sources. On the 31 March *World News* had published a long extract from Togliatti's report to the Central Committee of the Italian Communist Party. It was much more detailed and a good deal more sophisticated than George Matthew's article of a fortnight earlier and it greatly stimulated both speculation and discussion within the British Party. It was not, however, until the first of two articles by Harry Pollitt (*World News* 21 April 1956) that the British Party were given a summary of the secret speech, although Pollitt gave no indication that his article *was* based upon the text of the secret speech. The detail was made public gradually in various publications round the world. The American *Daily Worker*, for example, reported on 14 April that it accepted the information relating to the destruction of Jewish culture in the Soviet Union after 1948, and the deaths of many Soviet Jewish intellectuals. It was later revealed, on 22 June, in a Resolution at a secret session of the National Congress at the end of March, that the British Party had regretted the absence of a public statement on the Khrushchev speech. The leadership of the British Party continued, however, to appear to be ignorant in their public statements of either the facts, and their significance, or of the growing ferment within their own party among the ordinary rank-and-file. There were some quite remarkable examples. In the May issue of *Labour Monthly* Palme Dutt in his 'Notes of the Month' gave over his attention to what was headed 'The Great Debate'. 'What', he wrote, 'are the essential themes of the Great Debate? Not about Stalin. That there should be spots on any sun would only startle an inveterate Mithra-worshipper ....'

From my own correspondence of these days it would seem that I began to appreciate the political significance of the Khruschev speech during the second half of March, and from this time I was in daily contact with my friends and especially those within the Historian's group. There were increasing complaints about the refusal of the Party press to publish critical or questioning letters and articles. On the 19 March I wrote a long, private letter to Harry Pollitt, still General Secretary although soon to retire, and it exhibited my basic beliefs, not least in the importance of a Party organisation. I quoted to Pollitt the recent comment of a personal friend and colleague who was in the Labour Party: 'I feel less like working with Communists than ever before: how can I ever seriously believe your political line again ?' I then set out the answer which I would give, either in private or in public. The acknowledgement of our many mistakes was central to our political position within the Left of the labour movement, while I continued to accept the necessity for an organisational structure, with, of course, genuine democratic procedures.

I sent a copy of this letter to Christopher Hill who acknowledged it with the comment that he and Bridget had written in not dissimilar terms to Arnold Kettle and the *Daily Worker*. At this time Christopher would have been the obvious person to have contacted. We all regarded him as the senior member of the Historian's group, a historian of growing reputation and a man of notable integrity: characteristics which have remained throughout his life. Arnold Kettle taught literature at the University of Leeds and was a member of the national Cultural Committee of the Party. He later moved to the Open University.

Looking back on these early days it is interesting that I did not make contact with Edward and Dorothy Thompson until early April. We had been friends for half a dozen years or so, but not close. Edward was not, as I recall, a member of the Historian's group but may have attended the odd meeting. I thought of him as a literary person, certainly with a considerable historical understanding as his large volume on William Morris clearly showed. This volume was not widely reviewed but serious Marxist historical writing was only beginning to appear in bookshops. Even Christopher Hill, who had been at Balliol for many years, found some initial problems in publishing his first major work on the English Revolution until Maurice Bowra reminded Oxford University Press that they had in their time published works on mediaeval history by Roman Catholics.

It was working on Ernest Jones that first brought me into touch with the Thompson family. Sometime around 1949, after I had been in Hull for a couple of years or so, I made contact with Dorothy Thompson, who was herself collecting material on Chartism, and one day I took the train to Halifax, changing at Leeds. It was a journey that has remained in my mind. I was steeped in Chartist history and now here I was, seeing the towns and villages where I knew there had been Chartist groups and gatherings, with wonderful names such as Sowerby Bridge, Hipperholme and Luddendun Foot. Edward met me at Halifax station and took me up to their house which overlooked part of the town. Edward was active in the Yorkshire peace movement and at some point became a member of the Yorkshire District Committee, and Dorothy I sometimes met at meetings of the Historians group. She was also active politically in addition to her commitment to a young family. I must have written to them early in April because on the 4th I received in reply what I soon accepted was typical of Edward's style of correspondence. The typewriter sometimes ran away with him but reading his letters once more after over forty years has made me appreciate again what a remarkable personality he was. His letter of 4 April began:

Dear John,

Thank God for your letter. Never have I known such a wet flatfish slapped on the face as our 24th (National Congress). It is the biggest Confidence Trick in our Party's history. Not one bloody concession as yet to our feelings and integrity; no apology to the rank-and-file, no self-criticism, no apology to the British people, no indication of the points of Marxist theory which now demand revaluation, no admission that our Party has undervalued intellectual and ideological work, no promise of a loosening of inner party democracy, and of the formation of even a discussion journal so that this can be fought out within our ranks, not one of the inner ring of the Executive felt that he might have to resign, if even temporarily. The whole old gang back ....

This letter, which went on for another thee pages, single spaced, was the beginning of our collaboration which produced *The Reasoner* and *The New Reasoner*, and helped encourage a political if somewhat diffuse movement which became known as the 'New Left'. It is not the purpose of these memoirs to offer a detailed history of these closing years of the 1950s and early sixties. There have already been at least a couple of books and a number of articles, and before a close account is again written we need access to the papers of several leading personalities of these years, as yet unpublished or unavailable. Edward's own papers are in the Bodleian, not yet fully catalogued and their listing has particular problems in that he rarely put a specific date on his letters. This can in part, but only in part, be remedied by reference to my own still incomplete files of correspondence which are available in the archives of the University of Hull, and open to bona fide research workers. My purpose here is to discuss certain of the matters which I think important or misunderstood or not sufficiently developed in the quite considerable literature which has so far been published.

From the time of Edward's letter quoted above we began a correspondence that was almost on a daily basis; and what we did not put on paper we discussed on the telephone or talked about at our somewhat infrequent meetings. I still did not own a car and Halifax was not a very easy place to travel to by train. More important, perhaps, in terms of the time I had outside my university work, was the book that I was preparing for publication. This was the Dartington Hall project, to be published by Routledge, and its title was finally agreed as *Rural Depopulation in England and Wales 1851-1951*. I was working on the proofs during the summer of this tempestuous year.

The most important problem we were concerned with in the early days of our collaboration was the difficulty that we had, as did everyone else who tried, in getting anything published that related to the secret speech. At this time (April/May) I was writing to party officials at King Street and those at the *Daily Worker* urging an open discussion of the many new facts about life in the Soviet Union and arguing that we required serious theoretical analysis of why, in a socialist

society, these things should have happened. There were minor successes: I got a
letter in *World News* on 19 May which was really the first to raise in some detail
the political and theoretical questions that were troubling an increasing number
of ordinary party members. Edward and I were joined by Ken Alexander, an
economist at the University of Sheffield, and our two families, with Ken, made
up what may be described as the inner group of dissenters and discussants in
Yorkshire. (Alexander, whom we both liked, was to move to Scotland where he
had a very lively career in Scottish academic and industrial life; ending up with
one son, four daughters and a knighthood.) At this early stage we tossed around
many different, and confused, ideas within the context of our refusal to accept
anything but an open debate on the implications of the secret speech.

It was not until the second half of May that we appear to have begun consideration of independent publishing. I wrote to Edward and Dorothy saying that
Constance and I, with other friends, had been discussing possible pamphlets,
beginning with 'Communism and Liberty', which was to be followed by the
problems of the secret speech. During June, however, we were always constantly
reminding each other of the likely accusations of factionalism. What comes out
very clearly from the correspondence of these summer months is our recognition of the importance and the value of an organised Party in the struggle for a
socialist Britain, and it was a recurring theme throughout our letters. The idea of
a factional group or, beyond that, of an independent political organisation, was
never considered throughout all our long hours of personal discussion or almost
continuous correspondence.

The first number of *The Reasoner* was ready by the end of the first week of July.
A month earlier the full text of Khrushchev's secret speech had been released by
the American State Department and it was published by the *New York Times* on
5 June. Nearly a week later, on 10 June, the London *Observer* gave over the whole
issue to the publication of the speech – some 26,000 words – to the fury of many
of their readers whose weekly chess, gardening, bridge, etc. columns were not to
be found. Later the *Manchester Guardian* produced a booklet of the complete
speech in thirty-three pages.

We no longer, therefore, had to rely on excepts from the foreign press and our
main purpose in this first issue was to underline the backwardness, timidity and
narrow bloody-mindedness of the leadership of the British Party in their refusal
to offer the opportunities for a serious analysis of the history of Soviet society.
The *Reasoner* was a duplicated journal of thirty-two pages with a rather nice
heading under which appeared a quotation from Marx: 'To leave error unre-
futed is to encourage intellectual immorality'.

We opened this first issue with two editorial leaders. The first was an explanation of why we were publishing. We emphasised that we were a journal for
discussion and that it was no part of the aim of the editors to encourage the
formation of political factions. We continued :

It is now, however, abundantly clear to us that the forms of discipline necessary and valuable in a revolutionary party of action cannot and never should have been extended so far into the processes of discussion, of creative writing, and of theoretical polemic. The power which will shatter the capitalist system and create Socialism is that of the free human reason and conscience expressed with the full force of the organised working class. Only a party of free men and women, accepting a discipline arising from truly democratic discussion and decision, alert in mind and conscience, will develop the clarity, the initiative, and the élan, necessary to arouse the dormant energies of our people. Everything which tends to cramp the intellect and dull their feelings, weakens the party, disarms the working class, and makes the assault upon Capitalism – with its deep defences of fraud and force – more difficult …. We take our stand as Marxists … History has provided the chance … for the scientific methods of Marxism to be integrated with the finest traditions of the human reason and spirit which we may best describe as Humanism ….

Our second editorial commentary, 'Taking Stock', brought the general argument to the immediate problems we had been concerned with in the months since the secret speech. This was followed by a long article from Ken Alexander on 'Democratic Centralism', an issue and a problem which inevitably was to run through all our subsequent discussions. Then a splendid polemical piece from Edward, an answer to an article by George Matthews. The rest of the English side was taken up with four largely critical letters and the last section was a collection of documents from other communist parties. Important sections of the American Communist Left had been lively in these early months following the Khruschev revelations and we printed an extract from *Jewish Life*, an American communist paper which expressed its and its readers horror at the history of Jewish persecution. The Editorial Board acknowledged that they were aware at the time – 1948 – of the closure in the Soviet Union of Yiddish theatre, schools and press and of the general shut-down of Yiddish culture, and they went on to explain why, in the years before the secret speech, they remained dumbly uncritical. The final document was a long translation from the Polish writers' journal, *Nowa Cultura*, translated by our good comrade Alfred Dressler, who was on the academic staff of the University of Leeds and whose death we were soon to mourn. The date of the Polish extract was the 22 April: another reminder to our British readers of the obduracy of our own leadership and of their refusal of a serious debate on the evils that had been revealed.

We published about 650 copies of *Reasoner* No. 1 – that number included a reprint of three hundred – and began immediately to receive a large number of letters from all over Britain. We had a small advertisement in the *Daily Worker* but our request for a further notice of our reprint was refused. The Collet's bookshops in London and Glasgow took copies, with a refusal from the Collets in Hull on the grounds that we were likely to be disciplined for going outside the Party press. Within a few weeks the Party machinery began moving against us. That, of course, was hardly unexpected but much more important, and encouraging, beside the hundreds of letters we were to receive in the month that followed publication, was the support expressed for our initiative by some of the well-known personalities in the Party. These included Lawrence Daly who had already resigned from the Scottish Party and who was to become an outstanding industrial militant, Hymie Levy the mathematician, Doris Lessing and Malcolm McEwen of the *Daily Worker*. What soon became clear was that the criticism that was immediately levied against us: namely, that this was a typical effort of a small minority of intellectuals, was denied by the broad social spread of the correspondence we received.

During July and August we were subject to growing pressures from the Yorkshire District Committee, whose secretary Bert Ramelson, I had met in India. In 1956, once the crisis had begun we were inevitably in constant communication with Bert. This was especially true for Edward, who was a member of the District Committee. I think it fair to describe Bert as being quite reasonable, in personal terms, with both of us. He arranged a special sub-committee to listen to the criticisms we were making prior to a full meeting of the District Committee. I was unable to attend the sub-committee for family reasons. We had arranged a fortnight's holiday on the coast in a friend's cottage and Constance, who throughout was always helpful and wholly supportive, on this occasion was firm against the disruption of our holiday. I thought her attitude reasonable and told Bert these things in a letter which enclosed the statement I would have made had I been present. Later in the month I attended the full meeting of the District Committee. The central question in all these discussions with the Party officials was their insistence that independent publication of the *Reasoner* kind was impermissible and contrary to Party rules. We were finally summoned, in the closing days of August, to appear before a specially convened Political Committee.

Edward met me at Doncaster so that we could travel together to Kings Cross. The second issue of the *Reasoner* was well on the way and for us the only important question was whether we should publish the third. We had a full session before lunch and were then expected to present our final statement in the afternoon. Harry Pollitt had resigned from the General Secretary's position immediately after the British Party Congress in late March. He had been in poor health for some time and on the 25 April he suffered a haemorrhage behind the eyes which meant that he could not read for about three months. This meeting of the Political Committee, at which he took the chair, was one of his first engagements after the more or less recovery of his eyesight, but his health continued to worsen and he died in 1960.

John Gollan, the new General Secretary, was of course present, and he was joined by, among others, Palme Dutt and Johnny Campbell. Edward and I made separate statements and one of the striking things about the general discussion which followed was that no member of the Committee talked about the social and political structures within the Soviet Union and why it was so important for the whole membership to appreciate how the crimes described by Khruschev could occur in a society that called itself socialist. We were talking into very thin air and nothing we said would have any impact or relevance. We broke for lunch and then we both, separately, made a statement which refused to deny the principle of open discussion. We then left to catch our return train home. Pollitt asked each of us to put our decision in a letter to him.

I suppose we must have told them that the second issue of the *Reasoner* would soon be out. The decision of the Political Committee was that we must cease publication, and that was all. What this meant, we assumed, was that the Party leadership would accept our second number but that any further publication would mean either suspension for a period or outright expulsion, and the latter would be the more likely. The second number was a considerable improvement in general interest.

Among the more supportive was Doris Lessing. She had been in London for about half a dozen years, having joined the Party in the early fifties. Her second volume of memoirs starts with her arrival in Britain from Africa in 1949 and, although not as lively or as interesting as her first volume – indeed I found much of it boring – it rambles around her political life in a muddling kind of way, and naturally includes 1956 and after. In two places she notes that she had forgotten she had ever written to Edward Thompson, being reminded by Dorothy Thompson's offer to send her copies of the letters she had written to Edward. These years are obviously much confused in her mind. We were in contact after the publication of the first issue of the *Reasoner* and she sent us a long letter for our second number in which she offered her total support for independent publication, and 'the attitude of mind represented by the *Reasoner*'. And she ended her letter with a passionate statement of her political position wholly contrary to her account of herself at this time in her memoirs: 'We have all been part of the terrible, magnificent, bloody, contradictory process, the establishing of the first Communist regime in the world – which has made possible our present freedom to say what we think, and to think again creatively'. (29.7.1956)

No doubt Doris also forgot that she was on the editorial board, for the two years or so of its quarterly existence, of the *New Reasoner* which began publication in the summer of 1957. We began meeting in her flat in Warwick Road when Edward and I were both in London and it was there we first met Clancy Sigal. Doris had a second letter in the third and final issue of the *Reasoner*, the main import of which was a comment on the relations between the leading group in any political organisation and its ordinary membership, and it needs to be said that her comments, and the many conversations we had with her in these months and during her years on the editorial board of our later journal were sensible and helpful. No one would have guessed from these years that in her autobiography, written forty years later, she would have described joining the Communist Party as 'probably the most neurotic act of my life'.

Alongside her letter in the second issue of the *Reasoner* was a well-argued piece from Ronald Meek, an economist then in Glasgow, also on the much debated question of independent publication. This was followed by an essay from Hymie Levy on 'The Place of Unorthodoxy in Marxism', a large section of readers' letters, a cartoon from Gabriel of the *Daily Worker* (which naturally we regarded as highly significant), as many extracts from our readers' letters as we had room for, and ending with two major documentary essays: a long discussion from a Polish cultural journal and the lengthy editorial comment from a recent number of the New York *Monthly Review* which was edited by Leo Huberman and Paul Sweezy.

It was a good number and we printed nearly a thousand copies, and as before we sold out within two or three weeks. We did all the work ourselves, greatly assisted by our wives and a solid group of helpers in both our towns. For this second number (as indeed for all the three issues) Edward typed the stencils. There were forty pages in this issue, single spaced and Edward typed the 40,000 words in five days. The stencils were then sent by train to me, where I picked them up at the main station in Hull. By the time of the reprint of the first issue I had arranged with a friend who was a businessman – a fruit importer on the Humber docks – to use his office duplicator. I would set off in the evening about seven o'clock, on my bicycle, with the stencils and reams of foolscap paper, and start duplicating on a machine that seemed to misuse its ink too often, and I turned the handle of the duplicator every night until eleven or midnight . And so to bed, after bringing back all the sheets that had been duplicated. For the second number all this took ten evenings and one long weekend. The sheets were then laid out on a very large table in what we called our playroom and volunteers in the final stage would put all the sheets in numerical order and staple around 1000 copies. It was tedious and very tiring work. The third issue, planned for 1500 copies – which was about as many as the duplicator would take from each stencil – took me a fortnight's evening work and then a complete weekend when I had to work through the whole night.

There were special problems with this third issue. It was again what we thought was a good issue. The opening article was a brilliant polemical article from Edward: 'Through the Smoke of Budapest'. Russian troops were in occupation but at the time of writing Russian weapons had not been used. In his article Edward very properly wrote that no one could know what the future would be. His long piece was followed by a wide-ranging discussion from a number of readers on the problems of democratic centralism, very much the centre of the discussion about the future organisation of the Party. We had an unexpected essay, also on democratic centralism, from G.D.H. Cole. We had made no request nor did Cole tell us he was writing it. It just arrived and we were naturally happy to publish a contribution from this outstanding socialist intellectual. We also had our first article on the Soviet Union in this issue. R.W. Davies, who was to become a very well-known specialist on the Soviet Union, wrote a commentary on the Soviet Purges and Trials of 1937-8. Our last pages were taken up with a long editorial statement which reiterated our well-known position as to publication and we then went on to explain why this third number was to be our final number :

1) The indefinite continuation of *The Reasoner* in this form might make it possible for the 'Case of *The Reasoner*' and of ourselves to be turned into a diversion from the central issues of the discussion rights of the whole membership.
2) There is an urgent need now for a serious Socialist journal freed from the atmosphere of dissension, with a wider and more representative editorial board.
By our ceasing to publish *The Reasoner,* the E.C. has the opportunity to take steps adequate to the political crisis and itself to initiate the formation of such a journal. If the E.C. does take this step, it will bring to an end the situation within which individuals have been forced to act upon their own initiative. The E.C. has already lost much of its moral authority over the membership; it is its duty to begin to remedy the situation which is now critical. (31 October 1956)

There were other reasons why we decided to cease publication. We had hundreds of letters in our support but there was also a considerable body of hostile opinion. The opposition to us was mostly political and it was growing but there were signs of unpleasant sectarian comments: questions about our financial backing for example. And in my own Party branch in Hull, when the whole evening was given over to the question of independent publication and the relationship of individual members to the top leadership, one comrade happily characterised the *Reasoner* group as 'running dogs of imperialism', a phrase coined in translation from the Chinese Communist Party at this time.

I must not suggest that this kind of vituperation was in common use, but there was no doubt that opposition was hardening against us; and it meant that rational discussion was not likely to be possible if we continued publication.

The comments I have quoted from our final editorial were written at the end of October. History now began to intervene in our parochial affairs. At the end of July the Egyptian government had nationalised the Suez Canal Company, the main shareholders of which were British and French. Their two governments immediately began secret negotiations with Israel, and on the 29 October Israel invaded the Canal zone. A few days later British and French troops landed at Port Faud and Port Said. There was an immediate collapse of sterling on the world market, the United States not having agreed to the original advances Britain had made, and with the support of the Soviet Union in the United Nations the Americans forced a total withdrawal by December.

Meanwhile events in Hungary moved to a crisis. On the 4th November Budapest was shelled and while there was some resistance it was soon overcome, and

Kadar became head of state. I was duplicating the final pages of the third number of the *Reasoner* over the weekend of 3ʳᵈ and 4ᵗʰ November and very obviously we could not send out this issue without taking full note of the Hungarian tragedy. I was in the office in Humber Street and Edward was at home in Halifax and we both wrote drafts and adjusted them over long telephone conversations. The final editorial we added to the front of the original issue. The argument was blunt and passionately worded, and we ended in these terms:

> The E.C. of the British Party must at once:
> 1) Dissociate itself publicly from the action of the Soviet Union in Hungary.
> 2) Demand the immediate withdrawal of Soviet troops.
> 3) Proclaim full and unequivocal solidarity with the Polish Workers' Party.
> 4) Call District Congresses of our Party immediately and a National Congress in the New Year.
> If these demands are not met, we urge all those who, like ourselves, will dissociate themselves completely from the leadership of the British Communist Party, not to lose faith in Socialism, and to find ways of keeping together. We promise our readers that we will consult with others about the early formation of a new socialist journal.
> In attacking Budapest the Soviet Union has struck a blow at the moral authority of the international working-class movement. Only the political demands outlined above will give the right to Communists to play a part in ending British aggression in Egypt, and in restraining those Western generals and politicians who will see the present situation in Eastern Europe as an opportunity to unleash a new war.
> Sunday 4th November 1956.

It was quite clear to us, and to everyone else, of course, that some disciplinary action would be taken against us. A resolution of the Political Committee suspended us for three months for disobeying their specific instruction to cease publication, and after long and very intense discussion we decided to resign. It is not easy nearly half a century later to convey the difficulties we had in coming to this decision. Throughout the *Reasoner* months we had always emphasised that we were not involved in any factional activity; our concern was the democratisation of the Party relationships between the elected leadership and the ordinary members; we were fully cognisant of the necessity for a disciplined political organisation in the serious struggle within capitalist society. We recognised and warmly appreciated the comradeship we had both experienced within the British Party and, with all its problems and faults, we could see no alternative within the political structure of the United Kingdom. At the same time, and I am now offering my personal position, there were growing misgivings concerning the nature of the communist political structure. The considerable discussion we had initiated about democratic centralism had not produced for me at any rate a viable alternative. More immediately important, by the end of August 1956, and following our meeting with the Political Committee, which had greatly shocked me, I was beginning to consider more seriously than ever before the intellectual rigidities of the members of the Political Committee. The Soviet attack on Budapest advanced these concerns to a critical point, and there is no doubt that for many members of the Communist Party it was the Hungarian events which brought about their resignation. The numbers were never exact but about seven thousand had resigned by the end of the year, and in social background they were representative of all groups within the Party. These included some important trade union leaders, including John Horner of the Fire Brigades Union, Bert Wynn of the Derbyshire Miners, Bill Jones of the Transport Workers, Dick Seabrook of USDAW and a considerable number of other working-class militants. My pre-war friend Don Renton was among them.

There was a mix of reasons why I did not find it easy to leave the Communist Party. There were some members, of course, whom I positively disliked, and mistrusted; others whom I tolerated; but most, whatever their social background, were comrades in the full meaning of the term: friendly, dedicated and self-sacrificing. Not all by any means were wholly committed, and that must be expected; but the British Communist Party, small though it was by comparison with the movements in France or Italy, had a solid base in the working class and quite a large group of intellectuals who were not dilettante but serious in their political and intellectual work. I still regard it as wonderfully fortunate that I was of the generation that established the Communist Historians' group. For ten years we exchanged ideas and developed our Marxism into what we hoped were creative channels. It was not chance that when the secret speech of Khruschev was made known in the West, it was members of the historians' group who were among the most active of the Party intellectuals on demanding a full discussion and uninhibited debate. It must be emphasised again that when we began the *Reasoner* the idea of resigning from the Party was not in our minds and it was only in the months that followed that we recognised, with both reluctance and dismay, the basic conservatism not only of the leadership but of many of the rank and file. The central political problem, certainly for me and I have no doubt also for Edward, was the recognition that the achievement of socialism was never going to come about without a seriously organised opposition, the members of which must accept a tighter discipline than that of the Labour Party. It was the degree of acceptance that has always proved very difficult to determine, hence the constant flow of expulsions and resignations from the various groups on the Left in the past half century.

One of the political consequences of the internal debate inside the Communist Party in 1956 and succeeding years was that a number of former members, mostly intellectuals, were attracted to one or other of the Trotskyist groups. The best known, and at the time the most lively, was the movement associated with Gerry Healy. He had been one of the leading personalities in a minority faction within the Revolutionary Communist Party which Jock Haston had led during the years of war, and when the RCP dissolved itself in 1949 Healy moved stead-ily to a dominant position within the small Trotskyist movement. What is no-table during 1956 and succeeding years was the attraction Healy exercised over a number of former communists, mostly intellectuals. At the time I found this quite extraordinary. Trotskyism was anti-Stalinist, of course, but their creeds were dogmatic, inflexible and sectarian to a quite remarkable degree, and it was precisely against the intellectual rigidity and dogmatism of the British Commu-nist Party that the *Reasoner* had developed its central arguments. Healy was a firm exponent of his version of political purity and the trail of ex-members was to become somewhat crowded. Towards the end of 1957 I had a couple of hours with Healy and sent my impressions in a longish letter to Edward and Kenneth Alexander. We met for a coffee in the Partisan, which had not yet bankrupted itself through its own incompetence. I noted in my remarks that he had

> a flexibility of mind abnormal in a Trot, and with an undoubted sense of realities. At the same time he is at least three-faced and one never knows what his real posi-tion is, since he adapts himself very skilfully to his audience …. I've met him three times now, and the thing that stands out is the way he has to boost his own morale, and give a strong impression of confidence and know-how to those who listen. Since he operates on the thin margin of the movement he has to blow everything up in order both to convince himself and his followers that they really are part of something. And all this he does quite skilfully….

The Socialist Labour League, which Healy founded in 1959, with *Labour Re-view* and the fortnightly *Newsletter* (edited by Peter Fryer in lively fashion for a while), continued for the next decade or so, but more or less destroyed itself by its sectarianism, with Healy in increasingly dogmatic and bullying attitudes. Its failure to understand the radical student movement of the late sixties deepened its political isolation. The final collapse came with the revelations of Healy's sex-ual activities, and the highly exclusive Workers' Revolutionary Party (founded in 1969) shrivelled.

Edward and I had spent most of our time since our resignation in planning a new publication. There was the usual stream of correspondence between Halifax and Hull, but now we were working on what we hoped would be a high level quarterly. The editorial committee for the first issue comprised Ken Alexander, Doris Lessing, Ronald Meek and Randall Swingler. The last named had been close to Edward on various cultural projects in earlier years after the war, and he greatly respected him. Randall and I only met in late 1956 and we also took to each other.

Ronald Meek belonged to a younger generation, nearer in age to Edward than myself. I don't think either of us knew him personally before the first *Reasoner* was published, to which he immediately found himself sympathetic. He was a lecturer in economics at the University of Glasgow (later Professor at the University of Leicester) and during the last quarter of 1956 we both received a four page duplicated publication entitled '*THE RHYMING REASONER. A Journal of Indiscretion,* Edited by W. McGonagall. The most effective antidote for the poison of self-alienation is self-laughter. K. Marx'. The first number was dated September 1956 and the second, now enlarged to eight duplicated pages, in November 1956. The place of publication was the Elysian Fields, for McGonagall had died in 1902. He had been a self-styled 'Poet and Tragedian', a weaver from Dundee, and his unscanned doggerel and agonising rhymes made him a favourite butt with his Scottish audiences.

So here was Ronald Meek, much taken with the *Reasoner*, offering poetic versions of our political problems. He produced two issues of the *Rhyming Reasoner* and they have become difficult to find in second hand bookshops. He was out of Britain for a large part of 1957 but he remained on the board and was always helpful. A very agreeable man, much liked. The first number of the *New Reasoner* appeared in the summer of 1957. It took us quite a long time to agree, both before and after we received the material. One of the most debated was a piece from Doris Lessing. It was evidently the first part of a novel. At one time she had said she was going to write a novel for us in instalments. Whether this was an instalment I cannot say but in her memoirs she refers to it as unfinished. We all spoke of it as 'Excuse me', its full title being *Excuse Me While I'm Sick* and both Edward and myself were against publication. Randall, on the other hand, said the first part was very funny and should be approved. Our discussions took up the usual mass of paper, Doris was obviously very reasonable and for the second number produced what I have always thought as one of her most brilliant short stories: 'The Day that Stalin Died'. This was already advertised in the first number, so the disagreements must have been amicable.

I have re-read the complete ten issues of the *New Reasoner* and it still seems to me a very lively and imaginative review. We explained in the first number that the journal would carry material of three kinds: theoretical and analytical articles, documents and commentary on the international scene, and 'a wide range of creative writing – short stories, polemic, satire, reportage, poetry, and occasional historical or critical articles – which contribute to the rediscovery of our traditions, the affirmation of socialist values, and the undogmatic perception of social reality'.

The first number was published with a dull cover and on rather poor paper. It had around 140 pages and this was to become our normal size. Its contents, I think it reasonable to suggest, were as good as anything the Left were capable of at the time. Hyman Levy opened with a critical essay on 'Soviet Socialism' in which among other areas of discussion he compared the Czarist background to the Russian revolution with the evolution of bourgeois democracy in western Europe; and he ended with the arguments that the *Reasoner* had used in the matter of the attitudes that all socialists must take towards the revelations of the

Khruschev speech. This was the central theme, expressed in different contexts, which dominated this first number. There was the final section of a long article by Jean-Paul Sartre from *Temps Moderne* which bitterly attacked the degeneration of the French Socialist Party under Guy Mollet, followed by a comprehensive analysis of Stalinism in the Soviet Union and Eastern Europe. Oher articles included a review of the Hungarian situation from Peter Fryer who had originally been a reporter in Hungary for the *Daily Worker* in 1956; a very critical review of Andrew Rothstein's short booklet on the Soviet Union and Socialism by L. Hussey (Brian Pearce); an Open Letter to Shostakovich by the musician and composer Bernard Stevens; and most important, a very long article of 38 pages by Edward on 'Socialist Humanism', written with his usual verve and intellectual liveliness.

This first number was not all an analysis of Stalinism. Peter Worsley, a social anthropologist, if that is the way to describe a scholar of such wide cultural interests, gave us a quite remarkable essay on Mau Mau. Critical analysis of Kenya under British rule was not unknown, for there were already the writings, among others, of Norman Leys and Peter Evans, but no one had previously written of Mau Mau with the understanding of millenarian cults that Peter Worsley offered. His own study of Australian aboriginal cultures and those of other Pacific groups had just been published, and the analysis that he began in this first *New Reasoner* has remained a necessary discussion point for later, more comprehensive surveys. Of the cultural pieces we published there was a short story 'Behind the Brick Wall' by Tibor Dery, one of the great Hungarian dissident writers of his generation, and work by three different poets : Adam Wazyk's 'A Critique of the Poem for Adults', translated from the Polish by Alfred Dressler; 'Song of the Gillie More' by Hamish Henderson, who taught in Edinburgh; and four poems by Tom McGrath. It was Edward who knew and greatly appreciated the poetry of Tom McGrath. He was quite unknown to me, and, I would guess, to most of our English readers.

There were other shorter pieces, among them an interesting essay from Eric Hobsbawm – 'Dr Marx and the Victorian Critics' and a short note from me of a few pages, mainly a critique of Palme Dutt and his too dogmatic analysis of Indian independence. We were to publish nine more quarterly issues before the *New Reasoner* amalgamated with *Universities and Left Review* at the end of 1959.

The two and a half years of the *New Reasoner* ended in the closing months of the 1950s. It had been an interesting, very mixed decade in its politics, beginning with the political exhaustion of the 1945 Labour government, the turmoil over Gaitskell's increased allocations for a large-scale rearmament programme and the imposition of charges on the National Health Service. As I remarked earlier university students and the young in general were notably uninterested in radical ideas in these early years of the decade. There was, however, a vocal Left within the Labour movement, always restrained at national conferences by the block of the big Unions. Nye Bevan, not always consistent in his political tactics, remained the dominating personality on the Left. It was rearmament in general, and German rearmament in 1953 in particular, that gathered a serious opposition against the leadership, but only in the second half of the decade did nuclear weapons become the issue which brought mass demonstrations onto the streets. It is interesting that nuclear bombs were largely absent from ordinary people's consciences from the end of the war until the British H-bomb tests at Christmas Island in the Pacific during May 1957. The next landmark was the Brighton conference of the Labour Party in October. There were sixty-six resolutions calling for the unilateral renunciation of the H-bomb by Britain. The composite resolution was moved by Harold Davies and opposed by Nye Bevan, speaking for the Executive . He was now shadow foreign minister, living in a very uneasy relationship with Hugh Gaitskell, who had succeeded Attlee in the leadership, and his speech at this Conference astounded his friends and comrades on the political Left. It was generally accepted as a poor speech by his standards, but crucial was the rejection of the unilateralist argument in words that have remained in public memory. His future political standing with the Left would never be the same. This was the famous passage:

> If you carry this resolution and follow out all its implications and do not run away from it you will send a Foreign Secretary, whoever he may be, naked into the conference chamber. Able to preach sermons, of course he could make good sermons. But action of this sort is not necessarily the way in which you can take away the menace of this bomb from the world.

It was from this year, 1957, that the Campaign for Nuclear Disarmament (CND) very quickly became a mass movement. The first national march was from London to Aldermaston but in the years which followed it started in the Falcon Field, Aldermaston, over the Easter period, and ended in London. Until the early 1960s CND encouraged the largest demonstrations of any during the decades after the end of the Second World War. Constance went on several of these marches as well as one which crossed the North from the east coast through Hull to Liverpool.

Aldermaston, and the moral position it symbolised, attracted a very wide range of people of different social groups and above all the young. Naturally the *Reasoner* group and the ULR, now located at the famous address in London of 7 Carlisle Street, were all very active in the movement. It would not, I think, be correct to accept wholly the judgement of Peggy Duff, that CND 'swallowed up' the New Left as a political force, because this assumes that the New Left was, or could have been, a major political force. There is an argument here. It is often suggested that those who brought together the *New Reasoner* and the *Universities and Left Review* failed to develop a lasting political organisation, but that this was ever a serious objective is not tenable. What is overlooked is that we were deeply aware of the overriding strength of the labourist tradition. How else could one explain the considerable shift of so many ex-communists, without serious hesitation, into the Labour Party? The Labour Party had always had an open radical opposition within its own ranks – it was several decades before the 'New Labour' of the 1997 general election – and now, at the end of the 1950s, with CND *and* a successful anti-nuclear resolution at the 1960 Labour Party Conference, there was some, but not much, choice for anyone who really wanted to remain in active, practical politics.

My own position, however, was always clear. The Labour Party was not for me. I was conscious that in the coming decades a detailed critique of Labour's policies both at home and internationally was going to be necessary if we were ever going to curtail, and maybe severely diminish, the dogged conservatism of the movement in its fundamental postulates. I always maintained friendly relations with my comrades in the Labour Party – or at least most of them – as with most of my former comrades in the Communist Party. One of the deeply regrettable aspects of the history of socialism in the twentieth century – one could of course go back well before 1900 – has been the bitterness and sectarianism among the Left groupings towards each other. As each decade has passed I have been increasingly aware of the self-indulgence and sectarian stupidity of the consciously simon-pure on too many matters, large and small. I am not suggesting that I myself was always good tempered or fair in my critical comments, either spoken or written, but I have usually been aware of the importance of remaining comradely and receptive in the many heated discussions the Left has so often debated, and not seldom wrangled.

There were other developments that have also to be considered when analysing the position in radical history of what became known as the 'New Left' after the merger of the two journals. The communist Historian's Group had always emphasised the importance of 'history from below'. We argued, very properly, that the struggles of the ordinary people for civil rights and against their economic exploitation had always been neglected in the teaching of history. It was during the first decade after the war that there was a steady increase in the research and writing of the history of the labour movement in Britain. Edward produced his massive study of William Morris in 1955 (later revised and re-issued), Eric Hobsbawm his important pioneering study *Primitive Rebels* in 1957; Asa Briggs edited in the following year the very useful collection *Chartist Studies* and he and I began to plan a collection of essays in honour of G.D.H. Cole's seventieth birthday. But Cole died on 14 January 1959 and it became a memorial volume when published in 1960.

I have listed these titles – and the list is not conclusive, for it omits, among others, the beginnings of labour studies by Henry Pelling and others outside the orbit of the labour movement – to make the point that, just as it is necessary to appreciate the importance of CND in these closing years of the decade, so involvement in historical research for some of us was occupying a great deal of our time. A more or less automatic reaction to the growing output of serious writing on the history of the British labour movement was the formation of a national society which would bring historians together for critical discussions. We were fortunate in the appointment of someone as interested in social history as was Asa Briggs to a chair in history at the University of Leeds. I was encouraged to write to Asa suggesting that he might wish to become president or chairman of a newly formed society, and he was happy to accept. The Society for the Study of Labour History was to be of long-term usefulness in its encouragement of a steadily increasing sophistication in teaching, research and writing.

I have a nice story concerning the origins of Edward's classic work, *The Making of the English Working Class*. In July 1959 R.W. Harris, the Master of Studies at The King's School, Canterbury, wrote me a letter at the suggestion of Asa Briggs. Harris had been asked by the publishing firm of Gollancz to edit a series of historical texts suitable for sixth forms and undergraduates. He was enquiring whether I would be interested in writing a book on working-class politics in the 19th century. In reply I expressed my regrets, because of other commitments, and then proceeded to offer two names of suitable authors; and this is what I wrote:

> The first is Edward Thompson, who is an extra-mural lecturer at the University of Leeds – the author of a very large tome on William Morris – and who would, I have no doubt, fit your requirements very well. I choose my words carefully when I say that in my opinion Thompson would do a better job than anyone in this field. I would add a warning. He is a very busy person, and if you are interested in him, and he accepted, I should insist on a firm time table. I do not want to give the impression that he is unreliable. Emphatically he is not, but on the contrary extremely efficient; but he is an extraordinarily vigorous and lively individual who carries on many things at the same time, and you will need a firm assurance that he will meet your deadline. Let me add, if this really sounds too frightening, that I should offer the same advice in relation to both Asa and myself whose circumstances are, in this particular respect, similar ….

In his reply to my letter Harris said he had missed the William Morris and indeed had not heard previously of Edward. The latter accepted Harris's offer, and in the autumn of 1963 there appeared a volume of just under 450 pages. In the preface to *The Making* Edward included this sentence: 'Mr R.J. Harris showed great editorial patience, when the book burst the bounds of a series for which it was first commissioned'.

What is so remarkable about this story are the dates. It took Edward under four years to produce his great work, during a period of intense political activity. He was still editing the *New Reasoner* when he accepted the offer from Harris; he was almost immediately involved in the Daly election campaign which I discuss

below; and from the beginning of 1960 he was a leading figure in what was now
called the New Left. The lights must have burned through many a long night in
the house at Halifax.

Our circle of acquaintances and friends inevitably enlarged during these years.
I use the plural because in the five years or so after 1956 Edward and I were in
close contact throughout and none of our important political decisions were
taken in isolation, although occasionally we did not always agree. In the second
half of 1959, during the months of our final number of *The New Reasoner*, we
became involved with Lawrence Daly and the Fife Socialist League. Lawrence
Daly was born in the same year as Edward. He went from school into the mines
when he was fifteen. He became part-time NUM lodge official in 1946, chairman
Scottish NUM Youth Committee 1949, and Workmen's Safety Inspector at his
colliery, Glencraig, in 1954. In 1946 he was on a trade union delegation to Russia
and he published a pamphlet on his visit. He joined the Communist Party in his
teens. In these early years he was the most interesting and intellectually lively of
any working-class militant I have ever met.

Lawrence left the Communist Party in the summer after the secret speech of
Khrushchev and it was sometime later that he contacted us. By this time he was
already establishing a new political base in his own area. In industrial West Fife
the Communist Party had a 25 per cent drop in membership during the first
year after Khrushchev and this higher figure was no doubt in considerable part
due to Lawrence's own resignation.

Lawrence and his comrades had read all three issues of the *Reasoner* and were
to be subscribers to the *New Reasoner*. In February 1957 they had the foundation
meeting of the Fife Socialist League. A month later a constitution was adopted
which had as its central resolution the building of a democratic socialist society.
Activity continued through 1957, and then in 1958, as local elections approached,
the League debated whether they should make a challenge to the labour-com-
munist tradition in the West Fife coalfield. Ballingry, which was Lawrence's own
division, seemed the obvious choice. He had already stood on two occasions
while still in the Communist Party, and been defeated in straight fights with the
Labour candidate. In the 1958 elections a new Communist candidate was standing and the Labour County councillor, as did most public opinion, predicted
an overwhelming victory with a divided vote on the Left. The results astonished
everyone. Lawrence won 1,085 votes, Labour 525 and the Communist Party 197.
Elsewhere in the region the Communist Party did better than usual.

It was above all a tribute to the wonderfully vibrant personality that Lawrence
presented, and after the May 1958 elections Lawrence held every six months a
public meeting in Ballingry in which he reported on Council affairs and listened
to his constituents. Prior to these meetings the League circulated to every tenant
a bulletin outlining the main issues that had been debated.

By now Lawrence and his comrades in the Fife Socialist League were in close association with ourselves in the *New Reasoner* group. They continued with the grass roots politics of their early days – in June 1958 they organised pit-head meetings to protest against the execution of Imre Nagy – and the next year came the prospect of some action in the General Election of 1959. Should the League support Lawrence as an independent socialist candidate? There was no problem of allowing the Tory in – this was Willie Gallagher's old constituency – but a split vote was always anathema to your average Labour voter. Edward and I argued the question at length and communicated our agreements and disagreements to Lawrence. The outcome was that we accepted an independent candidature and promised on behalf of ourselves – not the *New Reasoner* editorial board for there were differences of opinion – that we would help financially and practically.

I wrote a Note on our decision to support the Socialist League's independent candidate in the final issue of the *New Reasoner* which came out after the general election had been held, in which for the third time Labour was defeated. Naturally Edward and I discussed the issue at great length with Lawrence but it was the members of the League who took the decisive vote. I ended my quite short article in the *New Reasoner* with an insistence that there were special circumstances in West Fife and that there could never be, at least at the present time, an automatic decision to present candidates against the Labour Party. Any decision in other parts of the country would depend on the nature and character of the local political situation and I argued that it would be unlikely to see anything comparable in other parts of the country. But the future might be different, and I ended by emphasising that any decision 'will not rest upon a simple assertion that what is not favoured by the Labour Party organisation is in itself wrong for socialists and the socialist movement. With a Labour Party dominated by Mr. Gaitskell and a world dominated by nuclear weapons, no socialist can give that answer'.

There was another reason why Edward and myself encouraged Lawrence to stand in the General Election and it was an argument with which he himself was in full agreement. I don't think we put the matter on paper, at least I can find nothing in my own correspondence, nor did we make it public. The Scottish NUM was dominated by the Communist Party with a leadership that was tough and militant. Lawrence was a renegade in their way of thinking, and they would go a very long way to diminish his political appeal. We all agreed that a lively campaign and a decent result would make Lawrence much better known throughout the mining districts, and so it proved. He was elected General Secretary of the Scottish Miners in 1964 and General Secretary of the National Union of Miners in 1968.

We had promised our full support to Lawrence in 1959. He needed a great deal of clerical help – addressing envelopes and so on, and he needed money. During the period of the election campaign Edward and myself, in different weeks, went up to Fife to stay with Lawrence and help with the usual activities, including speaking at meetings. And I brought back to Hull a large file of electoral lists in order to address the envelopes which enclosed Lawrence's campaign address. There were eight or nine volunteers who had already helped with the *Reasoner* and some who were what might be called permanent part-time workers: Joan Knott for foreign correspondence (she was a city librarian) and Joan Welton, the wife of the business friend who had lent me his office duplicator, who, among many chores, distributed the *New Reasoner* pamphlets. As for money, we received donations from all over the country and we more or less covered the electoral costs. Halifax, of course, set up the same kind of organisation and I think between us we addressed most of the electors' envelopes. Lawrence did as well as could be expected, with just under 5,000 votes, beating the Communist candidate by 1,000.

The Daly election campaign had taken a great deal of our time, but during these weeks we were also deeply involved in the negotiations and planning of the merger of the *New Reasoner* and *Universities and Left Review*. The first issue of *New Left Review* was to appear early in 1960 with Stuart Hall as editor and with Gabriel Pearson, Charles Taylor and Ralph Samuel as his closest editorial colleagues. Roderick Prince was Business Manager. There was a much larger editorial board which brought together the main personalities of the two original journals. I became the first chairman and Edward succeeded me later.

There is no doubt that the new journal was well received. We had assumed a sale of the first number of round about two thousand copies, although ULR had mostly sold more, and the first issue's circulation of the new title was around 8,000. The early months were hopeful and encouraging but difficulties very soon showed themselves. During the next two years our problems accumulated and led, towards the end of 1962, to a new editorial board and a quite different journal.

The history of these years of the New Left – a title that came into general use in about 1959 – has already been much written about, though there are still important collections of original documents, especially correspondence, that have not yet been made available. I ought to make the point that I myself was a supporter of the idea of a merger in the year or so before it took place. It was debated at great length by Edward and myself, and we had at various times our usual qualifications, although we ended in agreement, but the man to whom I was now beginning to come very close intellectually was a firm opponent from the early days of discussion. This was Ralph Miliband, with whom we first made contact during the first half of 1957, and whose intelligence and sharpness of mind we very soon began to appreciate. As I now accept the problem, although it has been obvious to many and it is not a new thought, the merger represented the coming together of two different traditions which always remained different in certain important areas of thought and practice. There is no doubt that the differences in our background and traditions were an important factor in the serious problems that later showed themselves. It is difficult sometimes to be precise on these matters but it meant that even without a conscious statement of differences, the approaches to practical matters as well as to some political issues were often conducted in different ways. Certainly the exploration of disagreements, compared with the roughness of argument often used between Edward and myself, were not always easily assimilated and here is a matter in which I must accept an important measure of blame. I ought to have offered much more support to Janet Hase (the administrative secretary) and especially to Stuart Hall, the editor. Stuart went on to have a successful academic career and he has remained politically very committed. He has always been an attractive personality and, although we have seen relatively little of each other in the decades which have followed, it has always been a great pleasure to meet him again. He is an extremely nice man, highly competent and reliable.

What I have only realised since I began writing these memoirs are the complications within my own working life during these years of the late fifties and early sixties. I mention them here not in any way to offer excuses for my failure to take a more sustained interest in the internal matters affecting New Left Review, but only as an indication of the general liveliness on the Left. I do not at all presume that my affairs were different or more concentrated than any around me. But within the half dozen years from the period of The Reasoner I was editing with Asa Briggs the essays for the Cole memorial volume; reading in detail the draft of Ralph Miliband's Parliamentary Socialism; involved in the Lawrence Daly campaign; helping in the formation of the Society for the Study of Labour History; continuing as chairman of the local Tribune Society (of which more later); the normal university teaching commitment with increasing numbers of students and the introduction of a new course – a comparison of Japanese with British industrialisation – and, a very big 'and', Constance had our fourth child in 1960 (it was not an easy birth). The background to all these happenings was, of course, the editing of The New Reasoner and the merger with New Left Review.

As already noted, working life for me, as for all those closely involved, could never have been easy within the somewhat diverse traditions of the personalities of the NLR, but we were also affected in other and sometimes crucial ways by the developing politics of the early 1960s. I have remarked earlier upon the expansion of the anti-nuclear movement, and while I do not believe it completely swamped the New Left there is no doubt that 'the Bomb' was the most important political, and populist, issue in the early years of the 1960s. There were two episodes of major importance, although in global terms hardly comparable. The first, in 1960, was the Labour Party annual conference in early October at Scarborough where it was already considered likely that Gaitskell would lose the debate on defence policy. Stuart Hall brought up to the Conference several of his colleagues on NLR and produced a daily commentary sheet, arguing in particular against the nuclear bomb and NATO. Gaitskell made the outstanding speech of his political career and although he lost the vote, it was by a much smaller margin than had been anticipated. His famous words that he would 'fight and fight again' for a reversal of the decision were to be fulfilled in the following year's Conference. The debates, and their aftermaths, confirmed for many over these early years of the sixties that there could be no serious politics outside the Labour Party. The tide of public opinion was already moving towards Labour and although the General Election of 1964 only gave the Party a very small majority, it was the end of thirteen years of Tory rule, with Harold Wilson as Parliamentary leader following the death of Hugh Gaitskell in mid-January 1963.

The second nuclear issue, of world significance, was the Cuban missile crisis in October 1962. Most historians seem to accept that for a few days there was the possibility that the world would be swept into war and possibly nuclear exchanges, although there are considerable differences in their emphasis. My personal memories of the Cuban crisis are still vivid. While neither Constance nor I considered that it was likely to be nuclear war, it was notable how many among my university colleagues, including those whom I always thought of as apolitical, were now moved to the edge of serious apprehension. The nuclear crisis confirmed for many the importance of the control or abolition of nuclear weapons and undoubtedly encouraged support for CND in general and the newly established direct action Committee of 100 in particular.

These weeks of the Cuban crisis covered the same period during which the final arrangements for the takeover of NLR were being worked out. The story has been told in several places. Financial problems were now without question of major importance although they were only the final deciding factor. The NLR, now under the control and editorship of Perry Anderson, broke with the tradition and approach that Stuart Hall, with all his many problems and difficulties, had broadly established within what may be called the first New Left, and it was no longer a journal in the same intellectual and political milieu. The change was not for the better.

There was another 'happening' during these years that must be noticed. On the 23 May 1959 I received a letter from a student at Fircroft College in the Selly Park district of Birmingham. Fircroft was an adult training college which, like Ruskin, could award a two-year certificate to its mostly trade union students who were then eligible for university entrance. The college was largely funded by the Cadbury Trust. The student who wrote to me had already been interviewed by Peter Worsley and myself and he was expressing his thanks for our acceptance of him for the next academic year. His name was Harry Newton.

I assume that I must already have known Harry had been in the Communist Party, which he had left during 1956. He came from Leeds where for a time he had been employed by the Gas Board and had led a strike of meter-readers before applying to go to Fircroft. I obviously liked him from the beginning of our acquaintance for I early fixed him up in lodgings with a close friend of the family. This was Margaret Palfreman whose husband, a man Constance and I were both very fond of, had died suddenly about five years earlier, leaving quite a young family. Margaret's house was in the next avenue to ours, a matter of a few minutes walk; and Harry stayed with her the whole three years of his university course.

He entered immediately into our somewhat loosely organised but very active political group, of which Peter Worsley and a young political scientist called Bob Dowse were my closest friends. Harry was privy to all the inner politics of the New Left and I talked our problems over with him without inhibition. I should explain that I was already in the habit of exchanging political ideas with my adult students. I had, during most of the 1950s, given at least one lecture a year at Ruskin College in Oxford, and I had come to an arrangement with Ruskin that I would take up to six of their students, after they had passed their diploma, into our degree course. I doubt whether we ever had as many as six in any one year, but from the late fifties through to 1968 we always had a goodly contingent of Ruskin and other adult students. For most of these years about one quarter our student population for the B.Sc. (Econ.) degree was above the age of twenty-one on entry – the definition of an adult student.

On the domestic front Harry had no difficulty in establishing relationships within my own family, and the children loved him. For Harry the door was always open, and there was always a place at our table for him. His memory, for all our family, remained lively and affectionate.

Harry finished his degree in the usual three years and then left Hull, and at this point he might have found his way to another planet. There was no further communication or contact with him. And no contact either with Margaret Palfreman, his landlady, who had been so kind to him. It was very odd, and I thought it odd, but life was very busy during these years. In the years to come I heard occasionally snippets of news of Harry – even that for a time at any rate he was living at Selby, half an hour by train from Hull. I heard that in 1970 he had been appointed to a lectureship at Fircroft College and also that he was in some way connected with the Institute for Workers Control at Nottingham. Around 1975 I learned that Harry was in the middle of a considerable upheaval within Fircroft College and that he was being supported by Labour MPs and socialist intellectuals, including Edward Thompson, but again I was very busy and I did not even communicate with Edward. Sometime around 1980 – I am not sure of the year – I heard Harry on the BBC radio, delivering as a Quaker a quite bitter denunciation of communism and all its evils, and while it greatly saddened me with its sectarian diatribe I shrugged my shoulders and told myself that too many of the flesh, even better flesh than Harry, had gone this way. But I was sorry, for I remembered how much my family had enjoyed Harry's company and how they still recalled with such pleasure his squat, stumpy figure coming into the house.

Harry died in 1983. He had been ill for some time and suffered a final stroke.

On the 20 February 1985 a documentary TV programme made by 20/20 Vision for Channel Four was banned by the Independent Broadcasting Authority on grounds of internal security. The following day, however, *The Guardian* published the full story. It was a whistle-blowing account by Cathy Massiter who had been an MI5 officer for over a decade and who had left the security services about a year previously. She spoke at some length about the targeting of leading members of the National Council for Civil Liberties and CND. These included Patricia Hewitt and Harriet Harman for the NCCL and Bruce Kent for CND but the name that was to invoke a wave of protest, indignation and fervent denial of wrong-doing was our former student, Harry Newton. Cathy Massiter informed us that Harry had been an informer for MI5 since the middle fifties and she especially emphasised his work within CND. She had herself been in the headquarters of MI5 for about a dozen years and her information was mostly of the seventies and early 1980s. There was no specific mention of the University of Hull.

The naming of Harry as a spy for the security services produced a quite remarkable response by many of his former friends. Most letters seem to have been published in *The Guardian* but there was a lengthy defence of Harry in the ILP *Labour Leader*, April 1985, signed by, among many others, Liz Newton, Harry's widow. I, too, found it very difficult to believe at first, although his total rejection of contact with us in Hull for the first time made sense, and there was one, but only one, comment that had always remained in my mind and which at the time I had found somewhat odd and curious, although I put it down to naivety.

Edward Thompson was as shocked as we all were and he wrote a very sensible, and compassionate letter to *The Guardian* (2 March 1985) which included the following:

> It is absurd to invite people to express 'disbelief' when they are not allowed to view the accusation or to pursue the evidence. I also knew Harry Newton, off and on, for 30 years, in the adult education and other movements. He was an unlikely agent. But then, as an historian of such things, who has looked into what traces of such espionage as survive in the public records when they are opened after 100 or 75 years, I know that agents always are unlikely persons.

Edward continued by asking for an immediate public enquiry which he then went on to say we would not get. There has not been a great deal of new information that has been helpful with the exception of a long article in the journal *Lobster* (No. 28) by Don Bateman, who was a well-known member of the ILP. He came from Leeds and knew Harry from just after the war. In August 1972 Bateman spent a week with Harry at the ILP summer school held at St. Andrews and during that week Harry 'displayed again his great personal hostility towards the

CP'. I had myself no idea that Harry had this anti-communist phobia, and had I not heard him on the radio in the closing years of his life I should have found it difficult to believe. Apparently this was expressed, no doubt in only one of a number of examples, in his belief that Bruce Kent was a crypto-communist.

Naturally, there was always the understanding that the internal security forces in all countries infiltrate any dissident group, whatever their politics, although it must be said that the Left in Britain seem perhaps more conscious of the iniquities of American and other societies in this regard than those of their own. But there were examples. The *Sunday Times*, in late January 1982, published the story of Betty Gordon, who had been an MI5 agent inside the Communist Party and had 'come out' of her own accord. She was active at least throughout the 1950s, and was a very close friend of Betty Reid who was well up within the hierarchy of the Communist Party. Betty Gordon herself had been employed not only in King Street but in certain other of its associated organisations, and while the date of her disclosures came at a time when the Communist Party was already on the way to disintegration, it was an illuminating story. As was that of Harry Newton, and for myself there are now no doubts about his involvement as an agent. I have never attempted to obtain any confirmation through governmental records, mainly because during the long years of Thatcherism there would have been no point in making such a request, and since New Labour came to power I have been waiting for several years for a new Access to Information Bill. So far the indications look mostly bleak. It would be interesting, perhaps saddening, to see what Harry really thought of the family which had welcomed him so warmly.

Part 5: **The Academy and Politics to Retirement**

University life in Britain began to change towards the end of the 1950s. The low birth rate of the 1930s had meant that the potential numbers of students declined to the mid-fifties and the special arrangements for wartime members of the Armed Forces had more or less come to an end. My own University College experienced a fall in total numbers in the middle years of the decade and certain planned investments in additional buildings were cancelled. During the closing years of the decade, however, attitudes began to change, against the background of increasing numbers in the eighteen plus age groups. The established University Colleges became Universities, the Robbins Committee on Higher Education was being planned and the idea began to be considered of a group of entirely newly established universities on green-field sites. Sussex was among the first with Asa Briggs who left Leeds to take the Chair of History. The decade of the sixties were exciting, lively years in higher education. They included also the foundation of the Open University, the formation of which came originally from the innovative mind of Michael Young.

My own subject of economic and social history was still within the department of economics. When Hull became a University in 1956 we had kept, more or less, the syllabus we had been teaching for the London External degree in Economics. This included two compulsory papers in economics and one in economic history, as well as an optional special subject of three papers in history or other specialisms such as statistics or sociology. As the number of students increased in the Economics Department so the numbers requiring economic history became steadily larger and at the same time the demand for our course in social history, from the Social Studies Department, also increased. We obtained our third lecturer early in the sixties and by the end of the decade we had seven in our group, still within the Economics Department, which now had two full professors.

The University began to remedy its very low proportion of senior staff by the appointment of eight senior lecturers towards the end of the fifties. I was among this group and happened at the time to be a lecturing staff elected representative on Senate. In those days Senate was a much more powerful body in universities outside Oxford, Cambridge and London than it was to become from about 1990 (a time of greatly increased bureaucracy in most university institutions). There was a very long discussion in Hull concerning the appointment to senior lecturer and much solemn debate from the older professors – most of whom were carried over from before the war – about the importance of establishing careful rules in making these promotions. And then, a couple of items later on the agenda, there was a resolution about the title of 'emeritus' being attached to retiring professors. At that time it was the practice, in at least some of the older universities, and it may have been universal, to award the title only to scholars of accepted reputation. Our old men, however, were obviously quite certain that the practice should be automatically followed on every retirement from an academic chair, and there was no argument from the professorial ranks, most of whom were due for retirement in a very few years. So I spoke up, and after making a comment on our lengthy discussion of the academic criteria in the matter of senior lecturers I asked the Vice-Chancellor, who was in the chair, whether it was not usual in other universities to offer the title only to certain of their retiring scholars. There were a couple of somewhat muffled comments from the body of Senate and then the resolution passed *nem con*. Naturally this exchange added to my reputation as a difficult, and for some, unpleasant radical on the Left. I must note that in spite of my own active role in university affairs and my well-known political position, I was among the first group of Senior Lecturers and one of the first two Readers to be appointed in the 1960s. My misadventure with my Personal Chair is a story I tell later.

The expansion in student numbers occurred when my own career also offered new directions. My book on Rural Migration was to bring useful dividends in terms of academic contacts and outside conferences. The year after it was published in 1956 there was the foundation meeting of the European Society for Rural Sociology at which it was decided that their first Conference should be around the subject of rural migration. Some thirteen European countries were represented at the University of Louvain, in Belgium, in September 1958 and I read my first paper to an international conference. Two years later I was offered a somewhat more exotic experience, although intellectually not quite comparable.

Monaco is an independent principality within France, with the Rainier family the ruling dynasty. The first Rainier was evidently seriously interested in marine biology and the family connection with science continued through the twentieth century. In 1960 a French research institute in Paris persuaded the sitting Rainier to subsidise a conference on migration, and I was invited. I flew to Nice and then by car provided by Monaco to a luxury hotel in Monte Carlo next door to the casino. The conference, which was in mid-May just before the opening of the season proper, was to last eight days and at our first meeting – with only about a dozen participants – I began to realise what a muddle it was going to be. I was the only historian among the speakers (the chairman was a well-known French historian, Louis Chevalier, but he took little part in the discussions) and the rest were scientists of one kind or another except for an American sociologist, who was regrettably dull. Some of the scientists were very lively. I made friends with an Italian biologist of about my own age. He had been to Cambridge after the war and spoke excellent English. The food at lunch and dinner was wonderful; so good that on the last night, with my Italian friend and a couple of others, we took ourselves off to Nice to sit in a small restaurant facing the sea and eat a simple meal of pasta. We were invited to a reception at the Palace where we knew we should meet Her Serene Highness Grace Kelly. Prince Rainier had married her a few years earlier. We were ushered into a large room where His Serene Highness and his wife were waiting to receive us. There were two queues, the one for Grace Kelly a good deal longer than that for her husband. My Italian friend and myself were asked by the major-domo if we would like to meet His Serene Highness, and we politely indicated that we would prefer to stay in the line we were in. I cannot remember anything of the ten minutes conversation we had with Grace Kelly except that we agreed afterwards she was efficient at what must be such a boring business. I do remember how beautiful she looked and I can still see her in the eye of my mind, some forty years later.

With my Italian friend the pleasures of Monte Carlo were cheerfully explored. A visit was arranged to the maritime museum which Jacques Cousteau, a famous name in those days, apparently used as his headquarters and we had a guided tour around his large aquarium. Naturally we had a couple of evenings in the Casino and on the last day we went shopping, my friend in the really expensive quarter where I went to find him after my own modest purchases. He was standing before a longish line of different sized parcels at one end of which was an especially large one. 'Ah John', he said, patting this large bundle, 'You may think this is for my mistress but you would be wrong. It is for my grandmother'.

Intellectually for me it was a total useless conference since there was no one at all interested in my migration problems, and the scientific problems of the migration of certain insects, etc. were not matters I really understood. This was the second of many international meetings, most of which were helpful in terms of the range of scholars who attended. The papers presented were, by contrast, a mixed affair, with the balance tilting towards the negative.

My migration studies continued to bring me invitations to discussions and conferences, both in the UK and in Europe. There was now a European section of the United Nations concerned with social/sociological problems, including problems of migration within and between national states. In 1963 I found myself chief rapporteur to an international group which was to spend a month looking at rural problems in the Italian South. We started with three days in Naples and then travelled over selected areas and projects and finished in Rome, where our four subject groups presented their reports. Inevitably the personnel were of mixed nationalities and all pleasant, but of differing abilities. My last job, back in England, was to edit the final reports and try to ensure some kind of reasonable agreement between them. One of the chairman of a group was an English civil servant from the Ministry of Agriculture who sent back my edited report with the comment that he would have been delighted had his group found themselves willing or able to discuss the sort of analysis that I had provided. The other chairmen – they were all men – took my editing as given. I cannot believe that our month's travel around southern Italy exercised much influence upon future rural policies, but I understand the Casa per il Mezzogiorne, the organisation we were mostly concerned with, has only recently closed.

There was one other foreign visit in this period of the early sixties. Every year, in early autumn, there assembled an international school at Alpbach in the Austrian Alps. Alpbach was not very far from Salzburg and had been the centre for this school since soon after the end of the war. Originally it was organised by upper-class conservative anti-fascist groups as a statement of their dissociation with the strongly Nazi trends in Austrian society before and during the war. The village was evidently chosen because it had originally been the centre of silver-mining operations and there were five or six large inns already suitable for students and tutors, as well the houses in the village. Each year there was a subject for the main discussion with quite small groups of about fifteen to twenty students. All told there must have been several hundreds: students, tutors and visitors. The groups met for a couple of hours in the mornings and there were sometimes optional lectures in the afternoons or evenings; and, of course, a wide variety of social life. It went on for about three weeks and had become well-known, especially in central Europe. Almost all the teaching was done in English.

I was asked to give one of the three plenary lectures over the first weekend. The subject for the year was leisure and work, with the emphasis, so I was informed, on leisure. So I gave my lecture and then later the same day met the group which had decided to join my morning meetings. I was giving an historical survey from medieval times of the meaning and content of leisure in different European societies and by the end of the first week – not least because I became known as a generally unstuffy character who actually made jokes (so I was later told) – my group became somewhat crowded. The students were interested, interesting and very lively – most in their early twenties.

It was a very pleasant affair. I had two encounters that are worth a brief mention. At the first weekend I met the British Cultural Attaché in Vienna who had not been to Alpbach previously and was there with his wife and two daughters. I was the only English scholar there among the French, German, Italian and Dutch – to mention only the most numerous – and my university was HULL! The frustration endured by the Cultural Attaché was grievous. He just brought himself to be introduced to me, and then forgot I was around. The American Cultural Attaché invited me to lunch, as did the French and the Dutch, but not the snob-ridden Englishman who clearly only recognised Oxbridge as the English universities worthy of recognition. My other encounter was with Arthur Koestler, who lived in the same valley as Alpbach. Some Austrian friends had arranged a dinner for Koestler and myself and one or two other visitors. Koestler, who was to sit next to me, arrived late, half drunk and spent his time trying to discover exactly what my politics were, especially in relation to the Soviet Union. He didn't get much response, continued to drink heavily and then left the table as suddenly as he had arrived. We then all had a pleasant evening.

There were some very impressive tutors among the different nationalities. Alain Touraine, who was already well known as a sociologist, was indeed an extremely lively personality (and very good also on the dance floor) and I made especial friends with Franco Ferraroti, who had the chair of sociology in Rome. By the end of the first week I was taking breakfast every morning with Franco and his American wife, and later, on a couple of occasions, Franco invited me to Rome to give a paper to his research seminars.

Edward Thompson and I had first made contact with Ralph Miliband in the spring of 1957 and he joined us on the board of the *New Reasoner*. Ralph and his father had escaped from Belgium on almost the last boat from Ostend, after the Nazi invasion of Western Europe. His mother and sister remained in a village south of Brussels for the whole of the war before they too came to England. Ralph entered LSE during the early part of the war, then served in the Navy (mainly listening to German naval broadcasts in the North Sea), obtained a very good First when he returned to his studies, and became Harold Laski's last outstanding student (Harold died early in 1950). Apart from his doctorate, which was a massive document, Ralph wrote very little for publication during the fifties and this was probably due to the general political atmosphere in which he found himself. He moved in Left circles at LSE but unlike many of his political contemporaries he never became a member of the Communist Party. Ralph had become friendly with Isaac Deutscher and while not fully accepting Deutscher's political views he could never approve the Stalinist position. He always said later that it had been the *New Reasoner* group that gave him the intellectual comradeship and encouragement to write and within a year (1957-8) he had begun work on one of the most important books on the politics of British labour in the twentieth century.

Parliamentary Socialism summed up for many of the New Left and the radical generations that were just coming into politics an analysis that made sense of the years since the formation of the Labour Party at the beginning of the century. The last chapter – 'The sickness of Labourism' – was especially important for an understanding of contemporary politics in 1960, the year the book was published. Re-reading this final chapter offers a notable introduction to the politics of New Labour following the election victory of 1997. There was, Ralph wrote of the late 1950s, 'a new revisionism, to which the new Leader (Hugh Gaitskell) was ideologically and politically committed, which claimed not only that nationalisation was an electoral liability to the Labour Party, but that in a "post-capitalist" society, it had actually come to be largely irrelevant'. And a few lines on he underlined the importance for Gaitskell of the need to educate his Party 'into a final acceptance of the "mixed economy"'.

Parliamentary Socialism offers a critical understanding of the evolution of the Labour Party through the twentieth century. Although it was written in the late 1950s the analysis remains central to the history of the later decades of the century. The decades of the twentieth century to 1945 had been dominated by war and economic problems of major proportions. During these years the Left in the British labour movement was able vigorously to offset the labourist traditions of its leaderships although in terms of policies and final decisions the block vote of the trade unions was almost always the decisive factor. The ideas and ideals of socialism were always present and the change to more radical policies was never considered impracticable. It was the more or less full employment of the three decades after the end of the second world war that increasingly bemused the theorists of the Labourist tradition. We now had the approach to capitalist society beginning to be indicated in the quotations from Gaitskell cited by Ralph above. At this time Gaitskell's attempt to jettison Clause Four was unsuccessful but had he not died in 1963 there is no reason to suppose that he would not have continued his attempts. The trade unions, however, were still powerful and it is unlikely the full Monty of Blair's New Labour would have been completely realised. The word ' Socialism' continued to be heard in the side-alleys off the corridors of power for the next three decades after Gaitskell's death, although its purpose became steadily less meaningful.

It was not until the ascendancy of Blair to the Labour leadership that the completion of Gaitskell's adaptation to contemporary capitalism was achieved in words as well as long-established practice. 'The liberation from capital is nowhere on the agenda of politics'. So Ralph Miliband wrote in the opening sentence of the final chapter of his last book published only after his death in May 1994. *Parliamentary Socialism* had provided a necessary introduction to the general understanding of the decline of social democracy in Britain, and *Socialism for a Sceptical Age* surveyed the consequences forty years on. After the 1960s, when there was much youthful radicalism around, the conservatism of British society had steadily reasserted itself, greatly assisted by the years of the Thatcher governments.

I mentioned above that these closing years of the 1950s witnessed a general increase in research on the history of the labour movement as well as in the radical history of other periods of British history. While I was reading Ralph's manuscript I myself was engaged, as I have noted, in a joint editorship with Asa Briggs of a series of essays for G.D.H. Cole's seventieth birthday. He died before the volume was published and it became a memorial to an outstanding socialist intellectual. This first volume of *Essays in Labour History* I have always thought the most interesting and the best balanced of the three volumes that we finally published. My own essay on the background to the Taff Vale decision of 1901 took me for the first time into legal history and it was republished elsewhere on a couple of occasions. Asa and I saw a good deal of Margaret Cole and after publication she offered us a number of Douglas's MS volumes containing names and brief biographical details of a large collection of members of the Labour movement, going back to its earliest days. The idea was that the volumes could be used to produce a Labour Dictionary of individuals covering the whole period of the movement's history. This was, of course, Douglas Cole's original intention. But Asa was about to leave Leeds to take the Chair of History at the new University of Sussex – he was later to become Vice-Chancellor – and declined the offer. I accepted it on condition that I could obtain a grant for a research worker. Through the influence of Margaret Cole and Julius Braunthal the Amsterdam Institute of Social History provided an initial sum which allowed me to employ Dorothy Thompson on a part-time basis for about two years. The shape and structure of the proposed Dictionary, however, worried me for most years of the sixties and the first volume was not published until 1972.

I have written at some length in the Introduction to volume 10 (published in the first year of the new millennium and the last under my editorship) of the main principles upon which the volumes of the *Dictionary of Labour Biography* are grounded and some matters need only to be remarked upon here. Let me emphasise again that the final structure of the Dictionary took me much longer to agree than I expected. This was, I would now guess, partly the result of the other activities in which I had became involved but there was also the fact that it was a new type of product compared with other kinds of Dictionaries. At least I knew it had to be different but it took me a long time to bring together all the half-formulated ideas that were circulating around my mind. One thing I was clear about. I was not interested in a parallel version of the *Dictionary of National Biography*. A record just of the members of Parliament, well-known intellectuals and the leading personalities of the trade union movement would miss the very large numbers of ordinary people who had given so much of their lives to their ideals. After the first volume was published in 1972 I decided that individuals likely to achieve a biography should be mostly excluded as well as those who were included in any detail in someone else's biography or MS papers.

I could take this approach since in the course of working on the first volume I decided that far from being a one volume project it could go on as long as the labour movement existed. So each volume could cover the whole period from the early labour movement, that is from about 1790 or thereabouts, to the present day, with every volume on an A to Z basis.

There was already a large-scale biographical Dictionary for France, edited by Jean Maitron from Paris, but organised on different lines. The *Dictionnaire biographique du Mouvement ouvrier francais* was divided into four periods: 1789-1864; 1864-1871; 1871-1914; 1914-1939. Each period was arranged in name order, and the number of volumes in each historical period would depend on how many individuals were to be included. Maitron, however, was not only concerned with the French labour movement. It was always his purpose to publish an international series, and during the 1970s I allowed myself to accept responsibility for a two-volume British labour dictionary which would be translated into French and published by Maitron's Institute.

It was through this connection that I first met François Bédarida who specialised in British history and whose friendship I greatly appreciated. Bédarida was a serious scholar who wrote most interestingly on modern British history. His Social History of Britain, 1851- 1975 was translated and published in 1979 and in a series *Les Inconnus de L'Histoire* he wrote what I have always thought a remarkable study of British socialism through the biography of Will Thorne. This biographical Dictionary I promised Maitron was to cause me a certain degree of stress and strain, and I regularly cursed myself for agreeing to the project. My two volumes were in collaboration with Joyce Bellamy and David Martin. The latter was first an undergraduate and then a post-graduate in my department, from which he moved to a lectureship in economic history at the University of Sheffield. David was to become a most helpful collaborator on both the French and the English Dictionaries. He has remained extremely well-read and could always be relied upon to produce his own sensible and scholarly biographical entries as well as critical commentaries on any MS entries that we cared to send him. He read the proofs for a number of volumes and over the years has been a wholly reliable collaborator.

Joyce Bellamy had been in the department of economics from the early 1950s as a research assistant. Then, at the beginning of the 1960s, she began a Ph.D. on the business history of Hull in the 19th and 20th centuries. Joyce was not an historian but an assiduous burrower of the facts of historical life and her doctorate, while lacking in theoretical understanding, has remained a useful source book on the business and commercial life of the city in the past two centuries. Some time in the late 1960s the University agreed that Joyce could become a full-time research officer working for the Dictionary. The discussions which produced this result went a long way towards solving a number of my problems. Decisions about the Dictionary all remained with me. What Joyce did was to answer our considerable correspondence, check the list of writings and bibliographies we always included for each entry, and arrange for the reading of proofs. She herself also always read proofs for the whole volume. In all work for which she was responsible she was meticulously careful and reliable. Six months before we were due to deliver the MS of volume one to Macmillans I decided that we must have a detailed index and it was compiled by two members of the University Library. No one I had spoken to, and I had consulted widely, had ever suggested the idea of an index to a biographical Dictionary but this was within a movement whose range and diversity were in very broad terms. Suppose, I said to myself, after the next few volumes, you wanted to find out how many coal miners were Primitive Methodists, an index would be helpful. So I drafted headings and sub-headings in considerable detail and the librarians were always encouraging and helpful. Many reviewers of this first and later volumes saw the point.

Publication of the Dictionary proceeded regularly but at different rates over the years. By that I mean that since I made myself responsible for the final draft of every entry that was published – there were of course many authors – how many years there were between the publication of succeeding volumes would depend on my own priorities. Over the years I mostly worked on the Dictionary only in the evenings and there were many occasions when I must have been behind the timetable that Joyce had organised. She never complained and this was among her many virtues. It was not that she was ever short of work – her correspondence alone was on a very large scale – and she worked a minimum of five and half days a week, and often at weekends. But while I regarded the Dictionary as a useful and important contribution to Labour studies, I was never going to let it dominate my own research and writing, although I wrote a good many entries and most of the Special Notes when they were introduced. My working relationship with Joyce was always pleasant and fully cooperative on both sides and it was extremely saddening when she had to retire effectively after the completion of volume nine. I write 'effectively' because she tried to continue for a year or so but her physical and mental condition deteriorated rather seriously. She had a series of minor strokes and her memory fell to pieces. Fortunately she had a reasonable private income as well as a pension and she was able to stay in her own house, and was satisfactorily looked after. One of her women friends, Audrey Hebb, practised in a truly compassionate way her Christian beliefs.

Volume 10 was published in March 2000 with the new editors already working on volume 11. I have sometimes been asked why Joyce's name preceded mine on the title page since all decisions concerning structure and content were mine. My answer was never a vehement one since I did not believe the matter important. I had noticed that in many science journals which published what was obviously mainly the research of the doctoral student the name of the professor responsible for supervision was almost always given first, and I was told that this was the normal practice, however much or little the professor had contributed. I recognise, of course, that scientific research is usually on a more collaborative basis than history or the social sciences, but again one must not generalise too sharply. I think the nearest answer is that I always assumed in our field of work names went by position in the alphabet.

Philip Larkin became the librarian of the University Library in 1955, and he arrived more or less at the same time as Brynmor Jones moved from the chair of chemistry to the Vice-Chancellorship. At the time I thought that Brynmor Jones' elevation was not in the interests of the University, since I was critical of what I thought were Brynmor's fairly obvious deferential attitudes towards the business men on Council; and this was the Council that had imposed the ban on Cheddi Jagan. But over time I changed my attitude towards him, and it was his attitude towards the Library that began my reappraisal. I mentioned earlier that the Staff Association had been developing a lively campaign for a much more generous financial approach to the requirements of the library, and Brynmor very soon responded in very positive ways. And I don't think at this very early stage – that is the late fifties – it was Philip's reputation. He was of course already becoming well known with the publication of *The Less Deceived* in late 1955 and within the University we all were aware that we had a poet with a fast growing reputation among our company. We also soon learned that we had also an efficient librarian who really knew what he was about, and it was a very welcome discovery.

I suppose we soon learned that Larkin's political ideas were on the Right but he almost never expressed his views in public – by which I mean during his working day. Like everyone else I found him courteous and pleasant and I got to know him rather better than most of my colleagues, partly because I was often elected to the Library Committee as a representative of the lecturing staff.

By the middle sixties I had began a project which was greatly to enlarge the University Library's usefulness, and in this I was much encouraged and supported throughout by Philip. I had been making contact for some years with the Amsterdam Institute of Social History. G.D.H. Cole had been quite closely associated with the Institute from its beginning in 1936 when, with the financial backing of the Dutch Co-operative movement, it acquired the archives of the German Social Democratic Party, which were housed in Berlin. I started going over to Amsterdam and learned to my surprise that Cole had encouraged one or two of our labour historians to deposit material in the Institute. Raymond Postgate, for example, who was Cole's brother- in- law, put in a collection of the 1926 General Strike posters. I thought this not very sensible if we wanted to develop labour history studies in Britain so I decided that it would be worthwhile to start looking into the problem. Obviously there were labour and socialist archives in various record centres – LSE came to mind immediately – and the papers of leading politicians would naturally get properly housed in most cases. The question was what happened to the materials of local and regional trade unions or the papers of activists below the top rank. I must have talked over the problem with members of the Society for the Study of Labour History, which was slowly building up its membership, and I cannot recall what was the first collection of papers and materials that I transferred into the University library at Hull. We did not have an archivist at this stage. My first really large archive comprised the papers, records and printed literature belonging to Jock Haston, a Trotskyist from the mid-1930s. His archive is especially important for the war years and the formation of the Revolutionary Communist Party but it also includes files on the Trotsky Defence Committee of 1936-8. His collection of manuscripts, journals, books and especially pamphlets was large and varied, and his materials are indispensable for the revolutionary groups to the Left of the Communist Party. Haston married Millie, one of the famous group of South African Trotskyists who came to Britain in 1938-9, and this archive has been used in a 1981 Hull doctoral thesis by Martin Upham.

Jock Haston's revolutionary politics began to moderate from about 1950 and he moved steadily to the right. He became Education Officer for the Electrical Trades Union after Les Cannon and others took over control of the Union from the Communist Party at the end of the 1950s. I got to know Haston just about this time, and I think it was through Stuart Hall. I can remember going several times to his house in south London, and I must assume it was the University Library which arranged the removal of all his records. I should emphasise that Philip Larkin wholly supported what I was doing. 'Saville's subversive archive' was a later description he happily used when he talked to me. It was the growing labour collection that was responsible for the employment of Norman Higson as archivist. He was full-time archivist for the East Riding Record Office at Beverley and he began working Saturday mornings for us, to become full-time a few years later. What has often been missed in the writing about Philip is his position as a librarian. He worked most of his life as a librarian from around 9 am until six o'clock or so in the evening, and during that working day in Hull he encouraged an efficient and very pleasant atmosphere among the steadily growing number of library staff. I knew this throughout the decades when I was myself a permanent member of the academic community, and it has been confirmed in many conversations I have had in recent years. One of the interesting things about Philip was that his very conservative politics did not confuse his role as a librarian. I have already written about his support for the Labour archive I was accumulating but there were other examples which I would guess are little known. It must have been in his early days when a Yorkshire regional scheme was introduced between all libraries in the county in order to develop specialised centres for certain areas of books. There was apparently some reluctance, notably among the public library sector, to accept the Dewey classification group (HX 56) which took in labour and socialist literature; and evidently Philip accepted this group without hesitation, as a good librarian should. There was a further indication of his scruples as a librarian in the later sixties when he introduced six special grants each year, in addition to the annual departmental grant, for the purchase of materials in selected research areas and allocated to named individuals who were already known for their work. My own research field in the general history of the labour movement was among the six. The grants were his decision and not discussed by the Library Committee.

One of the interesting and important collections that I acquired for the Library was unusual in that Philip had to agree to offer a negotiated sum of money for the archive. This belonged to the National Council for Civil Liberties which at the time I was talking with them had offices quite near Kings Cross station. I thought the £500 or £600 we handed over – I cannot remember the exact sum but it was around these figures – was a wholly reasonable agreement. They were a working organisation, engaged in what was an important and very proper civic activity. The Council had been established in 1934. Its original purpose was to appoint observers to monitor the arrival of the national Hunger March due to arrive in London at the end of February 1934. There had been a notable degree of police hostility towards the unemployment marches of the early years of the 1930s, and nowhere had this been more apparent than in London. The group that came together was made up of well-known public figures and their presence at the arrival of the Hunger Marchers – whose outstanding personality was Wal Hannington – undoubtedly encouraged a much more moderate approach from the Metropolitan Police. The National Council for Civil Liberties was now formally established, with Ronald Kidd as General Secretary, and his companion, Sylvia Scaffardi, in the position of Assistant Secretary. Their work was soon to be much more involved with anti-fascist demonstrations, where again the Metropolitan Police were a good deal rougher than many police forces elsewhere. Ronald Kidd is today the forgotten name of a man whose reputation deserves more consideration. The National Council, renamed Liberty in 1989, is still alive and active. It was agreed at the initial discussions that we would have the whole archive from 1934, and that every few years the NCCL would send its collected records for these years to the University. This particular collection is now of national interest.

It is, of course, a very large and varied labour and socialist archive and it probably ranks for its specialised subjects among the half dozen leading records centre in Britain. Of all the many items I was fortunate to acquire there are three sets of papers whose story I am always happy to tell. The first relates to Harold Laski whose death in 1950 was such a shock to his friends and former students. He was a quite prodigious letter writer and there are collections of his letters in many parts of the world. Constance and I got to know Frida Laski, his widow, through the Milibands, and although she remained active in left-wing politics, she became a lonely woman. In her later years she stayed a number of times with us in Hull and we greatly enjoyed her company. Granville Eastwood published a study of Laski in 1977 and he very kindly deposited his working papers with us. They included a number of interesting letters and interviews from former students and friends. I used to talk with Frida about Harold's papers and one day – this was in her London flat – she pointed to two quite large cardboard files and said: 'Those are the letters that Harold used to write to me when he was away. He wrote almost every day'. It was her quite firm intention that she proposed to destroy them before she died. It took me five years of gentle argument, in which I had inestimable help and support from Constance, before she changed her mind. I was in the same London flat when one day she just pointed again to the two files, and said: 'There you are. They are yours'. There were several hundred letters which are now in the Laski collection in the University archive.

The assembly of archival materials provide many different experiences; professional archivists will on occasion be ready to tell you of their more unusual stories. I have one here, as Tom Lehrer would no doubt have said. Some time in the later years of the 1960s Edward Thompson and I were written to by Jim Mortimer in his position as chairman of the Union of Democratic Control (UDC). Some months earlier the Executive Committee had taken the decision to disband the organisation on the grounds that after fifty years of political existence, new ideas and new forms of organisation were now required. The Committee was thoroughly aware of the importance of its archives, and during the previous summer it had advertised its impending closure and offered all its papers and records to any institution within the United Kingdom. I knew all this but made no bid, only because that summer vacation I thought I was too busy. My failure troubled me in the months that followed, and then there arrived the letter from Mortimer. The Committee had received a number of offers and they had reduced the applications to three: Nuffield College, Oxford; the new University of Sussex and one other whose identity I have forgotten. The Committee could not made up its mind and decided to take what they believed was specialist advice. So they wrote to Edward and myself.

Edward replied with the suggestion that although LSE had not applied at any stage, the papers ought to be offered there because they already had the records of E.D. Morel, the first secretary of the UDC and an outstanding activist for the first ten years of its life. It was a sensible idea, except that there was no one at that time at LSE who was much interested in this kind of history. Or so I was to argue. My own suggestion was even more out of line with what the Committee had requested. I wrote a paper setting out what records and documents I had acquired for the University Library, details of the teaching and research into radical history in my Department, and what I was proposing for the future. I quoted the fee we had paid for the papers of the National Council for Civil Liberties as evidence of the general support I had been getting from Philip Larkin. My conclusion was the obvious one that the UDC papers should come to Hull. There was an acknowledgement of my letter, and that was all for several months. Then, early in the New Year, Arthur Wood, the deputy librarian, took a telephone message from the present secretary of the UDC asking when the Library would be collecting its papers. Arthur asked how much was involved to which the reply was about half a shelf.

There had been no correspondence. Wood reported to Philip who then passed on the message to me. I immediately reacted with disbelief, and explained to Philip that I happened to have worked for six months in late 1937 for the UDC in their Victoria Street offices and that I had a rough idea of the extent of the records at that time. The UDC had been established the day after the First World War began. It brought together a number of active liberals, radicals and socialists for a continuously critical appraisal of British foreign policy, and it had remained very lively for its first ten years. And then, after the death of E. D. Morel in 1924, there was a short interregnum until in 1927 Dorothy Woodman became secretary. Dorothy was a woman of high intelligence and apparently boundless energy. She lived with Kingsley Martin and her international contacts were many, and reliable. I gave Philip a somewhat longer account than I have written here, and convinced him that there were important correspondents (Bertrand Russell, Ramsay MacDonald et al) whose letters should be searched for, and that in general the UDC over the years had generated a vast amount of paper which present and future historians would be interested in. He agreed that I could go to London – petrol being paid for by the Library. I had told Philip that my nose was twitching at the report that there was so little to be collected, and Philip said that a London visit was obviously necessary 'to help alleviate that twitch'.

I had a small Morris estate car, and found myself in front of a large South Kensington house of the upper-middle-class style of the closing decades of the nineteenth century. The UDC in my day had been in Victoria Street and after the war it moved to offices at the Holborn end of Southampton Row. And then, five years before my visit in 1968, it had moved again to this house in South Kensington. Here, on the ground floor, it occupied two corners of a very large room, with the third corner being taken by the Socialist Medical Association (whose records we later acquired) and the fourth corner, so I was informed, by the Eugenics Society. This last identification may have been incorrect.

The Secretary was there to meet me and the other corners remained unoccupied. The Secretary, who was now winding up the UDC, had been in post for some three years and had not therefore been around when they made the final move from Southampton Row to the present house. He showed me the shelf on which the records were stacked, and we searched all the cupboards, shelves, nooks and crannies, and found only the odd item belonging to the UDC. The secretary, a former official of the National Union of Railwaymen, was a pleasant man who, after an hour or so of our searching, was becoming sceptical of my reasons for making the journey from Hull. Or, as we were both beginning to recognise, there must have been a large-scale clearing out, most likely at one of the moves. With growing desperation I walked around the room once again, and in what I was told was the Eugenics section – which had better office equipment than the other corners, I looked again at a four drawer filing cabinet behind which was a very large, dark mahogany door. 'What is that, and does it lead anywhere?' I asked the secretary, but to his knowledge it had never been opened in the three years since he first came. I asked if we could look a little more closely, and with some reluctance he agreed. So we moved the heavy filing cabinet aside, and opened the door, which was not locked. Inside was a dark cavern. We had no torch, but after a few matches the cavern turned out to be a large dumb waiter. In the affluent days of this neighbourhood, which I took to be pre-1914, the peasantry had cooked in the basement and then sent the food up by the dumb waiter, from where presumably other servants brought the dishes to the tables. When more matches had been struck, and our eyes had become accustomed to the gloom, five feet of documents were revealed in the well of this domestic lift.

It took us another hour and a half to move all the records on to the tables in the centre of the room. I then put in as much as my car would take, and Philip arranged for the remainder to be collected by a London carrier which the University normally used.

The last collection I want to mention in any detail is perhaps the one I cherish most. It was quite unexpected and I have forgotten, if I ever knew, why it was given to me for our university labour archive. Victor Weisz (1913-66) better known as Vicky, was the outstanding political cartoonist of the middle decades of the century. His name goes alongside that of David Low. Vicky was charming, much loved by his many friends, and a serious manic depressive. I am not sure of the exact nature of his psychological condition except that it was serious, and recurring. Vicky committed suicide in February 1966. His fourth marriage to Inge Lew, some ten years younger than himself, was a joyous occasion and, so his friends thought and hoped, his salvation. They loved each other. Every morning before Vicky went to work he left Inge a note, almost always embellished with a pen and ink sketch. There are nearly three hundred of these notes and sketches: witty, loving, unpolitical from the most politically committed cartoonist of his day. They are utterly charming, and one year we used a suitable drawing for a Friends of the Library Christmas card. They were given to us by Eric Silver who first wrote an article about them in the *Observer* magazine (13 February 1993) and included a note about their future deposit in the University of Hull archive. Eric Silver had obtained them from Vicky's mother, who was living in Israel, and I rather got the impression that he had the kind of problem about their deposit that I had with the letters of Harold Laski. There was a further contribution. Vicky's second wife, Madame Lucielle Mondange, learned of the deposit and sent us a large number of illustrated letters Vicky had written to her in the middle years of the 1940s.

My pleasant relations with Philip Larkin continued until his death. I must, however, underline the point that in all matters in which I was somehow or other involved, he remained the dedicated librarian. Sometime in the 1970s we began to have arguments about the original copies of newspapers as against microfilm. There were beginning to be problems of space – the spectre that so often haunts librarians these days – and he talked to me about our copies of *The Times*. We had been given by the Prudential Insurance Company a complete set of *The Times* from 1848 on – this would be sometime in the late 1960s – and naturally the Library continued to buy and to bind each year's copies. By the mid seventies each year was taking four large and heavy volumes. We already had, of course, a considerable collection of newspapers and journals on microfilm, but the argument I was putting to Philip was that scholars who had to consult *The Times* – such a large paper – would always find the microfilm much more difficult to browse through than the original. And that we ought to have at least this one national paper in its ordinary format as our starting point. In due course the argument was settled. I went to a Library Committee meeting one day and there, at the end of the table, were four large volumes of *The Times* on top of which was a small reel of microfilm. When the item was reached on the agenda Philip explained that the microfilm contained the whole year's papers, as did the four large volumes; and would the Committee accept that over the future we should have serious space problems, and so on. The Committee naturally saw the point without argument. After the meeting Philip looked at me with the ironical smile that he was so often photographed with, and said: 'Sorry about that'. 'Bastard', I replied – and smiled back.

We never socialised after work. We got into the habit of lunching once or twice a term and occasionally we discussed matters arising in the coming Library Committee, and agreed how they might be approached. In the early years, before Monica came to live in Hull, I sometimes lunched with them both on what was then High Table. Constance and I met him at evening parties. but only infrequently, and sometime in the middle sixties he gave Constance a copy of his record *The Whitsun Weddings*, on which he reads his poems with a commentary. It was inscribed: 'For Constance – this droning: affectionately Philip Larkin'. Later I too had a record from him. I had been to the Hull Jazz Club, in a local pub, at which Philip talked about Pee Wee Russell, one of the musical joys of his life, and afterwards he sent me *Condon a la Carte* on which Pee Wee Russell played his clarinet in all of the twelve pieces. Philip inscribed the record: 'Musical education for J. S.'

We continued in this distant but friendly fashion to the final days of his life. His last years were not easy and three years or so before his death I had a note from him which at the time, and still today, I thought of as a continued insistence on the basic core of his politics.

Dear John, he wrote:

> Thank you for your note. Being in the hands of the media is like being in the hands of King Kong: even a stroking hurts. Am not looking forward to X this evening. I suspect he will remember my description of left-wing politics as idleness, greed and treason / Yours ever, Philip.

Now X was a leading politician of the Labour Party whom Philip could not have known very well. It was likely, I thought at the time, that one of the few left-wing intellectuals that he knew at reasonably close quarters was, of course, myself. So perhaps his comments were just to make sure that I dismissed any impression that he was going soft. I knew more about his personal life – or some parts of it – than most of his contemporaries, and I have read most of what has been written about him. I mourn him still.

Politics in these years leading up to the sixties remained on very lively levels. I did what I could to remain on friendly terms with my former comrades in the Communist Party, and with most it was not difficult. A.L. Morton was among those with whom I maintained close relations and his wife, Vivien, later became an efficient part-time research worker for the Labour Dictionary. There were exceptions and some attitudes continued to reflect the curse of dogmatism that has always afflicted too many of the Left during the past century. It is not that the Left is alone in its dogmatism, but it takes its own particular forms. At the 26th National Congress of the Communist Party in the early spring of 1959, around three years from the beginnings of the trauma of 1956, there was a splendid example of intellectual pomposity from someone who should have known better.
    The words were reported thus :

It would be very foolish for us to believe that most of the Leftish intellectuals, or for that matter most of the ex-Part revisionists, are wicked or insincere people. Their principal trouble is a persistent desire to have the best of both worlds, to have their cake and eat it – to retain the privileges of their position in bourgeois society while at the same time attacking bourgeois society and associating themselves with the Socialist movement. Our job is to convince them – through experience and argument – that Socialism is indeed the answer to their problems, their frustration and their hopes ….
(*Daily Worker* 30 March 1959)

The speaker of these stirring words, Arnold Kettle, was a member of the national Executive Committee of the Party and a lecturer in English at the University of Leeds. After the establishment of the Open University he became a Professor there in his subject. One is happy to record that he was able to receive some of the privileges that bourgeois society could offer. He was, without doubt, an intelligent scholar whose writings on English literature I have enjoyed.

The sixties remain a somewhat special, if chaotic period in the history of the twentieth century. It was a decade which had a particular resonance in the United States and western Europe. The long-term effects have not, however, proved quite so powerful as many contemporaries would have expected. Those who lived through these years tended to assume that there would be important changes within the structures of society and the place of the individual in society. The cultural impact of the new generation of playwrights and novelists in the later fifties, notably with John Osborne's *Look Back in Anger*, which opened at the Royal Court in May 1956, moved alongside the radical politics of CND and the New Left. There were other writings, including Shelagh Delaney's *A Taste of Honey* (1959), which encouraged and sustained the attitudes of a critical dissent which was expressed in many different ways By the last two decades of the century, however, conservatism in often different forms was already becoming dominant in many spheres of politics and culture, and this cannot all be attributed to the workings of the odious Thatcher or the collapse and disintegration of the Soviet Union. As I write the twenty-fifth anniversary of the publication of *The Red Paper of Scotland* (1975) is being announced for celebration at the University of Aberdeen on 1st December 2000. The editor of *The Red Paper* was a committed socialist who looked to the future to determine 'a massive and irreversible shift of power' to the working people. Gordon Brown, in this same issue, was joined by Robin Cook who insisted that we required 'a major re-ordering of the priorities of our society'. The radicalism of students in Britain died away in the closing years of the eighties, and Blair's New Labour Party took office after having renounced any major re-ordering by the ritual elimination of Clause 4 of the Labour Party's constitution. The record of the New Labour government, with a very large majority in the Commons, has confirmed the 'irreversible' shift towards a working relationship with corporate business. Socialist ideas and values are no longer matters for serious discussion. The exception has been feminism – hardly a new movement in Britain, where the name of Mary Wollstonecraft is still remembered, nor in the United States.

It was, however, in the United States during the 1960s that the feminist movement developed a militancy that encouraged the womens' movements in the countries of western Europe, although its national impact was uneven. De Beauvoir's *The Second Sex* had been published in the early fifties but some at least of the American activists relied upon less sophisticated analyses of their condition. 'Only women bleed,' I remember being reported from a speaker at a large demonstration in the middle sixties. There is no doubt that in Britain, as elsewhere, the position of women in society has steadily if unevenly improved and there is equally no doubt that much still remains unreconstructed, unfair and unjust.

My political life in the 1960s was on a somewhat less hectic level than the years of the *Reasoner* and the early *New Left Review*. My undergraduate teaching was about eight hours a week, no postgraduate students and a minimum of administration. I took over as chairman of a local discussion group, which met monthly at a local pub not far from the University. For most of its time we had a very efficient secretary in Chris Otley and for the five years or so that it continued from the late fifties, it was quite lively and more successful than most of the Left Clubs, and it lasted longer. The Left Clubs were a great disappointment. There was never in my mind, nor I think in Edward Thompson's, that we were in a position to begin to develop any sort of political organisation or party. I spoke at a number of Left Clubs all over Britain, and my general impressions remained somewhat sceptical of their future.

It can, I think, be explained. I noted earlier that many who left the Communist Party in 1956 just moved over and joined their local Labour Party. The successful unilateralist resolution at the Labour Party conference in 1960 was a great encouragement even though it was reversed the next year, and the succession of Wilson after Gaitskell's death confirmed the decision for many to devote their political time wholly to the Labour Party and end the long years of Conservative government. I have a personal story in this context.

The Labour Party had won the 1964 General Election with an overall majority of four in the House of Commons. This after three election defeats and thirteen years of Tory administration. The centre piece of Wilson's election campaign in 1964 was concentrated upon the importance for Britain of investment and support for science and technology. The Robbin's report on higher education of October 1963 had especially emphasised the need to encourage scientific and technical studies in higher education and there was a serious national debate on these matters. The Labour Party's campaign won their four seat majority, to be reduced to three with the loss of a by-election in Leyton. And then, in January 1966, there arrived a by-election in Hull North, the constituency in which we lived. The Labour Party candidate was Kevin McNamara, a contemporary of Roy Hattersley at the University in the later 1950s. He had read law and if I knew him it must have been only a slight acquaintance. Normally, of course, Constance and I always voted Labour, whatever the political position but now there was a quite new situation. Some members of the Left, mostly driven by opposition to nuclear weapons and the war in Vietnam, decided to put up an independent socialist and Richard Gott accepted their offer. So now the Saville mère and père were to have an interesting difference of opinion, though always, I am happy to report, on a pleasant and reasonable basis. I knew and liked Richard Gott. He was lively, a specialist on Latin America, never sectarian, and a wholly principled socialist. But while the Wilson government from 1964 had a mixed record, I thought their electoral position was by no means secure and there were issues which no Tory administration would ever agree to. The abolition of capital punishment had already been agreed in the House of Commons in 1965, and there was the promise of a more positive and liberal approach to race relations. While, like all on the Left, I could itemise matters in the Governments' record which were undesirable, I remained much concerned about the return of the Tories. I backed McNamara, and explained my position to Richard Gott.

Constance and our second son Richard, not yet at University, were vigorously with Gott, and our house in effect became his committee rooms. The by-election inevitably attracted national attention and we had a large number of journalists, including some high-level American scribes. Constance fed and watered them, and greatly enjoyed herself, as I did myself, surrounded by such lively conversation. We also naturally entertained many of the Left from all parts who came to give general support to Gott, and they were joined in the last few days by Edward Thompson who delivered a couple of his passionate and scintillating speeches to welcoming and attentive audiences, with many of our students among them, mostly without a vote.

McNamara won by a large margin. The size of McNamara's victory against the general trend of opinion polls strongly suggested that a General Election was now a practical possibility, and when Labour went to the polls in March 1966 its overall majority in the Commons increased to ninety-eight.

During the sixties my home town continued to present various political issues in which I became involved. One was a thoroughly depressing housing question which revealed the conditions in which too many of our people lived.

Lister Street had been one of the areas of Hull in which the middle-class professional groups had lived before 1914. The houses were large but with the movement into the suburbs and the country areas of the higher income groups in the years between the wars, Lister Street became an area of single rooms and flats. Rack-renting landlords now moved in, and by the 1960s it was mostly only the poorest families who were to be found, and their living conditions were appalling.

In the late summer of 1963 a tenant's committee was formed with David Kiddie, who lived in Lister Street with his wife (no children), as chairman. Kiddie, whom I didn't know, got in touch with me and asked for general advice and in particular for information about legal assistance. I am not quite sure why he approached me – probably through Stan Suddaby with whom I was to work closely during this Lister Street affair. Following Kiddie's request I went down to Lister Street and during the next couple of months I interviewed many of the families. I had never before seen such awfulness although I had not seldom offered similar accounts from contemporary 19th century sources in the lecture theatre. Lister Street had been an area of considerable disturbance and fights in the years immediately after the end of the Second World War; but there was the beginning of slum clearance in the fifties and by 1963 social life was much quieter. David Kiddie had formed the Tenants' Association and this had begun to take collective action. They began demonstrations to the Guildhall, to draw attention to their thoroughly wretched living conditions, and on their second demonstration they carried a full coffin on which was inscribed 'Bury the 1957 Rent Act'.

Under the 1957 Act it was possible for landlords to give notice to any tenant with only a minimum of legal hassle and following his initiative in forming the Tenants' Association Kiddie was served with a notice of eviction. Most of the landlords were absentee and employed agents to collect rents. Many were unpleasant, some exceedingly so, and this no doubt was responsible for the solidarity that the tenants of Lister Street showed with their chairman. I directed Kiddie to a very sympathetic firm of solicitors whose guiding spirit was a Quaker and Labour supporter. Leonard Bird was a well-known name in the town, and always helpful to those in need. There were various procedures to go through but the eviction order still remained and in October the time was approaching for the bailiffs to move in. By this date I had got together an assembly of support, with Robert Moore and Stan Suddaby among the most active. Robert was a sociologist who was later to occupy a chair of sociology at the University of Liverpool – an extremely nice man who became committed to the affairs of Lister Street. Stan Suddaby was a working-class socialist, very class conscious, rough and tough, and helpful.

Matters came to a head towards the end of October 1963 and after long discussions, and presumably contact with our solicitors (although I remember few details), we decided that Kiddie should stage a sit-in. He was already under judicial instruction to remove himself and his wife from their flat. On the 28 October his wife went to stay with a sister and Dave barricaded himself, with a brother-in-law, against the threatened eviction from bailiffs. Outside the house were dozens of university students alongside Lister Street neighbours from the Tenants' Association.

The students were undoubtedly important in encouraging the publicity we achieved. They were part of the radical movements which had overcome the political apathy of the first half of the fifties and which were to continue throughout the sixties. A week or so before the sit-in the Students' Union had agreed to allow me to address a meeting about Lister Street and I had an audience of over a hundred. When we were discussing the sit-in we had to recognise that the landlord's agents might attempt a forcible eviction, and we therefore organised a twenty-four hour rota of pickets outside the house. Most were students, and Robert and I took it in turn to cover the night watch.

The sit-in achieved a considerable publicity. We won after forty-eight hours. The solicitors for the landlords agreed that no further action would be taken until various legal appeals had been heard, so Kiddie was able to come out. And there, from my side, the story more or less ended. The Housing Committee of the Council had been stirred into action and the more urgent demolition of some parts of Lister Street was accepted and there were some improvements in general facilities.

I spent some time on another picket line. The National Union of Seaman had been subject to increasing discontent within its rank and file for many years, and we have testimony on this from Harold Wilson himself in his memoirs of the 1960s. The national strike began on the 16 May 1966. There had been an agreement in the previous year which gave the seamen just under £60 a month for a fifty-six hour week, and now the seamen were claiming a forty hour week (the hours agreement had always been abused by the employers) and a pay rise of twelve shillings on the basic wage. The strike lasted six weeks, with Wilson becoming more hostile as the weeks passed. He began using MI5 security material and in the Commons made his long-remembered speech about the 'tightly knit group of politically motivated men'. There were communists in leading positions in some of the strikes committees but left-wing Labour MPs (notably Eric Heffer and Michael Foot) were able to demonstrate to the Commons that Wilson's anti-Communist hysteria was founded upon a wholly misleading appreciation of the seamen's problems. The strike ended after six weeks.

My own local connection was in minor key. I already knew some of the active militants among the dockers, and through them I was introduced to the local seamen's strike committee. They had minor concerns about the possibilities of some strike-breaking activities, but they felt it necessary to organise picket lines at certain points along the seven miles of docks; so for three or four nights I went out for several hours along one or other of the pickets I was directed to. As far as I remember there were was no strike breaking activity, and certainly not on the lines that I was sent to. It was summer, and I learned a good deal about the working lives of ordinary seamen.

During the strike I was not in close contact with John Prescott. John had entered my department in the University in the previous autumn, and we were already in a friendly relationship but he was mostly involved elsewhere. In June 1966 he had largely written the pamphlet that became very well-known, a reply to the shipowner's case with the title *Not Wanted on Voyage. The Seamen's Reply*, and for most of the strike period he was operating at the national level or elsewhere in the country. The strike ended after six weeks but its conduct by Wilson was to have a not unimportant influence upon his reputation in the future.

The most useful political action in my own locality during this decade of the sixties was probably the organisation of a series of speakers' classes during the summer weeks for some six consecutive years. Organisation on the docks had never recovered fully from the devastating defeat of 1893. The local organisation of the T & G in the fifties, when I first got to know it, was a mixture of corruption and incompetence, the reasons why the stevedore's union was able to make inroads into membership. From the later fifties, however, there was developing a group of quite outstanding militants who from about the middle sixties were to promote a highly successful rank-and-file movement; and it was from a number of these that I recruited my speakers' class. The two most important members of the militant group were Walter Greendale and Wally Cunningham. The latter did not come to my class and I would guess at that time he saw no point in coming to listen to a middle-class intellectual. Walter Greendale was a member, however, and he it was who in later years was among the top ranks of the Transport Workers, becoming chairman of the national executive for four years in the early 1980s. I got to know them both well, and thought myself fortunate to become close to such remarkable personalities. Cunningham remained at the rank-and-file level, and in the most militant years on the Hull docks – the late sixties and early seventies – he seems to have been the central figure. For some wonderful years they had the shipowners over a barrel. At an Oral History conference in Hull I organised in the late seventies I persuaded Cunningham to let me interview him at some considerable length.

During situations when there was no progress with negotiations, Cunningham and his comrades would organise a 'no working' day. The decision as to which day would be chosen was left to Cunningham. On the day that he chose he would ring up at about three in the morning some three of four of his committee and tell them that the day of action was today. They would then ring their contacts on individual docks and by seven in the morning there would be pickets on every dock along the seven mile stretch, and when the workers turned up for their daily stint they would be told that it was a 'no work' day; and so they went home. By this time the workforce was wholly united. The directing committee would sometimes organise mass meetings in the City Hall with 1,500 dockers filling the seats. The political situation began to change in favour of the shipowners from about the middle of the seventies. Technical changes were largely responsible for restoring more discipline over the workers, with containerisation being very effective, not least in the reduction of numbers in the workforce.

And so to my speakers' class. I had of course taught many adult classes in the evenings for the Adult Education department, but never before a speakers' class. What I knew I had to avoid was a boring lecture on what to do and what to avoid; and in the end I decided that 'in the beginning was the deed'. When the first class assembled – about a dozen militant workers – I named two for the first proposer and seconder, and two more for critical comments. I gave then a subject and the whole class five minutes to make their notes, and then we began with the proposer and seconder being allowed three to four minutes. The critics followed, after whom I said my own piece, and we continued.

There were some who found this way of working somewhat trying, and apparently one or two had to be persuaded by their colleagues to come the next week, but on my second evening, everyone turned up. I had of course now given them a subject for debate, with speakers named, and on these occasions each of the main speakers had six minutes, and no more. On the last evening I took them into the big hall of the Transport Workers building, and each member had been given a subject he had to speak on from the platform to rows of empty seats. On the whole they said the six weeks had been useful, and almost all came the following year. For myself there have been few classes I have enjoyed more. The final year of the men's classes was followed by several evenings for women trade unionists, and I have long felt that I ought to have continued with more sessions.

Naturally, I followed Walt Greendale's career with great interest. He moved to senior positions within the Union and remained the man I had always known.

In personal terms I liked and respected him, and I have always thought of him and Cunningham as representatives of the kind of traditions of the labour movement in Britain that needed to be present in our highly-organised, class-ridden society.

My academic life became more varied and somewhat more intensive as the sixties moved along. It was in social /labour history that my interests were most concentrated, but throughout my teaching years I always also lectured in economic history, in the firm belief that it was essential to keep fully in line with the growing secondary literature. This middle quarter of the century was especially noteworthy for the expansion of the writing on economic history, with a notable increase in range and a much heightened sophistication.

I made one important teaching change in the compulsory course that all students reading for the B. Sc. (Econ.) had to take. In the early 1960s I decided that the modern economic history of Japan would offer an interesting comparison with British industrialisation, and this was in the compulsory paper that all students reading economics would have to take.

The most important teaching development of the sixties for me was the acceptance of post-graduate students. The former University Colleges had not normally been involved in post-graduate supervision – some science departments were the exception – and the practice in some departments was to send their brightest students away to an older and better known university. This was accepted by the department of History during John Kenyon's occupancy of the G.F. Grant Chair of History for most of the sixties.

My approach towards post-graduate research was much encouraged after the formation of the Social Science Research Council and its financial support, from about the middle sixties, of doctoral students. In my own subject – we did not become independent until the early seventies – our student numbers had grown considerably and academic staff had kept pace. I myself took on most but not all research students and by the mid-seventies, over the three or more years, there were about twenty theses in various stages of research and writing. Academic appointments were meeting the general growth in numbers during the sixties. I had a different, and closer relationship with most of my research students than with the undergraduates in my department. I don't think I neglected my history specialists and there were some, especially from the early days with whom I became very friendly, but inevitably, in a very crowded world I missed getting to know better some very interesting personalities. Nico Ladenis, for example, who has become one of our outstanding chefs, with a restaurant next door to the Dorchester in London, and to whom we gave an honorary degree in the later

1990s. And there was Roy Hattersley, a contemporary of Nico but not a history specialist within the B.Sc. (Econ.) degree, whose political career has been at a ministerial level and whose weekly column in *The Guardian* I always read. In the later fifties, when Hattersley was a student in the department, I would guess it was my political sectarianism that kept me from getting closer to him.

I had a few part-time research students, part-time that is, from the beginning. Among those I cherish are Marion Kozak – who married Ralph Miliband – and Tania Rose, the daughter of Morgan Phillips Price. Marion produced an excellent doctoral thesis on the condition and working lives of munitions workers during the First World War, with special emphasis upon engineering, and I have long blamed myself for not encouraging her to publish.

I was similarly fortunate with Tania Rose, who I got to know only when she began work. I had made contact early in the seventies about her father's papers – without success– but a few years later she wrote and asked if it was possible to register for a part-time postgraduate degree. I was off-putting because of the physical distance between us and suggested a number of scholars in London who would be helpful. To no avail, so I accepted her for a part-time doctorate, and it was a most helpful relationship. Her house in South End Green, Hampstead was three minutes walk from the local station through which ran the odd piece of rail which wandered through North London with its penultimate stop at Kew. The other side of the line from Kew Gardens was the Public Records Office, whose services I was to use intensively for the next twenty years.

Morgan Philips Price was one of the few foreign observers to hear Lenin declare the revolution in October 1917 and his papers are among the essential guides to Russian politics before and after the Bolshevik conquest of power. He was a radically minded liberal who went to Russia in 1914 to become increasingly sympathetic towards the revolutionary Left as the war years moved on. His dispatches became steadily more important to the *Manchester Guardian* and just as steadily more reprehensible to the office of censorship in London. By the second half of 1918 all Philips Price's despatches were put on the Censor's spike and he decided towards the end of the year to move to Germany, whose internal political situation was now increasingly disturbed. He stayed there for several years, married a young German and only returned to England when his passport, which had been proscribed because of his denunciation of the Allied military intervention, was finally returned. All this Tania Rose described in her doctoral thesis and a decade or so later she published *Despatches from the Revolution, Russia 1916-18*, most of which consisted of her father's unpublished articles, letters and documents: 'an extraordinarily valuable compilation', as Eric Hobsbawm summed up in his Foreword.

Working with research students is nearly always a highly useful educative process. There will at times be difficulties but the central problem of tutor and research graduate is the willingness of the former to engage seriously with the subject of research and the intellectual personality of the research student in question. I must not be pompous about this but in the 1970s, when I was a member of the Social Science Research Council, we visited university departments whose research students we funded, and our findings were not always satisfactory. Some colleges of both Oxford and Cambridge were among the worst examples of inadequate supervision and it must be assumed that it was the intellectual calibre of their postgraduates that carried them through. The relations between academic staff and research students were often closest and most friendly in the smaller departments of British universities, but this is not a statement that can be transferred without further enquiry into the intellectual level of their research theses.

In the sixties I began to act as external examiner in other universities for both undergraduate degrees and doctoral theses and from then on, for the next quarter of the century, I was occupied every year with outside work of this kind.

The undergraduate examinations were always useful exercises and so, of course, in a different way, were the post-doctoral dissertations and theses. Of these latter I sent back for re-writing quite a high proportion but in my whole career I only failed outright one candidate for a higher degree and this created a considerable furore. It was submitted again after considerable re-structuring, according to my suggestions, and I returned it once more for further re-writing before I accepted it. Oddly, I do not recall being asked on any future occasion by this particular university.

My most enjoyable external examining was with the University of Edinburgh. Scottish undergraduates took an examination after three years and then they had a fourth year with a further examination. In the nineteen seventies I went to Edinburgh seven times for their undergraduate degrees – three for the third year and four for the fourth (or it might have been the other way round). My journey by car always stopped at Newcastle, a city with excellent secondhand bookshops, and then I would go across country via Jedbergh and so to the handsome city of Edinburgh, also with very good bookshops. One of the many attractions of the University was its staff house, the most welcoming and generally attractive of any that I knew in Britain.

I always stayed with Victor Kiernan, the most erudite scholar I have ever met. Victor was a graduate of Trinity College, Cambridge – to which he went from the Manchester Grammar School – and on graduation in the middle 1930s he was awarded a Research Fellowship for five years. A condition of the Fellowship was a compulsory year abroad in the third year, the choice of country being wholly a personal decision. Victor chose India and for most of his years he lived in northern Muslim regions. He was in India when the Second World War began, and was thus contained there until after 1945. When he returned to England and Trinity College, where there was still a couple of years of his Fellowship outstanding, he then moved to Edinburgh University where he remained until his retirement from academic life.

I had first met him during the years of the Communist Historians Group but it was only during my examining visits that I really began to know him at all well. He was a charming host, and full of interesting conversation. We talked every morning for a couple of hours over breakfast, and I discovered later that Victor was in the habit of making notes after any conversation or formal discussion which he thought useful. We have remained in pleasant contact, my deep respect for him being wholly unchanged through the many years of our lives.

The closing years of the 1960s were remarkable for the radicalism within the student community in Britain, and the problem for the historian is not so much an analysis of why these unusual exhibitions occurred – even for a conservative country such as Britain – but why the fire burned out so quickly. Within ten years the era of Thatcherism had begun and it was not only the academic community in whom the fire had burned out. The decline of the many kinds of socialist thought and activity was striking characteristic of British life in the last twenty years of the twentieth century, confirmed by the electoral victory in 1997 of the Party leadership calling itself New Labour.

To return to the late 1960s, the changes in opinion from the lukewarm politics of the first half of the fifties was an uneven movement, affecting different groups in the community at different times. The anti-nuclear opposition got under way with the much publicised marches from Aldermaston to London and the successful resolution at the Labour Party conference of 1960. The Cuban missile crisis of 1962 was followed by the civil rights movement in the United States which had a notable impact upon liberal-minded opinion in western Europe. The 1964 occupation of Sproul Hall, University of Berkeley, in protest against the suppression of a civil rights demonstration on the campus, was the beginning of the radical students movement in the United States, and it merged into the growing opposition to the Vietnam war which was to dominate American campuses until the early seventies.

In western Europe radical ideas began to gather support among the student communities. In Britain it was not until 1966 that the consequences of a new kind of socialist agitation were to be demonstrated. A newly formed Socialist Society at LSE began to publish, somewhat intermittently, a journal, the *Agitator,* and in October 1966 it issued a biting criticism of Walter Adams, the new Director. Adams had been the Director of University College, Salisbury and the agitation against racialist policies in Rhodesia was the backcloth to the questioning of Adams's acceptance of the LSE senior administrative position. The agitation led to a sit-in, and at this time the student movement in western Europe was being rapidly politicised, with the May 1968 events in France as the catalyst. The political action and atmosphere in Paris, and elsewhere in France, was truly remarkable and remained for many years an influence upon those who were student activists at the time – even for those who had not continued in active politics.

It was at this point that the University of Hull moved into the national picture. The student community had naturally been influenced, in varying degrees, by the growing radical ideas in the country's universities, and towards the end of May 1968 a third-year student of politics and sociology with the name of Tom Fawthrop arrived back from Paris. He held an emergency meeting of a few socialists at which he gave his account of his experiences at the Sorbonne and it was agreed to call a more widely publicised meeting for the following Thursday. Two days earlier, however, Fawthrop tore up his examination papers before his fellow examinees and the lecturers, and on the Thursday there was the largest meeting the Socialist Society had ever organised. An eight demands programme was agreed, of which the most important was the unprecedented claim for equal executive power for the student body. All the academic groups and the administrative staff of the university should operate under the one man one vote system – it was still the days when 'man' read also 'woman' – and there were strong arguments for the total or partial elimination of examinations. On the 8th June, after days of wholly inconclusive negotiations, some 400 students occupied the administration building.

I was myself not a member of Senate at this time but naturally, with others on the Left, I followed the student agitation with the closest concern. There were a number of items within the agreed programme that I did not accept or agreed only in a modified version. I thought the idea of student parity within the University administration quite unworkable but I was firmly in support of a much more democratic structure within which student voices could be seriously heard. This would mean, as a first step, the presence of elected student members on departmental committees, and since some departments had no committees for even their own academic staff, this would require important changes within the whole university. And I was strongly against the naïve rejection of all examinations, although I accepted the introduction of assessed essays as part of the examination structure. What led me, however, to public support of the demands of the students was the unwillingness of Senate to examine the requests of their students at all seriously, and the outright refusal of influential members of Senate to listen to what their students were trying to explain. Among the fundamentalists were the historian John Kenyon, and Hanson, professor of theology. Hanson was among the most reactionary of the senior academic members of the University and could always be relied upon to damn any liberal proposal. He was, apparently, well-known for his scholarship on one of the Books of the New Testament.

The Vice-Chancellor went along with his senior colleagues, although my guess is that with more support he would have shown a more liberal attitude. The whole episode was, for me, a remarkable lesson in the fragility of anything approaching a liberal tolerance among the majority of the academic community. I was very surprised at the near-panic some of my colleagues exhibited, although I grant that the phraseology used by the more politically sectarian of the students was decidedly unhelpful to the achievement of any sensible outcome to what was becoming a bitter confrontation. With the decline in the influence of the Communist Party among intellectuals and the universities in general (but not for another decade among industrial workers) various groups of Trotskyists were able to make their often strident voices more clearly heard. There were, of course, sharp differences between them.

Among the academic non-Trotskyist Left there were inevitably serious discussions about the public expression of our support for an open debate on the student demands, and for our immediate backing to the occupation. I was still a Reader, although I had been told that a Personal Chair was being considered, and it was obvious to me that as the most senior academic I could be expected to initiate whatever demonstration was considered necessary. We were quite near to the end of the summer term and I had only one class of second year students. At my next lecture I announced to my class – I suppose there were present about fifteen – that my next lecture would be in the occupied building but that if anyone objected I would repeat the lecture in the usual lecture room. There was only one student who indicated that he was not willing to enter the occupied Administration building so I arranged for him to come to my study at 9 am on the day after my occupied building lecture, where I would repeat my text. I thought that this was the proper democratic way to go about matters, and I hoped it might be a further safeguard against any top Administration mayhem against me. It was my final lecture of the summer term.

When I first entered the occupied Administration I spoke for a short time and explained my position of general support with the qualifications mentioned above. There were only a few days left before the end of term and I found myself in increasing disagreement with the organisers of the sit-in. The radical movement among the students was now controlled by members of International Socialism, the organisation which received a considerable accession of influence in the closing years of the sixties. At Hull Michael Kidron was a national figure within IS, and being members of the same department, I knew him quite well.

Kidron I liked, but over the student sit-in I thought he was impossible. It was becoming clear that there was a growing opposition to the sit-in among the large number of students not inside the Administration building, and it had become even more clear how many of the academic and administrative staff were hostile.

In the last week of term I went into the occupied Administration building and spoke to the whole building. I explained my general support for the students, and then argued the case for an organised walk-out before the end of term. I emphasised that by continuing to stay inside the building they were neglecting to influence their fellow students, many of whom were now turning against them. There were only three more days to go before the beginning of the long vacation and that when they returned a large number of their present supporters would have graduated and would no longer be on the campus. In short, they needed to argue a strategy with the whole student body for the coming year, and that this would not be easy.

I was listened to politely but unconvincingly. The IS group were strongly opposed and it was they who were to lead the student radicals in the coming term. Not with much success, for the new generation which entered in the autumn for their first year were not notably aware of the political issues involved, and the IS themselves were not as understanding as the situation required. The radical tradition on the campus at Hull was by no means wholly eliminated among the students, for there was a sit-in for a few days during 1972 over the ownership of shares in the firm of Reckits. This was the time when the anti-apartheid movement was an important political issue – Peter Hain was probably the best known personality – but by the end of the seventies student life went back to its normal, mostly apolitical, existence.

There was one result of the 1968 student sit-in relating to myself that might be noted. As I mentioned above, I had been told that I was being considered for a Personal Chair in Economic History. At this time I was still within the department of Economics, which had two professors, and about a quarter of the second and third year students were specialising in economic history. However, following the events of the summer and my support for the students, matters began to look somewhat different. There was an internal memorandum, which I was not expected to see, which suggested that in place of a chair in economic history we should now consider a chair in econometrics, and this was what happened. My Personal Chair was delayed until 1972. And following my own promotion economic history became an independent department, with nine members of staff and a growing number of postgraduate students.

I must add a further comment about my own attitudes at the time, and I trust that I am not falsifying the record. The decision to cancel my professorial chair did not concern me unduly. The opposition to me personally was quite intense in some areas of the university and certainly this was the case with some members of my own department. One of the theories making the rounds was that I had been introducing, during the sixties, numbers of adult students from Ruskin College and that it was these wild trade union types who were among the leading figures in the student upsurge. It was quite true that from the late fifties, when I became responsible for student entry, I had arranged with Raphael Samuel, who was teaching at Ruskin, that I would be happy to take up to half a dozen Ruskin students who had completed their two-year course. I never reached six but we had two or three each year throughout the sixties until 1968. What was quite wrong was that the Ruskin students were the leaders of the occupation. They supported it, of course, but my general memory of them is that they were never very active in student politics.

My personal relations during the sixties and beyond with Ralph Miliband had become close. I was sort of best man at his marriage to Marion in the early years of the decade and our families have remained on the pleasantest of terms.

With the changes in the editorship of *New Left Review* in the early years of the decade the original *Reasoner* group, together with Ralph, found themselves out of sympathy with the political approach of Perry Anderson and his colleagues. Ralph and I agreed to publish an annual volume of essays which would take forward the ideas and approaches of the *New Reasoner*. Edward Thompson, who was wholly in sympathy, decided not to join the editorial group and this, I thought at the time, was because he wanted a change from editorial chores, and return to his own writing. His great classic had just been published.

The Socialist Register, published by Martin Eve of the Merlin Press, has continued annually to this day. We began to hand over to new editors after a quarter of a century or so, and it is now edited from York University, Toronto with editorial advisory committees in both Canada and England. Leo Panitch and Colin Leys have shown themselves to be very lively, very sympathetic and excellent scholars, and Ralph and I considered ourselves very well served. As indeed the journal had always been by Martin Eve, before his death in late 1998.

I wrote obituaries for both in *The Guardian:* a melancholy business, which keeps repeating itself in my old age.

I published a sharp critique of the journal *Encounter* in the founding number of the *Socialist Register:* criticism that was much needed. *Encounter* was intelligently edited and well received. To those of us on the Left it was obvious that its intellectual purpose was a sophisticated explanation and justification of the Anglo-American Cold War. Most of the 'difficult' matters of international thuggery were not commented on, and these included colonial butchery by the British in Kenya, among many others.

In later years it was revealed that *Encounter* and other journals were funded by the CIA and it made unpleasant sense. There has been much written about the Congress for Cultural Freedom, the organising body of these journals, and it was always accepted that *Encounter* was the most lively of all their periodical publications. I have read the writings of most of their political contributors; many I dislike, some I detest. Their literary contributors, by contrast, were often very lively and entertaining and it was these that made the journal so widely read.

The most useful account of the Congress for Cultural Freedom – written by someone who believed in its basic values – is probably *The Liberal Conspiracy* by the Australian Peter Coleman, published in 1989.

I have written a fair number of articles for the *Register* but most of my energies in this context have naturally been on the editorial side. Ralph and I were by no means always in agreement but this was inevitable. I resolutely refused to have a committee to whom we might turn for advice and counsel in the event of a firm disagreement between us. I had had sufficient problems in the closing years of *New Left Review* and the argument I used with Ralph was that if we really found ourselves with too many opposing views, then we should dissolve our partnership. But we never reached that stage, and for my part I remained wholly satisfied with our editorial relationship. Working with Ralph was in one crucial respect similar to working with Edward Thompson. They were very different personalities and their thought processes were not the same, but they were vibrantly alive and it was a pleasure and an intellectual benefit to have to confront their incisive and intense minds.

There were other reasons for my refusal of an editorial committee. I was entering upon what were to be twenty years of great pressures in my life, literary even more than political. Through my own particular areas of research I had become conscious of the need for access to 18th and 19th centuries out-of-print writings. The later 1950s had seen the beginnings of reprints of the classics of economics, and through Ralph I came to know Gus Kelley, who published from New York. Gus and I became friends and I persuaded him – it was hardly difficult – to move into the reprints of social history. I bought a lot of material for him, and for Gus as well as other publishers I wrote a number of Introductions to the reprints of important nineteenth century journals and books. These included quite lengthy essays for reprints of G.J. Harney's *The Red Republican* and *The Friend of the People*, W. E Adams, *Memoirs of a Social Atom*, the 1885 *Industrial Remuneration Conference*, the second edition Gammage's *History of the Chartist Movement* (1894), and Robert Owen's *A New View of Society*. I collected for Kelley separate volumes of the political pamphlets of Charles Bradlaugh and Annie Besant but with only short Introductions and bibliographical notes. There were others, including a longish introduction to the reprint of *The Life of Thomas Cooper Written by Himself*, which Leicester University published in 1971. I was especially interested in Cooper's early life since it brought back vivid memories of Gainsborough to which, after my very early years, I had regularly returned throughout my teens. Mrs Allison had died during the 1940s.

Throughout the sixties I continued on the committee of the Society for the Study of Labour History and for several years I was its chairman. It was during these years that I became quite closely involved with the Amsterdam Institute for Social History and I would take the North Sea ferry at least once a year. My particular contact and friend was Marcel van den Linden, and the seminars and discussions with very mixed groups of mainly European scholars were naturally enlightening and stimulating. It was in the second half of the sixties that I began to be asked to lecture in various universities in Europe – the United States came in the following decade – and for the next twenty years or so I could expect to broaden my knowledge of Europe's main cities and especially of its churches, always my particular interest. I used to tell myself that when I retired from academic life I would write a book on the churches and cathedrals of Burgundy, but my notes and jottings have never, to my considerable regret, been properly brought together and published. My serious interest in church architecture has always remained.

The decade of the 1970s increased what should perhaps be described as my general academic activities, in addition to my personal academic research. I had one major book – on Chartism in 1848 – ready to be put together but this had to wait until my retirement. I wrote a long essay for the third volume of *Essays in Labour History* – Asa Briggs had done most of the work on volume two and I was mainly responsible for this third, and last, volume. I had been invited to lecture at the American University in Egypt but was obliged to refuse because of my piece on 'May Day 1937' which I had to complete during the coming summer vacation to meet the publisher's deadline. I have always thought it one of the most useful essays I have written, much as I regretted missing Egypt.

There was one consequence of the political turmoil in many universities and colleges at the end of the sixties which we decided needed some countervailing action. We were getting reports of different kinds of political victimisation, and a small group, mainly centred upon certain of the academic staff of LSE, called a conference for the discussion of civil liberties within the world of the Academy. The most influential member of our group was John Griffith, one of the Professors of Law at LSE.

John's politics were somewhat different from either Ralph's or mine but what was crucial was his unshakeable commitment to academic freedom and democratic practices. He was also an extremely nice man. His academic reputation was considerable, one of his specialist interests being parliamentary procedures and constitutional matters, and in the newly established Council for Academic Freedom and Democracy (CAFD for short) his advice and good sense were always helpful.

Our first 'case', which received a fair amount of national publicity, was within the University of Manchester. I should explain here that when we formed CAFD it was with a membership arrangement with the National Council for Civil Liberties. The NCCL had been founded in 1934 and was a well-established organisation with liaison groups in many parts of the country. (I mentioned earlier that I had acquired the early papers of the NCCL for the archives of the University of Hull). The secretary of the NCCL when we joined with them was Tony Smythe, and he came with John Griffith and myself when we went to the University of Manchester, in late October 1970, for our first encounter with academic authority.

The 'petitioner', or however he may be described, was Anthony Arblaster, a political philosopher. I am not proposing to set down the details of the case but later we published a pamphlet highly critical of the practices within the academic community. A good deal of cant is always talked about 'the community of scholars', and 'the inviolable principle' of academic freedom and the like, without any reference to the situation in real life. In the Department of Philosophy at Manchester the result was great frustration and much unhappiness, and we recommended a judicial enquiry by the University.

I continued to be involved in the work of CAFD for the next twenty years. In the 1970s John Griffith and I, as the most active of our committee, mostly worked separately.

We sometimes published an account of our enquiries in pamphlet form. At the end of the decade I became chairman and my work changed somewhat. Most of the cases I was asked to deal with now came from post-graduate students. John was always helpful and his legal mind could always be relied on to offer reasonable judgements and practical suggestions. I spent several very pleasant holidays with John and his wife, Barbara in the Dordogne and, although as we have grown older we have had less personal contact, I shall always remember our relationship with respect and affection.

There are some very general comments that come out of my experiences of these years and I must add that these do not necessarily represent any collective agreement. I think that over these two decades, to the end of the 1980s, I was conscious that in any academic institution there would only be a minority of its full-time members who would be prepared to stand firmly, and publicly, against the arbitrary decisions of any of their seniors.

Naturally I was conscious of the problems which surrounded any one individual – matters of tenure, promotion and so on, and, as I have mentioned, we in Britain never suffered the iniquities that plagued American universities in the 1950s. The generalisation must remain, however. The absence of a genuinely liberal environment in too many areas of too many colleges and universities often made it difficult for wrongheaded, or unpleasant decisions to be reversed, and there were too many cases, in my own experience, when full justice was not done. I must not, however, in any way deny the usefulness of CAFD, and there are today a number of academics in place as a result of this outside intervention. As an organisation it began to wither towards the end of the 1980s but it has been succeeded by the establishment of CAFAS (Council for Academic Freedom and Academic Standards) in 1994. Its existence followed an important case at the University College of Swansea, in which Colwyn Williamson was a major figure. In the early stages of CAFAS John Griffith was his accustomed helpful advisor and at the time of writing, some seven years or so after its foundation, he is still involved in academic cases. Colwyn Williamson continues as a leading personality.

In my academic life during the 1970s, in addition to my working life in the

University, one of my extra-curricular activities was of an establishment character. In the mid-sixties the Social Science Research Council had been established
and from it came the Economic and Social History Committee. It was in 1972
that I was asked to join the Committee, a request that somewhat surprised me
given that my politics on the Left were well known.

I accepted, of course, since the SSRC had become important in the writing
and research of economic and social history. The national committee allocated
two research scholarships to those universities which had separate or defined
economic and social history departments and it had much encouraged research
in the general area of the subject. In the year that I became a member – I suppose
there would be nearly a dozen or so – it was decided that our committee would
visit those universities to whom research scholarships were awarded. We made
two or three visits a year. Our purposes were to enquire into the general nature
of the supervision offered and to discuss with the academic members of staff
how improvements in general into research might be helped. In all our visits
we talked first to the senior members of the department, usually of professorial
status, then the lecturing staff who were also involved, and finally to the post-
graduate students themselves. It was often highly illuminating. In very general
terms the most satisfactory arrangements came from the smaller departments
where the few postgraduate students were usually pleasantly integrated within
the department. What we did not consider was the quality of the research theses
produced.

The colleges of Oxford and Cambridge were mixed in their general organisation for research students, and our guess was that, since most of their students
we talked to were bright to very bright, the absence of regular supervision was
not of major significance. Some colleges were notably deficient in their arrangements for regular supervision. Our most extraordinary reception, in the seven
years I served on the Committee, was unexpected. The University we visited
was of middle size, not very old and with an excellent reputation. We first met
its four professors, whose reports were wholly satisfactory; then we went on for
the next hour to meet the remainder of the academic staff who were involved
in research supervision in relevant areas, and we were somewhat surprised that
only about half of the expected number presented themselves, but again with
satisfactory reports on the supervisory system; and finally, for an hour and a half
after lunch, we talked with a quite large group of post-graduate students. And
then we listened to a constant stream of complaints. We went back for a final
discussion with the professorial heads – this was our normal practice – and communicated our very considerable disquiet. On our return to London and after a
serious discussion, our chairman was asked to write a full report to the leading
officials of ESRC recommending the withdrawal of all postgraduate awards in
future years until we could be satisfied that adequate changes had been made.
There was, of course, a major row, and in the end – it was not our Committee's

decision – a cosy academic compromise was accepted.

I became chairman for my last two years on the Committee and was able, in my first year, to include the first woman in the annual appointments. I also began the occasional visits to two or three of the larger Polytechnics. There was at the time no suggestion of extending the grant of research scholarships to Polys but I was aware of the improvements in academic standards of the better known institutions. During my last year, in the early part of 1979, I was asked to stay on as chairman for a third year, but I refused. I had had a very busy decade and I urgently needed to return to my personal research and writing. At the time I was unaware of how sensible my refusal for a third term had been. Later in the year the obnoxious Thatcher was elected as Prime Minister and academic monies began immediately to be reduced or wiped out. My colleague, who had been vice-chairman, and was to take over, said to me towards the end of his first year that 'it had been a can of worms' he was administering, and financial assistance was to continue to decline until the present.

These were exceptionally busy years. In the late 1960s I had helped establish the Oral History Society and I later became its chairman for several years. The leading personality in this field of social history was Paul Thompson and from its earliest years he was a directing force. It was a growth area among historians and the Society has continued to have a lively existence. I was also in the chair of the Labour History Society for a few years, and I continued, as a matter of course, to work both on the *Socialist Register* and *The Dictionary of Labour Biography*. The first volume of the latter came out in 1972 and the tenth in the early months of the new century, to be then taken over by new editors.

From the middle sixties or thereabouts I had been invited to lecture outside the United Kingdom and over the years I have spoken from platforms in universities and colleges in Italy – Rome, Florence, Milan; France – Paris, Tours, Grenoble and Poitiers; Spain – Madrid; and Sweden – Stockholm. My more regular visits in Europe were Rome, Paris and, especially, Amsterdam, the latter with close relations with the Institute of Social History. It was the United States and Canada in which I stayed for longer periods. Beginning with visits to the editorial group around *Victorian Studies* at Bloomington where Martha Vicinus and Gail Malgreen were especially helpful and friendly. Most of my visits to the States ended by crossing the border to Canada where I lectured in the larger universities and became especially close to Leo Panitch at York University, Toronto. As has been mentioned, it was Leo, a close friend of Ralph Miliband, and Colin Leys who succeeded us as editors of the *Socialist Register*.

By the end of the 1970s, after my retirement from the SSRC, my academic time was coming to an end; and I retired from the University in the autumn of 1982. I was happy to do so, as I explain below. The opportunities for writing ought to be more easily available.

When I look at my academic life, which I so much enjoyed, it is necessary to emphasise what I assume has been obvious to those who have read the previous chapters. I changed some parts of my general approach to the politics of the Left, in the intellectual upheaval of 1956, but in certain crucial respects I remained fully conscious of what I owed to the communist movement. The principles of a consistent internationalism was a necessary and indeed essential part of all socialist activity, and there would be no argument on the Left. And I have remained a Marxist in my understanding of the world we live in. But the most difficult problem, which has greatly affected the history of all socialisms in the twentieth century, is the question of organisation, and the extent to which intellectual leadership can move down to the rank and file of the membership, and remain acceptable. I remain unclear on a number of issues relevant to this central question, but at the same time I am fully aware that only a disciplined organisation can expect to offer the serious challenge to the powerful order of capitalist society that is so urgently required.

Part 6: **Years of Retirement**

My life has been lived in a time of large and small wars; an epoch in world history when the destructive technology of war became rapidly more efficient and fearsome; with decades of brutal killings in many parts of the world, not seldom on an horrific scale. A century of blood and butchery: with the names of Vietnam, Israel and the Palestinians, Malaya, East Timor, Chile, Rwanda, and many other killings to be added to the years of the world wars, the monstrous evil of the Holocaust and the totalitarian viciousness and ravages of Stalinist Russia and Eastern Europe. The latest is the horrifying terrorist attack of 11th September 2001on New York.

When the Second World War ended the people of Britain, along with other nations in Europe, North America and Australia, began to live in peace with improving standards of living. For many in these mostly industrialised countries material improvements were tangible although for the poorer social groups always slow in their impact. In our own country there remained marked inequalities of income and health, and by the end of the century at least twenty per cent lived in conditions of social deprivation by comparison with their fellow men and women. While the Second World War had a considerable impact upon collective thinking, with the first majority Labour Government as witness to an enlargement of popular social demands, there has been a steady diminution over the succeeding decades, culminating in the many years of Thatcher and her Tory successors. The radical arguments for change have slowly weakened, the product of political incompetence within successive Labour leaderships together with ineptness and muddled thinking among the radical intellectuals.

We entered the third millennium, with the victory of New Labour at the polls in mid-1997 bearing a programme that rejected any suggestion of a socialist connection. The inroads of market thinking in the ideas of leading Labour politicians has been quite remarkable, and the intellectual and political opposition has been notably limited.

The embrace of business connections has been especially pronounced in Downing Street. Tony Blair has been an intelligent politician within certain unfortunate constraints. His knowledge of history is limited and his understanding of the traditions of the Labour Movement in Britain is minimal. The ministers in his government have not been noted for their administrative competence, and many public services are not likely to show major improvements over two terms of office. There will be some, with the National Health Service the most publicised. There are other problems beyond the specifically domestic issues, however, that are not seldom ignored, and require clarification. The fundamental hostility between the Soviet Union and the capitalist world was temporarily muted in most public respects during the Second World War, but was soon to find full expression in the politics of the Cold War. Against this background of global division there were two related problems for Britain in the post-war world. One was the disintegration of the Empire, and other was the emergence of the United States as the greatest power in the world, and what was involved for Britain in the so-called 'special relationship'.

Among the collective memories of the British people there are areas of darkness. For example, the crucial part which the Russian armies played in the defeat of Nazi Germany. The most serious part of the failure in the collective memory of our people is the result of American domination within world politics, both during and after the collapse of communism in Soviet Russia. Since the Second World War the United States, following direct or indirect intervention, has left a wide trail of devastation round the world. The Americans are stained with the blood of millions of Third World people, who have died to keep the world safe for the property owners of the world. And the United States have been actively supported by allies among the industrial countries – business corporations and individual states – as well as the corrupt and crooked among the indigenous peoples. The list of American interventions, often directly military, includes North Korea, the Dominican Republic, Grenada, Columbia, Panama. All the world knows of Vietnam, and there are other countries where American finance has been available for the elimination of radical movements. As noted above, during the decades of the Cold War the Soviet Union's supposed ambitions could be quoted as justification for the destruction of progressive movements in the colonial world, and after September 11th it has become very plain that 'terrorism' is a catch-phrase that will be used to justify any American counter-radical action in world affairs.

What is necessary, however, is to recognise that the British record of subservience to America in world affairs has been consistent through the post-war decades, and that we now have a Prime Minister in Tony Blair who appears to lack any serious understanding of the past half century, and is vocal in his support of America.

The history of these years is not, however, just a matter of support for the United States. Who, for example, remembers that it was British armed forces, within a month of the end of the war with Japan, which fought successfully to re-establish the French in Saigon and thereby to restore an area of colonialism in the general interests of the imperialist world? Or the 1953 overthrow of the government of Cheddi Jagan in British Guyana and the destabilisation programme a decade later in which the American CIA also played a major part? Everyone remembers the Suez fiasco, but there is also the shameful history of much of the decolonisation in countries such as Malaya and Kenya. In the post-war years, with the combination of relative economic decline and the shrinkage of Empire, Britain's politicians found it increasingly useful to persuade themselves that the so-called 'special relationship' fitted their requirements in the second half of the twentieth century.

The American intervention that particularly disturbed me, mostly I suppose because it was so widely reported and commented on, was their war against the Sandinista government in Nicaragua. The country was the largest in Central America and the United States had become involved in its politics from the early years of the twentieth century. In 1933 Anastasio Somoza won control and the Somoza family remained in power with consistent American support until mid 1979. The regime was brutally corrupt throughout the years of their rule and numerous guerrilla clashes broadened into civil war between 1976 and 1979. The Sandinistas won power and formed a government with other supporting groups, including the Christian Democrats. The early years were full of hope. The World Council of Churches commented in 1983 that while it was a great experiment still precarious and incomplete, it did extend 'hope to the poor sectors of society ... and for the first time offers the Nicaraguan people a modicum of justice for all'. A report from Oxfam two years later confirmed the general conclusions of the earlier Report. This was not a situation that any American government could accept anywhere in the world, and certainly not so close geographically. A genuinely democratic society within the poverty stricken peoples of the world might provide an example that could indeed be dangerous to the great business corporations. America therefore repeated policies applied to Cuba since the 1960s. When Reagan became President in 1981 Nicaragua asked for normalisation of their relationship on several occasions. To no avail, and it is to be much regretted that one has to add 'of course'. Reagan was hardly the man to exhibit decency in international relations, and the story of American knavery culminated in their support for the Contras, whose military operations can only be described as terrorism. It is a statement of fact to write of 'Washington's state-sponsored terrorism in Nicaragua'. The words are from Mark Curtis's book, *The Ambiguities of Power*, published by Zed Books in 1995. Curtis offers an analysis of British foreign policy that is probing, well-documented and highly critical. It is a sober text.

Throughout all these years I have supported the groups and movements which have condemned the American and Anglo-American interventions; with money, when I could afford it, with public speaking and with writing. My lectures on foreign affairs have been more frequent during the years of retirement. But of all these unpleasant and critical events the issue which has most disturbed me has been Israel and the Palestinians, although I have spoken in public only occasionally about my concerns. As I explained earlier, I had no awareness of the Jewish question until I went to University at the age of eighteen, and then I became quite closely involved. A number of my new friends were Jewish and our most active policy was to counter Moseley's fascists on the streets of London. My opposition to racism was strongly confirmed during my years in India and it has remained unchanged in its vigour to the present day. I have affectionate and vivid memories of the household of Chimen and Miriam Abramsky in Parliament Hill Fields when I went to London in my first decade of academic life, and I shall always be grateful for the intellectual stimulation which they offered in such friendly fashion. Throughout the years to the present some of my closest friends have been Jewish, although I never thought of them in this way, and I have rarely discussed the Israeli problem with them. But for me Israel and the Jewish orthodox attitudes towards the Palestinians have become steadily more important, and more distressing. My serious interest in the question began just after the war when Richard Crossman published his *Palestine Mission* in the late summer of 1946. The election of Ariel Sharon to form the government in Israel was as unpleasant a signal as the election of Bush to the American presidency. I regret deeply that I can foresee only continual violence, and in the long term, a combination of the Arab States against Israel. I am assuming that I shall not live long enough to witness one more terrible tragedy in the history of the Jewish people, and that this will be an occasion when their disgraceful and dishonourable policies towards the Palestinians will have brought about a bloody retribution. These are thoughts that darken my remaining years for I remain sympathetic and responsive to the Jewish people, highly conscious of their persecution through the centuries, and of their remarkable contribution to cultural and intellectual history. Of the Israeli policies towards the Palestinians, I can only observe and despair.

I retired from the University in the autumn of 1982. My contract still had one more year to run, but with the Thatcher government well in its stride there was a cutback of some twenty per cent in the University income. The Vice-Chancellor desperately needed early retirements and there was a reasonable capital sum for those who moved out. Those who had served in the armed forces during the war had until recently been allowed no compensation for the years when they could have been in academic employment, or in work of some kind. The AUT had been fighting a long battle, and a few years earlier the Treasury had allowed half the years of service to count towards the calculation of the annual pension. Normal practice allowed up to forty years of service for a full pension, and in my case, even with half the army service included I was still some three years short of a full pension. However, with the lump sum and various agreements about the Labour Dictionary, including a room in the same building as my co-editor Joyce Bellamy, I took my retirement rather happily. I should add that I was still being subsidised by outside foundations, the monies being administered by the University's Accounts department.

Three years before I retired I was presented with a *festschrift*, edited by David Martin and David Rubinstein. The former was a graduate and then a post-graduate in my department and he also worked on the Labour Dictionary. He had obtained a lecturing position in economic history at the University of Sheffield and, as I have already indicated, he was a most helpful colleague. David Rubinstein had been teaching in my department from about the middle sixties and we have always been on friendly terms. I was, naturally, much honoured by their confidence in me, and impressed with their choice of contributors. They included Asa Briggs, with whom I had co-edited three volumes of essays in labour history; my greatly respected friend Victor Kiernan; the distinguished economic historian Sidney Pollard; Margaret Cole; a group of former postgraduate students, and both editors. The most striking piece, for me at any rate, was a Presentation by Ralph Miliband: a survey of my life and career. The subject of the volume, around which the essays made their own individual contribution, was summarised in its title: *Ideology and the Labour Movement*; and it was rounded off with a complete list of my writings to date, which Joyce Bellamy compiled in her usual efficient way.

About the same time as this volume appeared I was invited on a seven-week tour of Australia, organised by former post-graduate students who had teaching positions in Australian universities. I mentioned earlier that while there always seemed academic positions in Australia (and, to a much more limited extent, in New Zealand) it was during the first half or so of the seventies that many of my postgraduates moved into Australian teaching jobs. I managed to obtain funds from the British Academy and a private Foundation, and flew to Perth via Bombay. I stayed a week in Perth, having been given some kind of short-term visiting lectureship from the University, in exchange for just one lecture, and then right across the Continent to Sydney, which then became the centre of my various excursions: to Monash, Melbourne, Canberra, a former gold mine north of Sydney and various journeyings in the mountains and the bush. Then back to Perth for the flight home. It was a great pleasure to talk with my former students and with many Australian historians. Academic life seemed to me lively, and with individuals such as Stuart MacIntye, whom I had known in England, it could not be otherwise.

I had two other long distance visits during these early years of my retirement. One was to Japan and this came about through Constance teaching English to foreign students. She had begun an evening class in English for students at the University around the middle of the 1960s. All nationalities, from the Near and Far East as well as Europe. She was always a sympathetic communicator and she maintained contact with quite a few after they returned home. For many years we had two or three of her students to lunch every Sunday. The University department of Economics used to receive three or four students from the Bank of Japan for a one-year stay. They came to Hull (as well as to LSE and Oxford) because we had a well-known specialist in banking, J.S.G. Wilson. In the late seventies, however, a Japanese student came to read for a full three year degree, and he failed his first year examination. Constance asked me to talk with his tutors, who all accepted that he was an intelligent young man, and that it was only his inadequate English that was responsible for his failure. In agreement with Constance and the student in question I wrote in considerable detail to his father, and assured him that we would take especial care with his English.

So Kantoro Tomiyama took his first year again. In his Final's examination there were 102 students who graduated and of these there were two Firsts, Kantoro being one of the two. About a year earlier we had learned that his father owned the largest toy business in Japan, and that Kantoro had been sent to England for specific business reasons relating to his future career. I should add that part of our commitment to his family was that he came to lunch every Sunday, so we had really begun to think if him as one of our own circle of relatives and friends.

The degree ceremonies were always held after the summer examinations in the City Hall, and all his family came from Japan to celebrate his success. And with the family was the young woman who had been chosen to marry Kantoro. The date of the wedding had evidently already been agreed and before the family left for home they invited Constance and myself to come to Tokyo for a fortnight over the wedding period. They would pay all expenses of travel and accommodation. They also invited Bob Chester and his wife. Chester, who was a social scientist, was also the Warden of the large student's hostel in which Kantoro had lived throughout his four years in Hull, and he had obviously been very helpful. So in due course we took the plane to Hong Kong and then to Tokyo. We were met in Hong Kong by a group of Constance's former students – she had them round the world – and we agreed to stay for a few days on our return journey. But now we flew to Tokyo and were met by Kantoro who took us to our hotel: a luxurious accommodation which overlooked the Imperial gardens. On the way from the airport he asked Constance if she would speak at the wedding reception, and for her this was a somewhat unusual request. She was a notably competent teacher, and it had always been obvious that her students found her very sympathetic, but public speaking of the kind that was now being asked was somewhat outside her usual practice. So she offered me, but Kantoro was insistent and it was agreed.

We presumed there had been a Japanese traditional wedding and we went to what was the equivalent of a public reception. There were some 800 guests, sitting at long tables in parallel lines to the top table, which was raised above the floor level, and this was where Kantoro and his bride were seated together with the 'go-between' who had arranged the marriage. There were some leading figures in the political and business world along the first row and we were half way along the second row. Apart from the families there were almost no women present. The food was French and excellent. The bride first came in an elaborate and strikingly colourful Japanese kimono, but about four or five times during the evening she went out and changed into different styles, including European.

Half way through this long ceremony Constance made her speech. She had been practising in our hotel room and was obviously word perfect but it must have been somewhat daunting, addressing this large congregation of men. There was an interpreter, since by no means a majority would have understood English. She spoke very clearly and pleasantly, and was warmly congratulated.

We had a most interesting two weeks. The Bank of Japan arranged a reception for Constance and when we first entered it was to meet a longish line of her former students, ranked in their seniority within the Bank. It was spring and cherry blossom time and there were celebrations in various parks. We went to Kyoto for a couple of days, travelling there at high speed in what was known as the 'bullet train'; everywhere we went the food was delicious, and people were always pleasant and helpful. I had a number of private sessions with various historians, mostly young scholars. Constance on one occasion was taken to a three hour performance at a traditional Japanese theatre. It was all most enjoyable and we flew back to Hong Kong for a couple of days sight-seeing and exotic menus.

We have always kept in formal touch with Kantoro and a couple of years back his firm were showing in a large exhibition in London. There must have been some other reasons for their visit – which I have now forgotten – because they organised a very large reception in the Banqueting Hall in Whitehall and Kantoro gave the keynote speech. It was a splendid occasion within this impressive and imposing building and we thoroughly enjoyed ourselves. The food was English, and frightful.

Within a year or so of this visit to Japan I was invited by the Indian Historical Association to spend a fortnight in Delhi and Calcutta. In Delhi I was to lecture at the Nehru Memorial Library and to take at least one session with postgraduate students whose research was in British history; and in Calcutta I was at the disposal of the University. I stayed first in Delhi, living in a very well-organised centre for visiting academics and thoroughly enjoyed meeting Indian scholars, some of whom I already knew. I had one long walk round the poorer districts and the memories of the war years returned quite sharply. It was Calcutta, however, which brought back the bitter impact of Indian poverty and the consequences of imperialist rule. My accommodation in Calcutta was a good deal more spartan than in Delhi, and I developed dysentery. I was ready to leave this crowded city with its many slums and but also with its many lively academics.

I had retired from academic teaching with the firm intention of bringing together a considerable amount of research material that I had been collecting over the years. But the Thatcher government was in power and one of her central concerns was the weakening of the industrial and political power of the trade union movement. Through the sixties and seventies the unions had been active and increasingly prominent, and opposition to their power, both alleged and real, was becoming vociferous. The climax of the Government's offensive against the trade union movement came with the year-long miners' strike of 1983-4. I wrote a lengthy analysis of the strike and its implications in the 1985/6 issue of the *Socialist Register,* having been much involved in the grassroots politics of this major confrontation.

There are some key dates to be noted. Arthur Scargill became national president of the miners in December 1981; Ian McGregor, with a notorious record of union-busting in the USA, took over the chairmanship of the Coal Board on 1 September 1983; and then on 1 March 1984 the Yorkshire area of the NCB announced the closure of the Cortonwood pit.

The National Coal Board insisted that this was a Yorkshire decision but it is unlikely that the NCB were not wholly involved. Pits were being closed down in other areas such as South Wales and Scotland but in terms of size these were less important than the central Midlands. Yorkshire still had 60,000 miners out of a national total of 180,000 and if the power of the NUM was to be broken, it could only come through a devastating onslaught on the Yorkshire area, which also now had the most militant miners' leader.

The strike was defeated in overwhelming and devastating terms and it effectively broke the power of the Miners' Union. Yet public support in the country at large for the miners was remarkably strong and the response from the mining communities, and above all from the women in the mining villages, was impressive and resolute.

Why did the strike fail ? It was a failure, it must be emphasised, that went beyond the usual repercussions of a working-class defeat. There were two major coal strikes in the twentieth century, and both had long-range consequences. The miners' defeat in 1926 was not remedied for the unions involved until the years of the Second World War. The 1985 failure not only reduced the national Union to industrially small proportions, but the years of the 1980s were witness to profound changes in the politics of the Left in Britain. The failure of the miners is a question that ought to be more carefully analysed than has often been the case, for it displayed aspects of British politics which demand a careful appreciation. The first is undoubtedly the politics of the Thatcher government, representing the intransigence of the propertied classes when they have felt themselves threatened. It is necessary to recognise again the concerns of the seventies when the strengths of the trade unions – much exaggerated, of course – were considered to be getting out of hand. Thatcher's legislative programme of her first administration was greatly welcomed, and her use of the coercive powers of the State in the many violent confrontations during the strike itself was widely approved among the propertied classes and the world of business. There was no limit to the money that was available. The intransigence of the Government was not wholly appreciated by the NUM and not at all, from their public statements, by the Labour leadership.

The crucial question of the opposition to the Government, first by the NUM and then by the Labour Party leadership within Parliament, and outside in the country, can only be answered in somewhat negative terms. During the year of the strike there was a growing amount of research into the economics of the coal industry that demonstrated the mistakes and incorrectness of the Government's statements about the coal industry. It was to be shown that Cortonwood, the pit which began the strike, actually made an operating profit in the year before the strike began. Andrew Glyn, of the University of Oxford, provided an analysis that was published by the NUM in the autumn of 1984. It was a serious, detailed critique of the Government's statistics but its findings were hardly ever used by Scargill or the NUM publicity machine in Sheffield. Throughout the year of the strike the weakness, amounting to a general incompetence, of the handling of the media by the NUM headquarters was an important factor in the whole dispute. In part this must be related to the personality of Scargill himself. He was undoubtedly a charismatic strike leader, wholly trusted by the rank and file and without question the most important single person to carry the miners and their families along with him, in this terrible year of deprivation and hardship. The leadership of a strike of the importance of this one required, however, qualities that Scargill unfortunately lacked. His role was twofold: to encourage and sustain his miners, and secondly, of quite central importance, to explain constantly to the public at large, notably through the media, the justness of his cause. What was needed was a group of dedicated specialists in the NUM headquarters who would work night and day explaining the miners' case and refuting the continuous propaganda coming from Whitehall. There was a gap, a very large gap, in the miners' case for the coal industry and there was also an absence of any continuous general criticism of the Government's handling of the dispute. In particular the Labour leadership was remarkably silent on one of the crucial issues of this year: the violence of the police against the picket lines. There was violence on both sides, but it was the 'police riot' at Orgreave that represented the powers opposed to the miners. Had it not been for the revelations of the solicitor who was representing a group of miners arrested on the day of the 'riot', set out in an impressive article in *The Guardian* on 12 August 1985, it is unlikely that the full details of this day would have become available. We are all greatly indebted to Gareth Pierce and her continued insistence upon the facts of police violence.

I must again emphasise the Labour leadership's failure to insist upon the Government's main responsibility for the violence of this year. It was the Falkland's war that had contributed materially to Thatcher's victory at the elections of 1983, although the extraordinary incompetence of the Labour leadership was possibly an even more important factor. During the miners' strike, with Kinnock now in the leadership, timidity was the notable characteristic of Labour's front bench. Kinnock was obviously fearful of the influence of the media's campaign against what was always described as the violence of the miners on the picket line. During the first ten weeks of the strike, after which there was a holiday for a fortnight, no debate was initiated by Labour's front bench. There were backbenchers who tried very hard to encourage a debate but Kinnock always refused.

The 31 July 1984 was Opposition Day in the House of Commons, when the Opposition chose the subject of the main debate. The miners' strike had now lasted twenty-one weeks, with its news filling the press and the radio and TV waves, and Parliament was about to adjourn for over two and a half months. Kinnock was concerned to avoid what the leadership decided was still damaging and so he settled for a long resolution condemning the general policies of the Thatcher government, with the miner's strike being referred to only briefly. What was missing in this whole debate was a serious analysis of the Government's gross misstatements about the economics of individual pits and the coal industry in general. The facts were available and were being steadily added to. There were academic and professional specialists whose expertise could have been used. In January 1985 the journal *Accountancy* published a devastating critique of the accounting methods of the National Coal Board. The article was a composite piece by five accounting specialists including the Price Waterhouse Professor of Accounting and Finance at UMIST. Their analysis offered a reversal of the Coal Board's position on the so-called 'uneconomic pits' and a rejection of the arguments used for closing individual pits.

As already noted, it was these economic arguments, capable of destroying the Government's justification for a number of pit closures, that were not used by speakers on the Left, either by the NUM or their supporters in Parliament, as well as arguments used at the popular level. The position north of the border was somewhat better. As in England there were academic researchers whose analysis offered the same broad conclusions, but in Scotland those involved in the work took it to the public domain, through the press and along the air waves. George Kerevan and my own son Richard, who taught at the University of St. Andrews, were able to make public their analyses of Scottish mining, through the press, radio and television. The Scottish area of the NUM was obviously much more conscious of the problems involved and they gave serious support to all who were arguing for a different outcome. In 1985 they published *The Economic Case for Deep-Mined Coal in Scotland* in which George Kerevan and Richard brought together their indictment of the National Coal Board and their suggested alternatives.

I have given space to this mining crisis, partly because in itself it represents the practices of the ruling groups in our country when they believe their position is at least somewhat threatened. It was also an important factor in the general decline of the Left in British politics characteristic of the closing quarter of the twentieth century. My own part in this year of the miner's strike was similar to many others: I spoke on about a dozen campuses, I collected money regularly for the Yorkshire miners and their families, and the only activity out of the ordinary was a BBC lunch time TV discussion on a Sunday, with Robert Maxwell and Arthur Scargill. This was the only time I ever met Maxwell – it was of course when he was still more or less accepted in public life – and I was not impressed. Nor, for quite different reasons, with Arthur Scargill, whose mind I thought lacked a subtlety required in this very difficult situation. And this was confirmed by the decision to continue the strike after the unusual offer by NACODS (National Association of Colliery Overmen, Deputies and Shotfirers) towards the end of September 1984 not to sign an agreement without asking for the signature also of the NUM. Now I accept that it would have been very difficult for the leadership of the NUM to sign, because the conditions of the agreement included acceptance of some pit closures, but it was nevertheless a deal that would have represented a situation, not of total victory, but one certainly to have allowed the NUM to continue as a serious force. As it was, the refusal to accept NACOD's very unusual offer was the beginning of a rapid decline of support for the strike within various mining communities. By the beginning of 1985 it was obvious that a disaster was now in train from which there was to be no recovery.

As I noted earlier, I wrote a long account of this year-long strike in the *Socialist Register* (1985-6: 'An Open Conspiracy: Conservative Politics and the Miners' Strike, 1984-5') and I have always thought this one of my better pieces on contemporary politics.

The miners' strike inevitably disrupted my long-term plans for historical publication. There were other interruptions in these early first years of retirement. I had a considerable number of postgraduate students in the last two decades of my academic career, and I continued with the supervision of those still in process of completion. I also accepted a couple of new doctoral students, one of whom became a close friend. This was Diane Kirby, who had read for an Honours degree in the American Studies department, and who was unable to obtain the finance for postgraduate study in the United States. Since there was no one in her department very close to her proposed subject – certain aspects of postwar international politics – the Department asked me if I would move in. Diane was an excellent student but obtained her doctorate in a notably dismal time for permanent employment in the academic world. I won't retell the long saga of disappointment she experienced, but what was so important was her refusal to be discouraged by the continued bleakness of academic life. Her part-time teaching jobs at York and Newcastle were very well received and then, after her years of dogged research (and publication) she got a three year contract at the University of Ulster which was then turned into a long-term contract By this time she had become a well-known scholar in the field of post Second World

War politics, with special emphasis upon the role of various clerical denominations in high-level political affairs. Diane, I should not forget to mention, was also a European water-ski champion.

I had, of course, continued with Ralph Miliband the editing of the *Socialist Register* and he and I continued our close relationship, so important to me throughout these decades. At the same time I must put on record that during the 1980s I found myself not always in agreement with him on certain important issues. I was somewhat dubious, for example, concerning the establishment of the Socialist Society in the early 1980s – largely a grouping of intellectuals in London, and later in the decade I was not involved in any way with Ralph's relations with Tony Benn, which were important to both of them. These were not matters which affected our personal attitudes to each other. I was also interested in moving out of the editorial seat of the *Socialist Register* – largely because of my historical work, but it was not until the end of the decade that I was able finally to retire.

I have, throughout my life, been fortunate both in my family life and in a wide circle of friends. Beyond the family I must first relate to Edward and Dorothy Thompson and then Ralph and his family. His sons have carried on the Miliband political tradition although almost inevitably with the differences between generations. Marion, as always, has remained helpful and affectionate, and I feel I have been a member of their family group since the day of the marriage three decades earlier.

There are many I have not mentioned. My quite numerous visits to North America, where over the years I lectured at Bloomington, Illinois, Yale, Harvard, Chicago, and UCLA, where I spent a very interesting ten days. The circle of acquaintances and friends naturally widened. My original visits were to the *Victorian Studies* at Bloomington, Indiana where Martha Vicinus and Gail Malmgreen were to become close friends over many years. Gail spent some time at the University of Hull. In Canada I lectured at Quebec, Queen's University, Kingston, Toronto, Winnipeg, and became especially close to Leo Panitch.

My English friends over the years have been many and I bow my head in apology because there are so many who have not been mentioned. I must not, however, omit one of my most treasured friendships. In around 1970 I had a postgraduate student whose subject was the 1930s unemployed movement and he came to me one day with the name of Frow. He had been reading the newly published *Daily Worker* and their accounts of the unemployed demonstrations in Manchester. The name Frow kept reappearing. I think I know his son, I said. My acquaintance was hearsay, and so I phoned Eddie Frow who revealed that the references were to him. He was an engineer, unemployed at the time (the early thirties) and an active Communist Party member. Our relationship soon became close. Ruth, his wife, was a school teacher and together they achieved one of the most remarkable collections of the twentieth century. Their house, when I first knew it, was covered with books, pamphlets and posters on every wall and in every corner. Each year, at least once a year, they would set off in their car, to explore the bookshops of Britain for materials of any and all kinds relating to the labour movement. At the end of the eighties Salford Council offered to rehouse the library with a pleasant flat at the top of the building for their own accommodation. And so the Working-Class Library – one of the great centres of research in labour and social history – became open to anyone with an interest. Ruth and Eddie were always helpful, and when Eddie died, not long after the celebration of his 90th birthday, Ruth has continued in her usual helpful way. Names to be honoured and remembered.

I have been privileged and much favoured in my friends. When I moved to Hull, I was only able to continue many of my academic enquiries in London, because Margot Jefferys, who lived in Highgate, offered me a room whenever my work required a visit. It was a blessing I have never forgotten. Margot was a medical sociologist, very lively intellectually, widely respected and a much loved friend to Constance and myself for many years.

The years which followed the ending of the Second World War were notably deficient in critical socialist writing – I exclude Crosland from this category – and it was not until Ralph Miliband's *Parliamentary Socialism* (1961) that serious debate began. The intellectual climate was propitious, with the anti-nuclear debate and the tumultuous aftermath of Khruschev's 1956 speech. If Ralph's book had been written two decades later much of the basic analysis would have remained but the pervasive influence of the Cold War would have been given a great deal more emphasis. Since he published, the archives of the Foreign Office and other departments, as well as the records of other Governments, have documented only too fully the anti-Soviet and anti- communist policies of the Labour Government from the beginning of its term of office in August 1945. The Foreign Office, with Ernest Bevin long-entrenched in his anti-communism, was perhaps even more single-minded in the first months than the United States. The starting point for Britain was naturally the colonial Empire, its continuing control a necessary part of Britain's status within the leading countries in world politics. The financial aftermath of the Second World War meant that American dollars, together with the dollar earnings from colonial tin and other raw materials and foodstuffs, were accepted as necessary, and subservience to the United States began to be put in place.

Labour in office and Labour out of government accepted levels of defence costs throughout the post-war decades that were higher than in any other western European country. The relationship with the United States continued to grow, and for Whitehall and many politicians on all sides it became a 'special relationship'. By the early 1980s there were 135 American military bases in Britain, most of them operational, and there were others either being built or planned. Of these, twenty-five were major operational bases or military headquarters, thirty-five were categorised as minor or reserve bases, and seventy-five represented facilities of various kind that could be used by the American military. There were also thirty housing sites for American personnel and their families. The term 'facility' covered a wide range of functions, and included intelligence centres, aircraft weapon ranges and a number of contingency hospitals.

There are also nuclear installations about which public knowledge, in the usual scattered detail, has become more aware in the last quarter of the twentieth century, much encouraged, of course, by the American plans for the new missile range which is a serious threat to world stability with the election of George Bush. My own increasing awareness of the American hegemony in world affairs was to exercise a close influence upon the historical approach to my own research and writing. I had, for a number of years before I retired, been increasingly critical of large parts of the writing of social/labour history. Too much, I thought, was becoming antiquarian and insufficiently probing of the political structures within which the various social groups were located. In particular, it was the nature and ideology of the different ruling groups that was absent from too many accounts of historical change.

My first book in my retirement years was based upon research that had begun over thirty years earlier, and it finally emerged as *1848. The British State and the Chartist Movement.* The new emphasis of my later years was upon the organisation of State power, and the political psychology of those who exercised this power. I was much more concerned, that is, with the class structure of society and the many ways in which modern society had developed institutional bodies and organisations to allow the propertied classes to exert influence and power and, in the last resort, effective mastery. As industrialised society became more complex, so the mechanisms of government, at local and national level, developed greater sophistication. And these were adjusted and fashioned to the basic structure of the ownership and distribution of capital and property.

Since my book on 1848 centred upon a European situation it also allowed me to consider in detail the relationship between the British government and the colony of Ireland. As I noted earlier in this volume, I myself rarely taught the economics and politics of Anglo-Irish colonialism, and I much regret that academics like myself have done so little to help dispel the historical ignorance in these matters that afflict most of our people.

Apart from political essays for the *Socialist Register* and two general texts, one on *The Labour Movement in Britain* (about 160 pages, and to my surprise my most commonly used text in public libraries) and a shorter commentary of just under

100 pages – *The Consolidation of the Capitalist State, 1800-1850* – I found myself increasingly concerned with the politics of internationalism in the second half of the twentieth century. In large part this undoubtedly was my reaction to the course of world politics, and in particular to the wars that followed each other in bloody succession. Since 1982 there were wars in the Falklands, Kuwait, Bosnia, Kosovo and, most recently, Afghanistan in which European powers and the United States were involved, with massacres, civil wars, conflicts over boundaries and tribal struggles in the underdeveloped countries of the world. African and Asian blood flowed freely, the weaponry, usually of a fairly simple kind, being mostly supplied by the armament firms of the 'peaceful' Western world on a very large scale. In Britain 'ethical' foreign policy, as interpreted by New Labour, was not conspicuous for any restraint upon the sales of arms on a global order.

In 1993 I published *The Politics of Continuity*, a series of essays concerned with British foreign policy and the Labour government in the first years of office after its victory in the summer of 1945. In a long essay on 'The Mind of the Foreign Office' I examined the political background, and the political attitudes which flowed therefrom, of the leading permanent officials; and the other essays concerned themselves with aspects of the first couple of years or so of Labour's approach to the world. These included a much neglected account of the critical attitudes of Attlee towards the traditional policies of the Foreign Office in respect of the Middle East, which were vigorously supported by Ernest Bevin, whose anti-communism I always strongly underlined. My final major piece – there were a series of shorter studies in the Appendices – was the forgotten intervention of Britain in Vietnam within a few weeks of the Japanese war ending. It is still forgotten.

This study, as with much of my other publishing, was delayed by the practical politics of current affairs, notably with the necessity of standing against the Anglo-American wars in the Balkans and the Middle East. My health has remained remarkably satisfactory, although I developed a kind of phlebitis during the Kuwait war, and I had to drag myself round to fulfil my obligations. I managed about a dozen meetings – about half were campus discussions, with the most critical against me being the Students Union in my own University. The phlebitis soon left me and has not yet returned.

These last twenty years or so have witnessed a steady decline in the politics of the Left, a phenomenon that apparently is common, in no doubt differing ways, to the industrialised countries of the world. In Britain the death of John Smith allowed Blair to move into the leadership of the Labour Party and organise, before the General Election, the removal of Clause 4 from Labour's statement of aims. I am writing this last section during the early weeks of the Labour Government following their second overwhelming victory at the General Election of the early summer of 2001: an achievement never before registered in such positive terms. What is already clear is that the Tory Party will be in serious internal conflict over a range of major issues, whoever becomes its leader.

I am writing the concluding words to these memoirs at a very unsettled period of history, with a whole range of questions on the agenda, The financial pages of the serious papers in Britain are much concerned with the future of the world economy, including, of course, that of the United Kingdom. We have so far avoided the experiences of Germany, for example, with those of Japan as much more remarkable. But Britain has a very marked decline in its industrial base, with a growing trade deficit, in part due to the continued high level of consumer spending. It would be surprising if unemployment did not begin to rise, and what in general is in question is whether Gordon Brown's insistence that we have eliminated the 'boom and bust' of earlier decades is likely to be achieved. If Britain does move into recession the social consequences within British society are likely to be widespread and certainly serious. In a rich country like ours – as elsewhere in other rich countries – there are already swathes of economic and social deprivation which are disgracefully ignored, and which can be expected to erupt into varying degrees of riotous turbulence. And as there are racial tensions already present, the turmoil will be the greater.

Politics in Britain are at an unusual stage. An economic recession will confront the New Labour Government with very large problems. That would be true for any government in power but Blair's administration had a very fortunate four years from 1977 with a not particularly competent managerial record. And it is an open question how capable it would be when confronted with very direct and serious economic and social problems. By the time this book is being read these questions may have become more explicit and, to some point, answered. The range and intensity of the world's problems, however, inevitably go much beyond the nature, however complex and difficult, of British society, with my personal conjectures about the global future deeply pessimistic.

These are memoirs of a political kind, and most of the private details of my life have therefore been omitted. There is little I propose to add. I have lived in Hull for over fifty years, in the same house in the Avenues district of the town. This middle-class suburb was begun in the 1870s and more or less completed in the 1890s and early 1900s. My own house, the middle of three, has a smallish front garden, a much larger stretch at the rear with a pleasant lawn on which we can enjoy meals whenever summer invades. In the front of the house, between the pedestrian footpath and the road, there is a very wide verge of grass, in my Avenue around three yards in width. All the four Avenues – some three-quarters of a mile in length – have trees, some very large, along their verges, and the general effect is still very pleasant, even with the growing number and noise of cars. Only along one Avenue, and not ours, is there a not very frequent bus service.

The gate at the far end of my garden gives way to what locally is known as a 'ten-foot' that is a small passage way for cars to be parked in their garages or householders to enter their property. Just across the side-road from my ten-foot is a short lane leading to a quite large group of Council allotments. In 1960 I began renting one and have continued to the present. The particular allotment I chose was planted for about three quarters of its length with fruit bushes: red and blackcurrants, raspberries, gooseberries and blackberries. At the front is a quite large area on which I can, and sometimes do, plant vegetables. Let me make it plain that I have remained an unskilled and, according to Constance, rather dumb labourer in the horticultural world, but the bushes have flowered each year and Constance has made many pounds of jam, and frozen the rest of the pickings. I have never been wildly excited by gardening, but mostly I have enjoyed the fresh air and exercise, and the pleasures seem to have grown somewhat with the advance of age,

My family life has been similar to other well-organised families, that is, with long stretches of pleasant life, interrupted at times with the usual social and personal displacements. Constance had four children. Graham, our eldest, is now a leading print dealer, specialising in political prints of the late 18th century, and maps before 1800. He is successful and very well known in the world of collectors. Richard, our second son, while teaching at St Andrews, produced a large-scale history of the Bank of Scotland from its beginnings in the 1690s and received a series of wonderfully congratulatory reviews. Our beloved Jane is a probation officer who is now a single mother with two lively daughters, Emma and Helen, who we are always delighted to have to stay. Our youngest son, Ralph, is the only member of the family who still lives in Hull and is happy to instruct me into the history of the world of theatre and music in the 18th century.

When Constance celebrated her 80th birthday some three years or so ago the family came together and bought her a third greenhouse. Exotic plants are one of her delights and certain of her cacti are very impressive. But she is a woman of many interests. She taught English to foreign students at the University for many years and we always had one or two for lunch on Sundays. I told earlier the story of Kantoro Tomiyama. About a quarter of a century ago she went to an embroidery day class and made very good friends who joined together to form the East Yorkshire Embroidery Society (EYES), and in recent years she has remained president. For about ten years from the late sixties she took a weekly discussion group into the local prison, which at that time was a high security jail, and it ended with a new Governor whose changes brought about the equivalent of a serious riot. The subsequent public enquiry found Constance explaining to the BBC TV that everyone knew trouble was building up – and that ended her permission to enter the prison. She continued to maintain some contacts both with former prisoners and sometimes their wives. Currently quite a fair part of her energies are devoted to Kurdish asylum seekers, there being a large number who have been 'dumped' in the town. 'Dumped' is unfortunately the correct word. The Home Office have been disgracefully incompetent.

And what of myself? I remain reasonably active in my study. My walking has become slower and somewhat less easy and I am going deaf. But for the rest I remain remarkably healthy and I am fully conscious of how fortunate I have been in matters of health throughout my whole life. A sporting youth, good food, interesting holidays, and above all my family and many friends to love and cherish. And no doubt my genes. I loved my mother and she remains in my memory, and I suppose it would be proper to offer a token bow to my Greek father.

I shall die within a few years having lived a privileged life for most of my years when compared with many of my own countrymen and women, and with billions of the world outside these islands. I have enjoyed much of my life while recognising my apartness from so much of the misery and bloodshed throughout the world. And I do not foresee serious change in the coming decades. What happens in the centuries which follow I do not pretend to understand.

Let me conclude my story with a low key pleasant family story. A few months ago I was eighty-five, and for my birthday my daughter Jane, who lives in Sheffield, and my son Richard, who lives in London, both gave me the same book, without, of course, knowing it was a second copy. It was Simon Jenkins' wonderful *England's Thousand Best Churches*, a very lively and interesting text with a collection of superb photographs. I keep it next to my place at the dining table and read one or two pieces each day. So now, having sounded my final composition on the misery the world will continue to suffer, I return to England's churches to comfort what, if I were a Christian and not an atheist, I would call my soul.

John Saville
January 2001

A Last Word

These memoirs were mostly written during the 1990s, but they also cover the second victory of Blair and New Labour, the questionable election of Bush to the American Presidency, and the coming to power of Ariel Sharon in Israel. The dire consequences of these three elections are steadily becoming apparent.

Blair's modernising ideas and practices are working their way through British society. Blair dislikes the House of Commons and is present as seldom as is practicable. His greatest asset is a remarkable verbal facility, to which he adds his religious piety. This smoothness with words has been continuously used to camouflage his conservative/liberal ideas and policies. Privatisation measures are preferred to a straightforward extension of the public sector. The army, for example, is, at the time of writing, waging war against Iraq, and it will be served by more private agencies than at any time in the past century: a fact that is not generally known.

In 1997 many were conscious of Blair's lack of understanding of, or sympathy with, the traditions of the British Labour movement. It must also be accepted that Blair lacked serious knowledge of the conduct of US foreign policy since the end of the Second World War. I refer not to the problems and conflicts of the cold war, but to the many ways in which American money, and arms, have been used in the service of reactionary regimes and movements, all calculated to withstand or offset the attempts to bring some decency into regimes of these kinds. It may be presumed, to quote one of the more unpleasant examples, that Blair would be unable to recite the story of US support for the Contras in Nicaragua.

On Thursday 20 March 2003 President Bush declared war on Iraq, passionately supported by Blair. There had been weeks of indecisive anticipation but it was always clear that Bush, and the hard-line group that surrounds him, was determined that the war should not be seriously delayed. The opposition to war throughout the world was growing, and outside the United States the only serious military support that Bush could rely upon was from the British Prime Minister.

It was not easy for Blair. Hans Blix, the chief weapons inspector, had insisted that some progress had been made and asked for several months more before a final report could be made. He was supported, in press statements, by his colleagues. Moreover, a declaration of war without a specific resolution from the UN Security Council is illegal. It is also contrary to the original spirit of the UN – not, of course, an argument that would make any impact on Cheney or Rumsfeld. In Britain a majority of international lawyers, excepting those within the Government, have declared the war illegal.

The usual journals and newspapers, especially *The Guardian*, are publishing critical commentaries, with John Pilger outstanding, particularly in his columns in the *New Statesman*. Tariq Ali, my long-standing friend from the Richard Gott days in the 1960s, has been putting powerful arguments against the war, in writing and on public platforms, and there have been many others along with him. We need, however, to match the mood within the country in serious organisational terms.

We live, in the spring of 2003, in a political situation that is unprecedented in my own long life. Before the declaration of war against Iraq there was growing opposition in the House of Commons as well as in the country at large. Any organised counter view was hardly visible. The Tory Party has rarely been in such a sorry mess, although inevitably most, but not all, supported the idea of war. The Liberal Democrats failed to offer anything approaching a robust opposition. Thier leader, Charles Kennedy, offered some acceptable comments, but he lacks the charisma required of a serious critic at the present time. There was certainly serious opposton on the Labour backbenches, and it will be historically interesting if this develops into an effective leadership.

According to the opinion polls, at the end of the first week of the war there has been something of a decline in the anti-war movement. This was to be expected, given that 'our boys' are now in the firing line. But this is going to be a war of increasingly heavy bombardment and there will be an increasing toll of deaths and injuries. And my reading of the opposition to the war is that it will continue to grow, not least within the British Labour Party. Blair is likely to split the Party, and what follows is open to a number of possibilities. On another level the alignment of the United Kingdom with the Bush administration will encourage increased terrorism against the British, at home and abroad, from some Muslim fundamentalists. Whatever the outcome of this war, the instability of the Middle East is almost certain to be enhanced. What has been striking during the weeks of debate and argument that led to this war has been the lack of serious attention to the most urgent problem of the Middle East, namely Israel and the Palestinians. There have been a few phrases from Blair, and we now have the 'road map'. But no one can yet believe in any serious change of US policy. This is an issue of the gravest importance, and if it is neglected the human cost will continue to grow.

Blair has made massive miscalculations in his international diplomacy. I must note again that it is his verbal skills that have bemused many people into a belief in his political skills and their justification. This acceptance of US policy on Iraq, and the war that it has brought about, will not be forgiven, and Blair will very properly be damned by history.

John Saville, March 2003

JOHN SAVILLE: Bibliography of Writings

NB   Book reviews and some ephemeral political writing have been omitted.

1. Editorial Works

1. *Democracy and the Labour Movement: Essays in Honour of Dona Torr,*
   Lawrence and Wishart (1954) 275 pp.
2. (with E. P. Thompson) *The Reasoner: a Journal of Discussion,* nos 1-3
   (July - November 1956)
3. (with E.P. Thompson) *The New Reasoner: a Quarterly Journal of Socialist
   Humanism,* nos 1-10 (1957-9)
4. (with Asa Briggs) *Essays in Labour History,*vol.1, Macmillan(1960) 363 pp.;
   vol.2 ,Macmillan (1971) 360 p.; vol. 3, Croom Helm (1977) 292 pp.
5. (with R. Miliband) *Socialist Register,* Merlin Press(1964,annually to1999)
6. *Studies in the British Economy 1870-1914: special number of Yorkshire
   Bulletin of Economic and Social Research,* vol. 17 (1965) 112 pp.
7. *Occasional Papers in Economic and Social History,* University of Hull,
   nos 1-8 (1969-1975)
8. (with J.M. Bellamy) *Dictionary of Labour Biography,* Macmillan, vol.1
   (1972) 388 p.; vol.2 (1974) 454 p.; vol.3 (1976) 236 p.; vol.4 (1977)236 pp.;
   vol.5 (1979) 279 p.; vol.6 (1982) 309 p.; vol.7 (1984) 301 p.; vol.8 (1987)
   309 p.; vol.9(1993) 328 p.; vol.10 (2000) 257 pp.
9. (with J.M Bellamy and David Martin), *Dictionnaire Biographique Du
   Mouvement Ouvrier International. La Grande Bretagne.* Paris, Les Editions
   Ouvrieres, Paris, Tome 1 (1979) 301 p.; Tome 2 (I986) 313 pp.

11. Books, Pamphlets, Essays and Miscellaneous

10. (with R.W. Gray) *A Preliminary Survey of Productivity in House
    Construction 1924-1937,* Ministry of Works Technical Notes, 10 pp. (1947)
11.'The Measurement of Real Cost in the London Building Industry, 1923-39'
    *Yorkshire Bulletin of Economic and Social Research,*vol.1(1949) pp.67-80.
12 'A Note on the Present Position of Working Class History' ibid. vol.4(1952)
    125-32
13.*Ernest Jones: Chartist. Selections from the Writings and Speeches, with
    Introduction and Notes,* Lawrence and Wishart *(1952)* 284 p.
14.'The Christian Socialists of 1848', *Democracy and the Labour Movement:
    Essays in Honour of Dona Torr* (1954) pp. 135-59
15.' A Comment on Professor Rostow's *British Economy of the 19th Century:*

Past and Present, no.6 (1954) pp.66-84

16. 'Henry Fielding (1707-1754)' *Labour Monthly (1954) pp.516-19*

17. ' Friedrich Engels et le Chartisme', *La Nouvelle Critique,*no.72 (February 1956) pp. 73-90

18. ' Czartyzm u voku rewolocki,1848', *Zagadrienia Nenki Historyeznej,* vol.2 (1956) pp.42-53

19.' Sleeping Partnership and Limited Liability 1850-56', *Economic History Review,* 2nd ser. vol.8 (1956) pp.418-33

20. *Rural Depopulation in England and Wales, 1851- 1951,* Routledge and Kegan Paul (1957) 253 p.

21.' The Welfare State: an Historical Approach', *New Reasoner,* vol. 3 (1957-8 pp. 5-25

22. (with E.P.Thompson) ' John Stuart Mill and EOKA', ibid, vol,7 (winter 1958-9) pp.1-11

23.'Rural Migration in England and Wales' in *Rural Migration: Papers and Discussion,* European Society for Rural Sociology (Bonn,1959) pp.58-63

24. 'Apathy into Politics', *New Left Review, no.4(1960)* pp.8-9

25. 'Henry George and the British Labour Movement', *Science and Society,* vol.24 (1960) pp.321-33

26 Review article of E.H. Phelps Brown, *The Growth of British Industrial Relations,* ibid (1960) pp.256-64

27. 'Trade Unions and Free Labour: the Background to the Taff Vale Decision' *Essays in Labour History (*ed. with Asa Briggs, 1960) pp.317-50

28. 'Some retarding factors in the British Economy before 1914', *Yorkshire Bulletin of Economic and Social Research,* vol. 13 (1961) pp.51-60

29. 'The Authorship of *The Bitter Cry of Outcast London,' Bulletin of the Society for the Study of Labour History,* no. 2 (1961) p. 15

30. ' Dictionary of Labour Movement Biography', ibid. pp.15-17

31. 'The Chartist Land Plan' ,ibid. no.3 (1961) pp.10-12

32. ' Henry George and the British Labour Movement: a select bibliography with Commentary', ibid. no.5 (1962) pp.18-26

33. ' Mr. Coppock on the Great Depression: a Critical Note', *Manchester School,* vol. 31 (1963) pp.47-71

34. ' Internal Migration in England and Wales during the past hundred years' *Les Deplacements Humains: aspects methodologiques de leur mesure* (ed. J. Sutter (Paris 1963) pp.1-21

35. 'Research Facilities and the Social Historian', *Library Association Record,* vol. 65 (1963) pp319-23

36. (with R. Miliband) ' Labour Policy and the Labour Left' *Socialist Register (1964) pp.149-56*

37. ' The Politics of *Encounter' ibid.,* pp. 192-207

38. 'Le radici storiche del riformismo laburista in Inghilterra' , *Rivista Storica del Socialismo, 13* May 1965, pp. 571-91

39. 'Henry Noel Brailsford', *Tribune,*vol.28 (24 July 1964) p.10

40. 'Labour on the Move', *Times Literary Supplement,*13 May 1965, pp.361-2

41. 'Labour and Income Redistribution' *Socialist Register (1965)* pp.147-62

42. 'The Background to the Revival of Socialism in England'. *Bulletin of the Society for the Study of Labour History*, no.11 (1965) pp. 13-19

43. (with J.W.Y. Higgs and G.A. Marshall) *Report of a United Nations European Study Group on Rural Social Development in Southern Italy* (Rome, 1965) pp. 1-23

44.' Urbanisation and the Countryside' and 'Development Problems in Rural Areas' in *People in the Countryside: Studies in Rural Social Development:* UN Study Group (1966) pp. 13-34 and 35-51

45. Review article of A.J.P. Taylor, *English History 1914-1945, Bulletin of the Society for the Study of Labour History*, no.12 (1966) pp. 49-58

46. *Pitt Jr., I Protagonisti della Storia_Universale,(1967) pp.309-36*

47. ' The Present Position and Prospects of Labour History, *North East Group for the Study of Labour History, Bulletin,* no. 1 (1967) pp.4-6

48. 'Trades Councils and the Labour Movement to 1900', *Bulletin of the Society for the Study of Labour History*, no. 14 (1967) pp.29-35

49. 'Labourism and the Labour Government', *Socialist Register (1967)* pp.43-71

50. 'How can the British Working Class Regain its Voice and Power', *Tribune, v*ol. 33 (7 February 1969) p.5

51. 'Primitive Accumulation and Early Industrialisation in Britain' *Socialist Register (* 1969) pp.247-71

52. (with Ken Coates, N. Harris and M. Johnstone) 'Britain: Prospects for the Seventies,' ibid. (1970) pp. 203-15

53. 'Some Aspects of Chartism in Decline', *Bulletin of the Society for the Study of Labour History,* no,20 (1970) pp.16-18

54. Review article: D.H. Aldccroft (ed) , *The Development of British Industry and Foreign Competition 1875-1914,* in *Business History,* vol.12 (1970) pp. 59-65

55. (with John Griffith and T. Smythe), *The Arblaster Case: the Findings of a Commission of Enquiry established by the Council for Academic Freedom and Democracy (CAFD) in October 1970,* 16 p.

56. (with P. Higgs) *Craigie College of Education: the Findings of a Commission of Enquiry established by the Council for Academic Freedom and Democracy in February 1971, 24p.*

57. 'Notes on Ideology and the Miners before World War 1', *Bulletin of the Society for the Study of Labour History,* no. 23 (1971) pp,25-7

58.' Oral History and the Labour Historians', *Oral History,* no.3 (1972) pp. 60-2

59.' Interviews in Oral History' ibid. no.4(1972) pp.93-106

60. *The Wakstein Case (* CAFD,1973) 12 pp.

61. 'The Wakstein Case', *Times Higher Education Supplement,* 30 November 1973, p. 14

62. 'The Ideology of Labourism', in R. Benewick, R.N. Berki and B. Parekh, (eds) *Knowledge and Belief in Politics: the Problem of Ideology,* Allen and Unwin (1973) pp. 213-26

63. 'Labour Prosopography', *Social Science Research Council Newsletter.*

no.20 (1973) pp.5-7

64. Review article of J.D. Foster, *Class Struggle and the Industrial Revolution*
    Socialist Register (1974) pp.226-40

65. *Marxism and History: an Inaugural Lecture,* University of Hull (1974) 19p

66 'The Twentieth Congress and the British Communist Party' *Socialist Register (1976)* pp.1-23

67. ' May Day 1937 '*Essays in Labour History (1977)* pp. 232-284

68. 'The Radical Left expects the Past to do its Duty', *Times Higher Educational Supplement,* 13 February 1976, p.15

69. 'Il socialismo e il moviemento operaio britannico', *Reforme e Rivoluzione nella Storia Contemporanea,* Piccola Biblioteca Einaudi, Turin (1977) pp.255-90

70. (with Alan Howkins) 'The Nineteen Thirties: a Revisionist History' *Socialist Register* (1979) pp. 89-100

71. ' Hugh Gaitskell : An Assessment ' ibid. (1980) pp. 148-169

72. (with Barbara English) ' Family Settlements and the Rise of Great Estates' *Economic History Review,* no. 4. November 1980, pp, 556-8

73. ' Valentine Cunningham and the Poetry of the Spanish Civil War' *Socialist Register* (1981) pp.270-284

74. ' Reflections on Recent Labour Historiography' ibid. (1982) pp.303-12

75. 'Historian' in the Fabian Tract(482) on Margaret Cole,1893-1980, pp14-17

76.(with Barbara English) *Strict Settlement. A Guide for Historians.* University of Hull Press (1983) 144 p.

77. 'The Origins of the Welfare State' in *Social Policy and Social Welfare*(eds) M. Loney, D. Boswell and J. Clarke, Open University,1983, pp. 8-17

78. ' Ernest Bevin and the Cold War', *Socialist Register* (1984) pp. 68-100

79. ' An Open Conspiracy: Conservative Politics and the Miners' Strike, 1984-5', ibid. (1985-6) 295-329

80. *The British State and the Chartist Movement,* Cambridge University Press (1987) 310 p.

81. . The Price of Alliance : American Bases in Britain', *Socialist Register, (1987)* pp. 32-64

82.. *The Labour Movement in Britain. A Commentary.* Faber and Faber (1988) 166 p.

83. (with Ralph Miliband and Leo Panitch) 'Problems and Promise of Socialist Renewal', *Socialist Register* (1988) pp. 1 - 11

84. ' Imperialism and the Victorians', *In Search of Victorian Values* (ed. E.M. . Sigsworth) Manchester University Press (1988) pp. 162-178

85. ' British Internationalism and the Labour Movement between the Wars' *Internationalism in the Labour Movement, 1830-1940,* (ed. Frits van Holtoon and Marcel van der Linden) Leiden, 1988, pp.566-582

86. 'Some Notes on Perry Anderson's 'Figures of Descent', *The Development of British Capitalist Society: a Marxist Debate,* (ed. Colin Barker and David Nicholls) Manchester 1988, pp.34-45

87. *The Labour Archive at the University of Hull,* The Brynmor Jones Library, (1989) 42 p.

88. *The Politics of Continuity. British Foreign Policy and the Labour Government, 1945-1946,* Verso (1993) 293 p.

89. *The Consolidation of the Capitalist State, 1800- 1850* , Pluto (1994) 91 p.

90. 'Edward Thompson, the Communist Party and 1956', *Socialist Register,* (1994) pp.20-31

91. 'The "Crisis" in Labour History. A Further Comment', *Labour History Review* (Winter 1996) pp. 322-328

92. 'The Trade Disputes Act of 1906' , *Historical Studies in Industrial Relations,* no.1 (March 1996) pp. 11-46

III Introductions and Prefaces

93. Introduction to 'Joseph Redman'(pseud. Brian Pearce),*The Communist Party and the Labour Left,1925-1929,* Reasoner Pamphlets No.1 Hull (1957) pp.2-7

94. Introduction to facsimile reprint of *The Red Republican and The Friend of the People,1850-51,* ed, G.J. Harney. Merlin Press (1966) pp. i-xv

95. Introduction to reprint of *Industrial Remuneration Conference: the Report of Proceedings and Papers* (1885) Kelley, New York (1968) pp. 5-44

96. Introduction to reprint of R.G.Gammage, *History of the Chartist Movement,1837-1854, 2nd ed. (1894);* and including Gammage's pamphlet: *The Social Oppression of the Working Classes: its causes and cure* (1852 ?) Kelley, New York (1969) pp. 5 - 66.

97. Preface and bibliographical notes to *A Selection of the Political Pamphlets of Charles Bradlaugh,* Kelley, New York (1970) pp.5 - 11

98. Preface and bibliographical notes to *A Selection of the Social and Political Pamphlets of Annie Besant,* Kelley, New York (1970) pp.v-xiii

99. Introduction to reprint of Robert Owen, *A New View of Society (1816)* Kelley, New York (1972), pp. 1-12

100. Introduction to reprint of *The Life of Thomas Cooper Written by Himself (1872),* Leicester University Press (1971), pp. 7- 33

101. Introduction to *Working Conditions in the Victorian Age: Debates from 19th Century Critical Journals,* Gregg (1973), pp. 1-19

102. Foreword to *Mutiny in the RAF. The Air Force Strike s of 1946.* Socialist History Society (1998) pp.2-6

103. Books to Be Remembered: (In *Socialist History.* Each book with 2-3 pages commentary). e.e.cummings, *The Enormous Room*(New York,1922) No. 18 (2000); Clive Branson, *British Soldier in India* (1944) No.19 (2000) Bert Birtles, *Exiles in the Aegean*(1938) No.20(2001);Jessica Mitford, *The Making of a Muckraker,* New York, 1957, London 1979) No.21(2001); John Peet, *The Long Engagement. Memoirs of a Cold War Legend* (1989) No.22 (2002) Ongoing each journal number

104. 'John Saville and the *Dictionary of Labour Biography*': Interview by Malcolm Chase, *Socialist History,* 19. pp. 71-81

Index